OUR FIGHT

ALSO BY RONDA ROUSEY
WITH MARIA BURNS ORTIZ

My Fight / Your Fight

OUR FIGHT

—

RONDA ROUSEY
WITH MARIA BURNS ORTIZ

GRAND
CENTRAL

New York Boston

Cover design by Dana Li
Cover photos by Eric Williams Photography
Cover copyright © 2024 by Hachette Book Group, Inc.

Grand Central Publishing
Hachette Book Group
1290 Avenue of the Americas, New York, NY 10104
grandcentralpublishing.com
@grandcentralpub

First edition: April 2024

Grand Central Publishing is a division of Hachette Book Group, Inc. The Grand Central Publishing name and logo is a registered trademark of Hachette Book Group, Inc.

The publisher is not responsible for websites (or their content) that are not owned by the publisher.

Grand Central Publishing books may be purchased in bulk for business, educational, or promotional use. For information, please contact your local bookseller or the Hachette Book Group Special Markets Department at special.markets@hbgusa.com.

All photos by Eric Williams unless otherwise indicated.

Library of Congress Cataloging-in-Publication Data

Names: Rousey, Ronda, author. | Ortiz, Maria Burns, author.
Title: Our fight : a memoir / Ronda Rousey, with Maria Burns Ortiz.
Description: First edition. | New York : Grand Central Publishing, [2024]
Identifiers: LCCN 2023050761 | ISBN 9781538757376 (hardcover) |
    ISBN 9781538768327 (signed edition) | ISBN 9781538768334 (signed edition) |
    ISBN 9781538757390 (ebook)
Subjects: LCSH: Rousey, Ronda. | Women martial artists—United States—Biography. |
    UFC (Mixed martial arts event) | Self-actualization (Psychology)
Classification: LCC GV1113.R69 A3 2024 | DDC 796.8092 [B]—dc23/eng/20231201
LC record available at https://lccn.loc.gov/2023050761

ISBNs: 9781538757376 (hardcover), 9781538757390 (ebook),
    9781538768327 (signed edition), 9781538768334 (signed edition)

Printed in the United States of America

LSC-C

Printing 1, 2024

For my husband and children,
I hope you're proud of me.

INTRODUCTION

Dear Reader,

Nice to meet you. You seem cool. Obviously, you have excellent taste in books. Since you've only read three sentences, you're probably wondering what this book is about. This book is one I wish I would have had on the worst day of my life. I like to think someone would have given it to me when I felt completely destroyed, and said, "I know you're not ready, but when you are, you should really read this—and not just because it has valuable life lessons, but also because it's amusing as fuck." (I'm trying to limit my swearing, but heads up, I definitely say "fuck.") You don't have to hit rock bottom to read this book. Just saying, if you are there, I know what it feels like to be sitting there with you.

This book is *not* about how sometimes the greatest challenges are blessings in disguise. This book is about how sometimes in life everything you have worked for comes crashing down and the only way forward is to rebuild it into something better. This is my story on my terms. It's all the things I wanted to say over the last decade but didn't because I knew my words would be edited and dissected and ripped apart until they meant nothing.

From the moment I burst on the MMA scene seemingly overnight— "overnight" is what they call it when no one has been paying attention to the decades of time and effort you put into perfecting a craft—I was unbeatable. I was beyond unbeatable. I was all but untouchable. Some people might say that's arrogant, but that's simply stating a fact, and whether people like it or not, or like me or not, doesn't change that fact. I walk out to my mantra "I don't give a damn 'bout my reputation" blasting, so I could not care less about what "some people" who don't know me think. I am known for being as brutally unfiltered in my words as I was for my style of fighting, and that's what you'll get in this book.

As the first female fighter in the UFC, I put together a back-to-back-to-back-to-the-fifteenth-power string of wins. Most were in mere seconds, racking up an impressive collection of records from fastest win, to fastest submission, to fastest title defense turnaround. I changed not only the face of a single sport, but transcended sports. I dominated both opponents and headlines. I appeared in two of the largest action franchises in history, *The Fast and the Furious* and *The Expendables*. I had a long list of endorsement deals—from Reebok to Pantene to Carl's Jr.—and an even longer list of companies that wanted me. I inspired. Whether it was inspiring love from my fans or vitriol from my haters, I inspired. That journey, that rise, that seeming invincibility, that was my story.

Then, on November 15, 2015, in Melbourne, Australia, it all came crashing down. The worst moment of the worst day of my life was broadcast worldwide.

And afterward, for days, it was replayed over and over, on an almost inescapable loop. Everywhere I looked there it was. On TV. On social media. In news headlines. On people's faces. I'm not sure which was worse: the looks of pity from people who care about me and didn't know what to say, or the looks of smug satisfaction from people who can't stand me, even when they've never met me. Imagine being asked about it, *endlessly* asked about it. By people who don't know you, but who feel like they have a right—no, more than a right, *a duty* to ask. That moment dissected and discussed by millions of people who have never met you. Your worst enemies brought out to weigh in on it. People cheering about it, celebrating it, laughing about it. People tagging you in pictures with trolling comments almost a decade later. How do you come back from that?

For a long time, I felt like so much of my life had been me—just me—against the world. My story was literally and figuratively fighting to achieve what so many people had said was impossible, from learning how to speak as a small child to blazing a path for women in the UFC. I knew that others felt that same way, as though they had been counted out and underestimated their whole lives, as if they too were always fighting.

But I never stopped to ask myself, What comes next? What about after that? This is that story. It is about how there are things in life unquestionably worth fighting for, but there is also so much in life to just enjoy that doesn't require constant struggle. It's about letting down your guard; the one thing that is fatal to a fighter, but essential to building real relationships. It's about identifying *your* people, whether they come into your life or they've always been there. It's about replacing the unachievable pursuit of perfection with the pursuit of happiness. Finally, it's about reflecting on the decisions you've made and knowing that making different ones isn't giving up but growing up. And it's interwoven with body slams, bruises, baby-making, and the occasional anecdote of zombie apocalypse–prep farming.

There is some element of truth to failures being blessings in disguise, but anyone who says that in the moment of misfortune is opening themselves up to being deservedly throat punched. For me, "blessing" is too passive. Instead, I like to think they're opportunities in disguise.

For a long time, I envisioned myself walking away from fighting undefeated. A future that no longer exists. But now I realize that had that been the actual outcome, I would have also been unchanged and unchallenged. I don't know if that means I would have been unhappy, but I can tell you that I am happier now than I could have ever imagined I would be.

This book is about facing your fears, even when you don't want to. But it's also about sometimes taking a minute to do whatever it is that you need to do to put yourself first before you face those challenges, and how that's OK too. (And that can 100 percent mean lying on the couch, crying, and eating Cocoa Puffs if that's what you need.) It's a book about figuring out what you want, not what's expected of you.

I don't think my story is that different from everyone else's. It's about resilience, the evolution of self, and coming not only to find but also to accept happiness. It's about chasing your dreams, facing failure, tackling transition, marriage, parenthood, and jumps off the top of the turnbuckle. OK, maybe that last part is slightly less relatable. But the not-as-relatable bits are what make things interesting.

Let's start with the worst day of my life…

1

his is the end. I will close my eyes. And then this will be all over.

I sat alone on the cold, gray concrete floor. Staring forward, blinking. Tears ran down my cheeks, but I was silent.

I couldn't even think about what had just happened. Thinking would make it real. I needed a minute. A minute to process. To try to put together the irreparably shattered pieces.

I walked out to the Octagon, the UFC's eight-sided cage. I had stomped out to Joan Jett's "Bad Reputation" blaring, the crowd at its feet, screaming. I hugged my coaches. I held out my arms to be patted down by cageside officials. I met my opponent in the middle. The official said, "Fight." I was hit. I tried to hide it, but the world swayed.

Then there was a bell. And my world ended.

A million lights burst before my eyes, but I couldn't discern which were real and which were visible only to me, the result of random electrical impulses caused by my brain being jolted inside my skull. I stood within a kaleidoscope of noise and light, a jumble of images and sounds that I hadn't figured out how to piece together.

Suddenly I was moving, as if caught in an invisible wake made by the large men in black shirts, ushering me through a human tunnel. I followed them, propelled forward only by muscle memory and an overpowering need to get away. It was as if I was drowning, breathless and kicking upward toward the surface that I wasn't sure was there.

At some point I must have passed through a black curtain into a cement, fluorescent-lit corridor lined by black cables. It was the only way I could have gotten to the small medical room, where my legs collapsed under me, as if they couldn't bear my weight.

I sat barefoot, covered in a layer of sweat and shivering. I could taste the blood in my mouth, my tongue against a gaping hole of flesh and muscle where my inside bottom lip had once been.

I could not yet comprehend the enormity of what had happened, but I felt it in every cell in my body. I had lost. But it wasn't just that I had lost. I was still in my body, stuck here in some kind of state between hell and living. Dying would have meant all of this was over. Dying would feel better than this.

I could hear noise in the hallway, laughter. I could hear an entire stadium of people cheering my defeat. Tens of thousands of people celebrating the worst moment of my life.

It was the most intense pain and misery and embarrassment and shame I had ever felt. I wanted to kill myself. I wanted to swallow a bottle of pain-killers, close my eyes, and end it.

Across the room, pressed against the opposite wall, as if trying to shrink themselves into the corner, stood the half-dozen athletic men who made up my team. Sadness hung in the silence. They stood, some blinking back tears, heads lowered as if attending a funeral. Their eyes darted around the room, glancing at me, concerned but afraid to linger too long. All of them except for one. The man who would become my husband locked his eyes on me and never looked away.

It wasn't a look of pity, disappointment, or sympathy. It was pure love.

He looked at me like he would do anything to take my pain away, even if it killed him.

Amidst overwhelming grief, as I looked back at him, my only thought became *You can't die, you have to live for me.*

And if he was living for me, I knew I had to live too. It would have been easy to end it that night. To escape the crushing pain I felt, and pass that pain to him and my family to bear instead.

But with that look I knew I loved him so selflessly, so completely, that I would endure anything to spare him the suffering I felt.

I didn't grin. But I bore it.

That night, after I was rushed to the hospital to sew the muscles in my lip back together, Trav held me while I sobbed in his arms for hours. And he said something to me I will never forget: "You are so much more than just a fighter."

All I had ever known was being a fighter. It was my entire identity. I had been fighting since the moment I was born.

I fought to live. I came out of the womb blue, listless, and not breathing. My umbilical cord had been wrapped around my neck, cutting off air for no one knew how long. The doctors worked quickly, but no one knew the impact those first breathless moments might have.

I fought to speak. As a result of my traumatic birth, I struggled to talk as I grew older. I knew what words I wanted to say. I knew what they meant and what they should sound like, but there was a disconnect between the words in my head and being able to get them out in a way that people could understand. I spent years in speech therapy to be able to find my voice.

I fought to overcome tragedy. The same year I learned to speak, my dad had a sledding accident. Sledding was the kind of thing that people have done millions of times for fun and been totally fine. But he broke his back and because he had a rare blood disorder, his diagnosis was terminal. Facing a slow, painful death, he took his life when I was eight. He was my hero and the greatest man I'd ever known, and he was gone.

I fought for sport. I started judo when I was eleven years old. My mom had been the first American to win the world judo championships, and I followed in her footsteps. Judo translates into "the gentle way," but it is often anything but. Ways to win include throwing your opponent to the ground as forcefully as possible, choking them unconscious, and breaking their arms (technically, you're *just* dislocating their elbows). I made my first Olympic team as a teenage underdog and my second as a serious gold medal contender. But both times, I went home without standing on the top spot of the medal podium. My soul ached as I listened to a national anthem that wasn't mine as they raised another nation's flag. I quit judo after my second Olympics, leaving behind a sport that I had loved because loving it wasn't enough.

I fought as a career. I hadn't set out to become a professional fighter, but in the gym I found solace and purpose after walking away from the sport that had defined my entire life. MMA presented another chance to chase greatness. A way to use my skills to prove that I was capable of being the best in the world. It was a place to channel my drive, energy, and hope. And in less than two years of training, I had taken not only myself to the sport's highest level, but elevated women to a level that no one had ever believed possible. No one but me, that is. Within four years of me first stepping into an MMA cage, I had changed the face of the entire sport. I ran up an undefeated win streak of fifteen fights, many of which were over in a matter of seconds. Until the moment I stepped into that cage in Melbourne, headlines everywhere asked, "Is Ronda Rousey the greatest fighter we've ever seen?" Now, with a single defeat, I had lost everything.

Fighting was all I had ever known.

"You are so much more than a fighter."

The words echoed in my mind.

2

had just turned seven years old and was learning the backstroke. You're supposed to count the number of strokes from the flags to gauge distance, so you don't run into the pool wall, but I hadn't yet mastered that. I was going as fast as I could, racing an older teammate in the lane next to me who didn't even know we were in competition. I was mid-stroke when I slammed my head full speed into the tiled wall. When I didn't come home after practice—our house was literally across the street from the pool—my mom sent my dad out as a one-man search party. He found me, wandering our small-town North Dakota neighborhood in my snowsuit, hair still wet, disoriented and trying to find my way home. That was my first concussion. It wasn't the last time I'd headbutt the wall swimming or crack heads with another kid going the opposite direction, but you always remember your first.

Five years later, I was a twelve-year-old orange belt competing at a tournament in San Diego. I hadn't been in judo long but was already one of the best local competitors. I was fighting in the boys' division, which added extra pressure. I had more to prove, and no boy ever wanted to get beat by a girl. In one of my first matches of the day, I hit my head landing on the mat after a throw. I got photo vision, like someone just took a picture of you with the flash. I blinked my eyes a couple times and kept fighting. I won the match, but not the tournament. I fought at least four more times that day, but I couldn't blink away the spots, the light in the room hurt to look at. I told my mom I had a headache. She said to tough it out and stay focused. On the way back to the car, I threw up in the parking lot. I remember feeling my mom was upset with me, disappointed. I silently vowed to tough it out if it ever happened again. Many years later, I can recognize the concussion symptoms all too well, but I was just a kid. I didn't say anything. I didn't want anyone to think I was weak.

For the next decade of my judo career, I endured several concussions a year. Sometimes, it happened in tournaments. Other times, in practice. I would go round after round at training camps against the best in the world, then return to my room, nauseous as I tried to force food down with my face, tongue, and fingers tingling and numb. All common signs of head trauma that I ignored. I would never rest or recover. I just trained through them. Any hit to the head would exacerbate the symptoms, extending the healing process. For ten years, I was experiencing concussion symptoms more often than not.

All my many judo-related concussions sort of blend together. One, however, stands out. The worst was at the 2006 Pan American Games in Buenos Aires. While fighting a girl from Cuba in the final, I got caught and thrown on the back of my head so hard, it knocked me out.

Sometimes, when your brain suffers a significant-enough trauma, one where it can't effectively process the information it is receiving, it creates a story so that the information makes sense. In judo, you don't knock people out the way you do in boxing or MMA, so I had never experienced that knock-out sensation. But you can choke someone until they lose consciousness.

I knew what it felt like to be losing and regaining consciousness. As I lay on the mat coming back to consciousness that day in Argentina, the only thing that made sense to me was that I had been choked and was breaking out of it. When the referee called the match for my opponent, I was convinced he'd thought I had tapped out from a choke. I would have died on the mat before I tapped out. I got up and tried to argue, "I didn't tap!" I didn't remember that I got thrown. Then I don't remember anything until waking up the next morning.

My weight cut for that tournament had been especially hard, and I later learned that dehydration is believed to play a factor in making you more susceptible to neurological injury. When you're dehydrated—like when you're making weight—you lose some of that fluid cushion in your brain.

A few years later, I left judo, but the thing about neurological injuries is you can never leave them behind. Your brain is not supposed to bounce around in your skull; it doesn't develop calluses, it accumulates damage. With every brain trauma you incur, the next one comes easier.

No one was talking about brain injuries in athletes yet. The studies and awareness around CTE (chronic traumatic encephalopathy, the degenerative brain disease that can be brought on by repeated head trauma, most commonly found in athletes who suffer multiple concussions) had not become mainstream. In a sport defined by toughness, a blow to the head was met with "Don't be a pussy!" not "Are you OK?"

When I started doing MMA, I had a lot to prove as a woman in the gym. I'd spar with world-champion strikers, but all too often, even with the smallest hits, I'd end up seeing stars. I endured photo vision and headaches for days afterward but said nothing. MMA is a sport where one of the things you are scored on is who lands more blows. I knew I couldn't take many hits. Instead of going out in the cage and banging it out like a Diaz brother, I needed to be so perfect I wouldn't be touched. The style of fighting I cultivated required me to be so dominant in my fights that my opponents hardly had a chance to blink, let alone swing at me.

I was well aware that concussions weren't the kind of thing most people counted in the dozens. The more I pushed my body, the more it started to push back. The more that I fought, the worse it was getting. Even when I was at my most dominant, if the other person touched me at all, it could be enough to give me spotted vision. I would get barely grazed and feel like I'd had my bell rung. My fingertips would tingle. My teeth would buzz. Just push through it, I told myself. I was embarrassed to admit the impact the tiniest taps were having. No one could know I was vulnerable. My seeming invincibility did a lot of the work for me, keeping my opponents on their toes. If they knew I was one solid strike away from hitting the canvas, it would make my job a million times harder.

In fighting, people talk about your "chin" with such reverence. They don't mean your physical chin, but your ability to take punches without it seeming to have an impact. They act as if the ability to withstand blows is simply a matter of will. That if you just want it badly enough, if you're mentally tough enough, you can withstand anything. If that was the case, I would still be undefeated.

Going from one fight straight into the next, I didn't have any time to rest, let alone reflect. But more than that, I think I was too scared to address the reality of my brain being pushed to the brink. I couldn't speak up and say, "Hey, I'm dealing with some neurological issues and need to rest" because that would mean admitting to myself I had a limit. And to do what I did, I had to believe I was limitless.

I was so ashamed that I couldn't merely will my way out of the evident physical deterioration that I didn't talk about it. As a fighter you never want to admit weakness, but you can't toughen up your brain. There's no callus that will form. No break that will heal back stronger. There's just an acceleration of the inevitable decline.

My entire MMA career felt like I was on borrowed time. How long could I be perfect? How long could I keep anyone from touching me? I had to believe it was forever. I had to believe I was capable of anything. I had to believe that no matter how hard things got or how heavy the demands, I could not only do it all but do it perfectly. I had to believe it because the only other alternative was if people found out I was already dozens of concussions deep, they'd know I was vulnerable. Then I'd be forced to face the music and leave the sport before I was ready to walk away.

I swore to myself never to be one of those athletes who should have retired sooner, the fighter that's hard to watch age. I owed that not just to myself, but to all the women in MMA. Having its greatest champion linger past her prime wouldn't be a good look for the sport. Being too proud to admit my brain had taken too much abuse wouldn't be a good look for me. For Us.

Some days, after training, I would sit on the edge of the ring, unwanted sparkles dancing before my eyes, and ask myself: How many fights can you get away with not getting hit once? For me, it turned out to be fifteen.

Heading into the Holm fight, I was running on the fumes of my dreams and into problems I couldn't train my way around. The harder I worked, the more my body and brain deteriorated. The more I physically broke down, the more insecure I became, and the harder I worked to overcompensate. It went on and on until everything just gave out all at once.

After my loss, people went around saying, "Ronda got exposed for having no chin."

That's bullshit.

I did everything that nobody else could, and I did it without even being touched.

I created the most effective and efficient fighting style that ever existed.

I was perfect. Until I wasn't.

3

As all true love stories begin, mine with Travis Browne started when my best friend Marina tweeted at him.

Travis was a top UFC heavyweight, so I had known that he existed before this moment, but this was the first time I actually *thought* about him. It was sometime in the fall of 2013, two years before we would find ourselves halfway around the world in a cold, concrete room in the depths of a Melbourne stadium. He had—and still has—a very large beard. Marina sent him a photo of birds living in Peter Griffin's beard, and that is how I first became aware of the man who would eventually become my husband. Of course, that was the furthest thing on my mind then. I was dating a guy who doesn't even deserve to be named, and Marina had a boyfriend who was one of the biggest losers ever. I fucking hated that guy and was on a mission to find her anyone else. I told her this Travis Browne seemed like a catch.

He was tall, standing six foot seven, had a shaved head and dark beard. His look was not uncommon in the sport, especially for heavyweights, but he had probably the longest and most glorious beard in the UFC at that point. What really made him stand out were large traditional Hawaiian tattoos running down one arm and up a leg. I thought they were cool. But that was it.

A few months later, he and I were both on the UFC's annual New Year's card in Vegas as 2013 rolled over to 2014. I was having a rematch with Miesha

Tate, my MMA archnemesis whose arm I had mangled in our previous meeting. I ran into Travis in the warm-up room before the weigh-in.

"I just wanted to say thank you for being so nice to Marina on Twitter," I said. "You guys are so funny."

And then I went into my zone. I made weight and again submitted Miesha. My professional record improved to 8-0. That night, at the post-fight press conference, I was seated between him and another of the night's winners, Uriah Hall, making jokes about balls as UFC president Dana White stood at the podium telling the media that I'd be going straight back into training camp to prepare for the fastest title defense in UFC history. Before I even had a chance to catch my breath, it was right back into fight mode.

Fifty-six days later, I knocked out Sara McMann in the first round.

In the fight, McMann and I came out swinging. She tagged me a few times in the first fifteen seconds as I was backing her up against the cage to close the distance. Taps like that should have been nothing, the kind of hits that as a fighter you just shake off, but not for me. I dropped her with a knee to the liver less than a minute later in what was declared the "performance of the night."

Afterward, the cageside doctor looked me over as is standard for every fighter after every fight.

"Great job, Ronda," he said.

"Thanks!" I said.

"I've just got to check you out real quick."

"Of course," I said, smiling. I knew the drill.

The post-fight exam is required, but not thorough. The goal is to triage major injuries and catch serious complications. They're not diagnostic checkups. "Medical" is typically a small curtained-off area that you stop by on your way back to your locker room. The extent of the exams varies based on the fight and whether you win or lose. Because I won in such dominant fashion, my exams were usually as quick as my fights. A quick check of my hands, flash a light in front of my eyes, look at any bruises that might be forming.

"Any concerns?" the doctor asked as always.

"Nope," I said. "All good."

"OK, well, I don't see anything that gives me any cause for concern, but obviously, you know the drill, look for signs of concussions, anything starts hurting later, anything changes, let us know or get it checked out."

I nodded.

I headed back to my locker room. Contrary to what the name might evoke, it was just a smallish dressing room with a workout mat on the floor and some waiting room–type furniture, a couple chairs, a couch, and a coffee table pushed up against various walls. I flipped off the lights that hurt to look at. My head was pounding. I lay down on the mat on the floor. Photo vision danced before my eyes. I knew I should be celebrating, but I didn't want to get up. I'd had so many concussions at this point that I'd lost count. This was just one more to add to that tally.

I certainly wasn't going to tell a doctor. It's not like I'd never fought injured. Hell, I don't know if I've ever fought *un*injured. I'd had multiple knee surgeries. I'd broken my thumb. I'd exploded a cyst under my knuckle. I never pulled out of a fight because of an injury because pushing through the pain was part of the job. The last thing I needed was to not be cleared to fight. The concussions were just one more thing to push through. I refused to think about what could have happened if the fight went longer.

After the McMann fight, I was running into people, and they would say, "I loved your last fight with Miesha." I'd correct them and say, "Well, actually I've already had another title defense since then." Now a decade has passed, and I've come to understand that no one's ever going to realize how active they kept me as champion. How fucking difficult that blink-and-you-miss-it turnaround was. Or how unbelievable what I achieved was.

Later that spring, around the time I went back into camp for my third title defense in six months, Travis came to check out our gym. He was coming off a loss and looking for a change. Glendale Fight Club, or GFC, was located along a generic stretch of road amidst LA's massive urban sprawl. It inhabited a small commercial space that was easy to miss if you didn't know to look for it, buried between a half-dozen car dealerships and the occasional small storefront. The gym had a front wall of windows that could just as easily have made it a nondescript second-hand boutique or tire shop. Inside was a row of boxing heavy bags, a floor covered in green and red grappling mats, a full boxing ring, a small-scale MMA cage, and some dated cardio equipment. It wasn't fancy or state-of-the-art, but it had everything you needed to train. The wall behind the ring featured a brightly colored larger-than-life mural bearing the words "Nothing is Impossible" and depictions of boxing legend Muhammad Ali on one side and GFC's Edmond Tarverdyan on the other as if they were watching over the room. Lanky with thick eyebrows and an even thicker Armenian accent, Edmond was one of those people who even when he was in his twenties looked middle-aged. He, like my mother, had a piercing gaze that could make you feel like either the center of the universe or an insect on the floor.

In addition to being the subject of the gym's artistic centerpiece, Edmond was its owner and my head coach. I had been training with him since I began a mission to do the impossible: tear down MMA's chain-link ceiling and create a place for women in the UFC. Back then, MMA trainers wouldn't give women time of day. There was no real money in women's MMA. Without the potential to make money off female fighters, few coaches saw any value training them. But Edmond at least let me occupy a corner of his gym to train for free. I busted my ass harder than any of the guys in the gym until he was forced to take notice. Since then, I had gone 11-0 in my professional fight career, ushered women into the UFC, and established myself as one of the greatest female athletes ever.

For the longest time, it had just been me and a bunch of Armenian guys at GFC. Then after I served as a coach on the UFC's *The Ultimate Fighter* reality show, it was me, a bunch of Armenian guys, two of the show's contestants—women's MMA pioneer Shayna Baszler and up-and-comer Jessamyn Duke, who had since moved to LA—and occasionally Marina.

Travis liked the way we ran things. Edmond had once been an amateur fighter but made the transition to coaching when he was still young and now had a small but growing stable of fighters and boxers. Travis had been training at one of those super camps, what we call a big-name trainer's gym that has dozens of fighters. Those places draw athletes based on the name recognition, but you tend to find you're just one face in the crowd without a lot of individualized attention.

Not only that, but Travis's gym was out of state and he had two little boys in San Diego who he wanted to be closer to. GFC was at least drivable. And so, he became another guy who trained at our gym.

I am all business at the gym. This is my place of work. I'm not there to fuck people, I'm there to fuck people up.

Moreover, it's a very family-type environment. The few girls that were there were like everybody's little sister. We weren't like those incestuous gyms where everyone's banging everybody. When I was training for the 2008 Olympics, I had the misfortune of being at a few of those places. It wasn't the reason that I didn't win the Olympics, but that kind of toxic environment certainly didn't help my performance or me as a human being. That was the culture we actively tried to discourage at GFC. The only hitting on girls in the gym happened during sparring and it was actual hitting.

Considering that, up until this point, the gym had basically been a bunch of Armenian dudes and me, it was an easy policy to enforce. Now, I love me some Armenian dudes and they love me, but we're just not each other's type.

The unwritten rule was in full effect when Travis joined as were my attempts to convince Marina to leave her boyfriend and date him. By this point, I was single, having sworn off dating because when it came to relationships, I neither had the time nor the luck.

One night, after getting home from practice, Marina and I began our evening ritual of taking bong hits in the kitchen and talking about our day. We had been friends since we were in our early teens, after we first bonded as two girls cutting weight in a sauna in Belgium at an international judo tournament. Born in Moldova and raised in upstate New York, Marina was the daughter of an Olympic-caliber powerlifting refugee who had to flee the USSR for being too Jewish at the wrong time in history. She had a slender but muscular frame reminiscent of a mastiff puppy hinting at the beast it would grow into one day, but also piercing blue eyes and gorgeous long brown hair that gave her a stunning Eastern European look. Marina was the kind of friend who would tell it to you like it is, but never judge. She had moved to LA shortly after I started my MMA career, and we'd been roommates ever since.

In yet another attempt to convince her to leave her tugboat sailor boyfriend, I started listing Travis's virtues. Ten minutes later, Marina looked me dead in the eye and said, "Yeah, sure, *I* should go out with Travis Browne." And I realized—whether in a moment of total clarity or an herbally altered higher plane of thought—that maybe while I was trying to sell him to her, I was really selling him to myself.

Travis had been training with us for a while when it was announced that his first fight as an official member of our team would be against my ex-boyfriend. My ex thrived on playing fucked-up mind games with me when I had a fight coming up and insisted we hide that we were dating so he wouldn't be labeled "Ronda Rousey's Boyfriend." As Travis headed into the match-up, I pretended it wasn't personal. I tried not to be overly involved or emotional. This wasn't my fight. I was hoping he would win, but I was in training camp, so I didn't really think too much more about it. That is until it was on live TV, and I lost my goddamn mind. Screaming at the top of my lungs, "Get him, Travis!" while punching the arm of the person on the couch next to me.

When Travis knocked him out at the end of the first round, I didn't think it could get any more gratifying. My ex covered up on the ground while Travis pounded away on him. The referee waved the match over. Then Travis, towering over the crumpled, semi-conscious body of my ex, leaned down and whispered something in his ear. His words were indiscernible to the camera, but I swore I could hear Travis's voice saying, "Ronda says fuck you."

When he got back to the gym, it was as if there had been a shift. You don't know why or how or when things changed, but things are just different.

Even though there was nothing going on between Travis and me, it felt like everybody in the gym could tell there was tension. When we would talk, everyone would stop what they were doing and listen. This suddenly noticeable silence hung where the clink and thunk of heavy bags being punched, the rapid-fire thump of the speedbag, and an unintelligible stream of Armenian wisecracks had existed only moments before.

One day I waltzed into the gym while Travis was training in the ring. "Hey, Travis," I said as the sound faded like someone had turned down the volume on a stereo. "I got this really funny beard meme. What's your number? I'll send it to you."

He walked over to the edge of the ring. "Oh, just show me."

I hugged my phone to my chest so he couldn't see it. "Give. Me. Your. Number. And I'll send it to you," I said slowly and with more emphasis.

I could see the lightbulb go off.

For the next six months, we communicated exclusively via beard memes. Ours was a very millennial love story.

Then, the stars aligned and the tour for my first book landed me at a signing at the Air Force base in Las Vegas, the exact city and the exact date Travis had a fight with Andrei Arlovski. The fight was back and forth, back and forth. Arlovski wobbled Trav. Then Trav came back and wobbled Arlovski. Then Arlovski came back and wobbled Trav. The referee called it for Arlovski on the second wobble. Trav stayed on his feet.

I was undefeated in MMA but knew the devastation of losing. From the time I had started judo at eleven years old, I had been focused on one goal—Olympic gold. I made it to the Olympics twice. As a seventeen-year-old, I had shocked the US judo world by coming back from injury to make the 2004 Athens Olympics team. I had planned to shock them again and to take gold even though probably only myself and my mom thought I stood a chance. But I lost two matches and was eliminated. Four years later, I headed to Beijing, the world silver medalist, no longer under the radar. I lost in the quarterfinal, and while I battled back to take home a bronze medal, it was consolation, not a victory. The pain of those losses has faded with the years, but it never completely goes away.

Watching from the crowd, I felt awful for Travis, but I was impressed by his heart. He was hurt, but he fought back. It was a hell of a fight.

After the fight, in the cavernous tunnels that thread under the floors of Las Vegas casino event centers, Edmond pulled me aside.

"You need to go talk to him," Edmond said.

"Me?" I asked, looking around as if he was clearly talking to someone else. "What the fuck am I gonna say? You're his coach. Why do I need to talk to him?"

Edmond stood there, stoic. "You always say the best things. If anyone can understand what this moment is like, you're the one."

"Fine, fine," I said, making it clear that I didn't feel like it was my place. To this point, our communication had been memes. How was it somehow up to me to provide some words of encouragement or consolation or whatever was expected in a situation where there is nothing that can be said? There were no beard memes for this situation, no words that make losing easier. Nothing takes away the soul-crushing pain of defeat.

We went up and knocked on the door of Travis's hotel room. The space was crowded but quiet. A small group of family friends sat on the bed. His wife, whom he had married in a quickie courthouse wedding a few months prior, glared at me when I walked in.

She'd been to the gym once or twice with Travis's dog, but I had never officially met her. However, it was clear through her pursed lips that she hated me. I had never thought about her before at all.

Travis stood there looking down at the ground. Edmond muttered some words of encouragement. Travis didn't say anything, so I said what I would want to hear if it were me.

"I know this sucks," I said. "Nobody knows how much this sucks as much as me. I trained my whole life to win the Olympics. And fell short—twice. I know this feels like the end of the world, but you don't have to wait another four years for another opportunity. And when that day comes, when you get your title shot, you're going to be more ready for that fight because of the lessons you'll take away from tonight."

I didn't even know where the words were coming from, they were just coming. His gaze remained fixed on the floor. I reached up and held his face in both of my hands, raising his gaze to eye level.

"Just know that I love you," I said. "I love you, and it's all going to be OK. I promise, and whether you can see it right now or not, we'll look back on this moment and be grateful for it."

I gave him a hug, then spun around to the rest of the room as if this had been a totally normal exchange.

"OK, guys, well, bye," I said with a half wave, walking out the door with Edmond close behind.

People often want to look back on relationships and romances recrafting the narratives into these beautiful, idealized versions of what happened as opposed to the messy, roundabout reality. I won't do that here, and that moment is not where our love story became a love story.

I'm not a sociopath who would tell someone in front of their wife that I romantically love them. I said the same thing to Davey Grant when I coached the Ultimate Fighter—in front of his fiancée—when he lost. "I love you and this is going to be OK." And I meant it then as a coach, just like I meant it with Travis as a teammate.

Of course, sometimes your words have repercussions in ways you never intended or imagined. In that moment, I unknowingly threw a grenade into their marriage. Albeit into what was already a post-apocalyptic level of destruction battlefield. But, as there weren't any beard memes conveying such, I had no way of knowing any of that at the time.

What I did know was that after losing a fight, everyone's trying to talk to you about the fight. And that's the last thing you want to talk about. I wanted to be someone who wasn't talking to him about the fight, and that's how we actually started talking.

The next morning, I did something I'd never done before. I texted Travis Browne.

"I just wanted to say hi," I wrote. "I hope you're having a better day today."

From Vegas, I set off to finish my book tour and Travis headed to Brazil. A week later, I sat in my hotel room in Denver, a blur of cities and signings making it feel much longer, texting with Travis. It was the last night of the tour, and I was ready to get back to my dog. To my own bed. To the gym.

"I can't wait to be home. We can finally get some face time," I wrote, my fingers aching from hours of texting.

The reply was almost instantaneous.

"Oh, sure, I'd love to FaceTime."

And before I knew it, the little green camera phone icon was ringing on my phone.

At the time, I thought that he read it wrong. But much later, Travis clarified, "Oh, I knew what you meant."

We talked until the sun came up in Brazil. By the time we hung up, all I could think was *Oh shit*. Oh shit, I like this guy. Oh shit, he's married. Oh shit, I cannot get caught up in a scandal. Oh shit, I don't even know if he feels the same way.

I told myself we had gone from teammates to friends. I rolled with that, and we just kept talking. About our days. About interests. About life. The kind of things you would talk to your friend about. And we let what we weren't saying stay unspoken.

It seems cliché because every story about someone finding love seems to start with "I wasn't thinking about serious relationships…" But I wasn't thinking about serious relationships. I had a career that was unrelatable to almost everyone on the planet and that consumed virtually all of my time and all of my energy. I had gone through a string of shitty boyfriends, and after a 0 percent success rate, I had basically given up on any sort of love life. The year before, I bought a house that could only fit me—a Venice Beach bungalow with a bedroom loft where the ceiling peaked at five foot seven—with the full intention of living alone forever. I had no room in my life, metaphorically or literally, for six-foot-seven Travis Browne.

I was slated to fight Bethe Correia in Rio that August. As always, we started training camp six weeks out, and we always did the first week at altitude.

From a scientific standpoint, there's significant value in training at higher altitudes where the air is thinner. Because there is a lower level of oxygen in the air, your body adjusts by making more red blood cells to ensure enough oxygen is transported to your muscles. Moreover, when you return closer to sea level, your body is even more efficient and effective at carrying oxygen to your muscles thanks to the boost altitude training provides.

But that first week in the mountains was as mental as it was physical. It was like the moment in a race where the starting gun is fired, indicating it's go-time. A discernible, location-based transition between training between fights and going into a fight.

The cabin we trained at in Frazier Park, in the mountains but not a ridiculous long drive from LA, was owned by the family of another athlete at GFC. While everyone referred to it as a cabin, it was more like a giant man cave in the woods. It was filled with vintage pinball machines, a pool table, foosball table, and a surprising amount of Marilyn Monroe memorabilia. The entire place smelled like pine, tea, and Armenian BBQ.

I looked forward to the first week of camp. There wasn't a full ring set up there, so we couldn't spar, but this time was more about making the mental shift into fight mode. I was starting to watch what I ate, but the diet to ensure I'd be able to hit my division's 135-pound limit wasn't yet underway. In the morning, I'd look out into the pines, drinking Armenian coffee and snacking on dark chocolate.

Beside the house, there was a small garage with workout mats and a punching bag. We'd start the day focused on striking, doing drills, hitting mitts, working the bag. After that, we'd work on strength and conditioning. One of the goals early in camp was to put on weight in the form of muscle.

In the afternoons, I would feed Monte, the lone surviving chicken after a bear got into the coop. If I felt up to it, I'd go hiking. If I just wanted to relax, I'd lay in a hammock and read. In the evenings, I'd do a grappling workout with whoever we had brought up to train with me, like my coach Martin who was an Olympic bronze medal wrestler or my longtime US judo teammate Justin Flores or whatever other bodies happened to be there.

At night, we'd feast on Armenian BBQ, huge servings of grilled meat, and watch old fights.

Wham! We were all sitting around watching a match one evening. On the TV, the legendary boxer hit the mat.

"And after that he was done," Edmond said with finality, as if there were no more of this boxer's fights left worth seeing.

"What, he just quit?" I asked.

"No, *kyank jan*," he said with an Armenian term of endearment. "He just took one hit too many, couldn't never take them the same after that. His chin was gone. Should have hung it up then. Can't even shit on his own these days."

I tried my best to hide my horror.

"So anyway, check this match out," he continued, turning his attention to the next fight.

But I couldn't focus on the back-and-forth playing out on the screen, wondering *When was it going to be one hit too many for me?* I shuddered at the thought, *Never.* I pushed the doubt out of my mind. I had to in order to stay sane. If I had to be so good that no one could ever land a clean shot on me, that's how fucking good I would be.

I wasn't an idiot. I could feel that my body and mind were running out of mileage, but I was still getting better with every fight. How could I walk away when I was then best I'd ever been?

It wasn't unusual for various members of the gym to join us up at the cabin for training camp. This time, Travis was among them.

While we had not addressed it, it was increasingly obvious there was something between the two of us. And it was clear that Edmond both had a sense of this and was not OK with it. It was as if Edmond had pulled everyone else aside— or maybe just said in Armenian—"Do not leave these two alone." Because there were not two seconds where we were unchaperoned. And so, we would sit next to each other on the couch, pressing our pinky toes together, and brushing elbows as we passed in the kitchen as if we were living in an episode of *Bridgerton.*

These moments, however, were few and far between as the purpose of training camp was to focus and prepare me for the fight.

Part of the ritual was that at night, after I went to bed, the guys would stay up late drinking and telling stories that were probably 99 percent bull-shit. The third day of camp I came down in the morning after what I could tell had been a raucous evening. Everyone was still asleep, sprawled through-out the house. Travis was lying on the couch. Alone at last. I went over, sat next to where he lay, said nothing, and gave him a hug. My heart was pound-ing so hard and fast I was afraid he'd feel it. There was a lot of tension and things unsaid at that point. One was that he was married. That was a line that although we seemed to be moving dangerously close to, I didn't plan on crossing. His beard was surprisingly soft. I had never felt it before. Afraid we might be seen and cause a scandal, I jumped to my feet and snuck back upstairs.

A few hours later, once the rest of the house had roused themselves hung-over or still half-drunk, Edmond said, very matter-of-factly, "Travis, we have other people coming up to train. You've got to go."

It made sense. He wasn't my size and was of no value in a training situa-tion. But I couldn't help feeling it wasn't purely logical.

"Yeah, sure," Travis said. "No problem."

He leaned in to give me a hug.

"See you," I said as casually as I could.

Travis went down the mountain. I went back to camp.

A week later, I was back home when Travis texted that he wanted to stop by. We had never hung out outside of the gym, and now he was coming to my house.

The roar of a large diesel truck announced his arrival before the doorbell even rang.

"Hi," I said, inviting him in. I was trying so hard for it not to feel awk-ward that it was awkward.

He came in, instinctively dipping his head as he walked through a door-way. His large frame seemed even bigger in my intentionally small house.

He cleared his throat.

"I just wanted to say this in person and not like a text or a phone call," he said. "But me and my ex separated. We're getting the marriage annulled. I'm telling you because I wanted to be completely upfront with you. To let you know. In person."

The last sentence hung in the air like a question.

"Would you like a tour of my house?" I asked. "Starting with my room?"

I led him to my little loft. He looked comical hunched at the foot of the bed. "It's easier if you just dive in." I demonstrated. "It's Tempur-Pedic, life changing." He dove in next to me. We looked at each other, awkward as could be. I felt like my mouth was frothing, like my spit was full of bubbles. I've never had that feeling before or since.

"I just got a new jacuzzi in the back too." I jumped up. He walked sideways down the steps of my loft because the stairs were too shallow to fit his feet.

I led him to the doorway, going on about my old Kit-Cat Klock as its tail swung back and forth, its eyes watching us. I wasn't even looking at him when he gave me the sweetest little peck on the lips. I was totally caught by surprise. He stilled like a deer in the headlights.

"Sorry," he said.

I smiled. "It's OK."

And from that moment on, Travis Browne and I have been together.

The next morning, after holding me all night, Trav turned to me.

"Listen, I'm not here to be your flavor of the month," he said.

I was flattered that he believed I was successful enough in this arena to have flavors of the month. But here he was, less than twenty-four hours into our relationship—could we even call it a relationship yet?—letting me know, "Don't go down this road unless you plan on going down the aisle."

My mind was focused on fight planning not wedding planning, but this—whatever *this* was—seemed worth a try.

It wasn't just two people meeting, but two people meeting at the right point in their lives. We both had already gotten to know who we were as people and what we wanted. We got to know each other first and respect each other first.

Even though it was only a few hours old, this relationship was different from any other I'd ever had. It was, I realized very early on, something worth fighting for.

4

Travis and I resolved to keep our relationship a secret at the gym, but we were so fucking obvious that it didn't even last a week.

My dating life had never been a problem with my fighting life. But this time, I had violated the one unbreakable rule: no dating in the gym. I would like to think that what happened next was because of that. It would make it simpler. Easier to justify. But it wasn't just about that. I don't know if it was even about that at all.

I hadn't been avoiding Edmond since Travis and I got together; I just hadn't been seeking him out. I knew what he was going to say, and I wasn't interested in hearing it. I had a fight to focus on. The optics of me and Trav getting together while he was still technically married was bad for me, bad for Trav, bad for Edmond by proxy. If word got out before my fight it would be an even bigger distraction. So, I pretended not to notice the daggers Edmond had been shooting me all week and did what I always thought would solve everything. I trained my ass off.

I can't even remember exactly how the argument that day began. By this point, arguing with Edmond had become so commonplace, it felt like it was embedded within our routine.

———

Edmond as a coach nitpicked, criticized, and argued with me not just about fighting but every detail of my life. Honestly, by the time I arrived at

Edmond's gym, I had spent over a decade being conditioned to take abuse in the name of training.

That part of my dynamic with Edmond wasn't much different than how I'd been treated by my many judo coaches including Jason Morris, Jimmy Pedro, and especially Big Jim Pedro. As a sixteen-year-old kid training for the 2004 Olympics, I lived with him in a remote cabin in the woods of New Hampshire. I'd wake up to Big Jim barking about how I was fat, a slob, and lacked discipline. By lunch, he'd be on rambling tangents about something he'd heard on Fox News. At training, the focus of his criticism shifted from my character to my judo.

I tried to say nothing. I sat there, listening to him rant for hours, day after day. Silence did little to diffuse the situation, but it was more effective than talking back. I started carefully weighing my words, figuring out how to respond in ways that would keep Big Jim from screaming at me. And I got good at it.

"God, look at your room," he'd say, surveying my less-than-tidy living space, pronouncing "room" like "rum" in this thick New England accent. "This doesn't embarrass you? Your mother taught you to be a slob. Of course, you liberals always make a mess of everything." He'd spit out "liberal" like it was the worst thing a person could be called. I was a sixteen-year-old girl who hadn't voiced a single political opinion and couldn't even vote. But apparently being female and from California was egregious enough.

I spent the better part of a year living and training my ass off with Big Jim. It was undeniable that I got a lot of individual coaching attention from one of the best coaches in the country. I was getting better than ever, but that came at a price: you had to take Big Jim's shit all day.

As the name Big Jim might suggest, there was also a little Jimmy. Big Jim's son Jimmy had won the world judo championships five years prior. He was the third American to do so, following in the footsteps of my mom, who was the first in 1984. While Big Jim in all his abrasive gruffness tolerated me, I felt like Jimmy resented me.

I did not worship at the shrine of Jimmy Pedro. I did not line up to kiss his world championship ring. (In fact, I was pretty sure they didn't even give out rings.) When I arrived at the Pedros' club to train, it was a very different judo environment than the one I had grown up in. My mom says all the time, "I won the worlds, and I didn't care if anybody else knew I was the best in the world but me." Her world championship gold medal seemed to travel randomly around our house, resurfacing in the kitchen "junk" drawer when what you really needed was a pair of scissors.

The Pedros' entire identity seemed to revolve around Little Jimmy's world championship achievement. Big Jim had coached Jimmy, and in turn, Jimmy had become a champion and now a coach. Their methods were not to be questioned. But I had a lot of questions.

"Why?" I'd ask.

"Because I said so," Big Jim would bark.

"I was thinking ..." I'd suggest.

"You were thinking? That's the problem." Big Jim would scoff.

Whenever Little Jimmy coached me, he seemed more concerned with getting me to recognize the presence of his greatness than getting me to improve. He used his attention like a weapon, focusing on you if you appeased him, ignoring you if you didn't. He had his favorites, and no matter how hard I tried or how much I succeeded, I was never one of them.

One day at practice, I was trying not to get pinned by Jimmy. He was twenty years more experienced and at least twenty-five pounds heavier, a world champion going against a teenage Olympic hopeful. He was trying to pry his leg out of my guard. I held with all my might, determined not to get caught. He pushed his shoulder into my jaw, focused his weight into that one spot, so hard that my jaw was dislocated. The injury would plague me for years, causing my jaw to randomly spasm and lock. I thought that was what it took. That he was making me tough. I popped my own jaw back in for the first, but not last time, went right on practicing. There were tears in my eyes but I trained even harder than before.

A few years later, I was back at the Pedros, training for my second Olympic team. I threw Jimmy in front of the whole class. Proud of myself, I laughed as I flew through the air with him and landed on top. He stood up as if it was fine. I smiled. He grabbed my gi like it was the Olympic finals. He moved me off the mat but didn't stop, throwing me into the benches against the wall. I winced as the corner of the bench jabbed into my shoulder, but I stood up as if I was fine. I was an expert at hiding pain at this point. He grabbed me again, this time throwing me hard into the table by the side of the mat as onlookers moved out of the way. Again, we got up. This time, he slammed me hard into the mat, right at the feet of the same people who had watched my throw minutes earlier. I refused to show any emotion but sobbed in the shower that night. I reasoned this was about making me tough and providing me with a valuable ego check. Coaches weren't supposed to be your friends.

At least I got his attention? I thought afterward. *Maybe this means he respects me even more now.*

Now I look back at those moments and can't help but wonder if it was really abuse.

When I was eighteen, I left New England and the Pedros to train at Jason Morris's club in upstate New York. Jason and Jimmy were rivals who pretended to be friendly while talking an insane amount of shit about each other.

Jason had won a silver medal in the Olympics almost twenty years prior and, like Jimmy, his entire life revolved around that singular accomplishment. Clubs like Jason's were the reason that I so readily embraced Edmond and GFC's policy against dating in the gym. You would have thought you'd stumbled into a Greek orgy the way the athletes there were drinking, partying, and bed hopping. A tangled web is woven when you've got a bunch of young people living together, training together, and having "no strings attached" sex. Where Big Jim demanded obedience and order, Jason's club lured athletes with the promise of freedom and fun.

But the two clubs competing for the US top judo talent weren't as different as they wanted to believe. Everyone was always kissing the coach's ass to get on their good side, constantly vying for their attention. But when it came to cutting you down, Jason's tactics were different. He used humor and sarcasm to belittle his athletes. Jason gave disparaging nicknames. He would smile as he said a remark that cut you to the core. Then he'd cover it up with a laugh as if it was a joke you just didn't get.

I walked away from all of them when I left judo after my second Olympics with the prime mid-twenties years of my career still ahead of me. With an eye to making a run at my third Olympics, I had entered at the Grand Prix Tunis, an international tournament in Tunisia. But even before my first match, I knew my judo days were over. The sports governing body had made changes to the rules to the point where the sport was becoming unrecognizable, and when I looked ahead, I felt nothing but dread at the thought of enduring four more years of misery for a single shot at glory. I just couldn't bring myself to do it, so I left it all behind at twenty-two years old.

I fell into MMA by chance. My friend Manny Gamburyan, who had done judo with me since we were kids, had transitioned to cage fighting. The US judo community had basically excommunicated me when I left the sport, and Manny was one of the few who kept in touch at a time when I was struggling to figure out what I was going to do next. He invited me to come train with him, just for fun. It was Manny who unwittingly set me on my course, when he mentioned offhand one day after training that if I did MMA, I'd beat every girl out there. And it was Manny who brought me to GFC for the first time, introducing me to Edmond, the coach that would be behind me as I made that a reality.

By the time I landed at Edmond's gym, it seemed normal to have a coach spend hours berating me. The line between pushing me physically and being abusive was so blurred that I didn't know where it was. In combat sports, where your trainer's job is to prepare you physically and mentally to beat the shit out of someone while defending yourself against them doing the same, that line is even harder to identify.

Big Jim grabbing me by the neck during rants about how women aren't as capable of defending themselves as they think they are. Edmond and I training mid-argument and him hitting me just a bit harder, escalating until it felt like he was really trying to hurt me. Those moments ignited a primal rage that made me fight back, made me want to fucking kill them. I would push myself to the point where I was willing to beat someone within an inch of their life with my bare hands. I'd feel like a killer. Defiant. Unstoppable. I became better, tougher, ruthless in the ring. Was this training? When does it turn into abuse?

At one point, I went on Jim Rome's show and displayed an entire thigh bruised various shades of purple from training with Edmond. A news head-line commented that my "visible bruising showed she's in serious fight train-ing." That sounded a lot better than the truth.

A few days earlier, Edmond and I had been bickering about something so insignificant that I couldn't have told you what even if you'd asked me that day. The UFC had just announced my signing. It marked a seismic shift in the sport since the UFC is MMA's highest level, the equivalent of the NFL to football or NBA to basketball, and had no female fighters. My amateur career had lasted just 104 seconds in the cage, as I went 3-0 before turning pro where my record reset. (In MMA, your record only reflects your profes-sional fights, not any amateur bouts you may have won.) In my first year in professional MMA, I racked up a 5-0 record, going from unknown in the sport to its champion after defeating Miesha Tate for the Strikeforce title. My ascent had been as captivating as it was rapid. People who had never watched MMA were tuning in, and they were tuning in to watch women. Ratings equated to dollars.

It was September 8, 2012, when Dana White told me he was signing me to the UFC as the promotion's first woman fighter. He brought me to Mr. Chow in Beverly Hills. It was the same restaurant he had stood outside almost a year before and mockingly laughed when a TMZ reporter asked, "When are we going to see women in the UFC?" "Never," Dana said, repeat-ing himself for emphasis. "Never."

He meant it as an absolute. I took it as a challenge. I knew women would never be viewed as equals in MMA unless they were fighting in the UFC's trademark Octagon and was determined to convince Dana to make that happen.

"I love this place. You've never been here?" Dana asked when we sat down. I didn't know the best way to explain that, until only a few months prior, I had been juggling working overnights at a twenty-four-hour gym, bartending, and training for amateur fights while living in a one-room apartment where sewage regularly backed up out of the sink, a lifestyle that left me neither the time nor the money to be frequenting dining establishments with checkerboard floors and white tablecloths, so I just casually said, "No."

Dana ordered and, over a table covered in plates of chicken satay, noodles, and glazed prawns, told me he was going to be signing me to the UFC.

"You won't regret this," I promised. "I will be there for anything you need. If you take this chance on me, I will die fighting my heart out for you. I will fight when nobody else wants to. I mean it."

And I meant it. Every day of my fight career from that moment forward was defined by that promise.

My MMA career before this was being in perpetual fight mode. Up-and-coming fighters tend to fight two to three times a year. For champions, it's maybe once or twice. In my first year as a professional fighter, I fought five times, going from unknown to holding the Strikeforce title, the top title in women's MMA at the time. I wasn't just winning decisively, I was dominating. No one had been able to take me past the first round. In fact, up until I turned Miesha Tate's elbow inside out for that Strikeforce title, no one had taken me past the first minute. Months later, I defended that title by arm barring Sarah Kaufman in under a minute with higher ratings and a bigger crowd. Right in front of Dana, who was sitting cageside to see if I lived up to the hype. Two weeks after that, I was sitting across from him in a fancy Chinese restaurant promising to be the best business decision he ever made.

As a businessman, if not a feminist, Dana saw the draw women could have and offered me a contract that would make me one of the highest paid athletes in the organization. My part in ushering women into the highest level of MMA had begun. Not only was I opening the cage door for women in the sport, but I was going to headline UFC 157. To headline a combat event means that you're considered the biggest star, the biggest bout of the night. A historic fight was on the horizon, the future of women in the sport hanging in the balance, and no matter what Edmond was upset about this time, we had to train.

We started practice, and Edmond started kicking the fuck out of my leg. It was like the infamous Aldo vs. Faber title fight in WEC (WEC—World Extreme Cagefighting—would go on to be purchased and absorbed by the UFC), where Faber took thirty-one punishing kicks to the leg. That was the kind of fight that hurt to watch. Only this was sparring. I stood there and took it, accepting his passive-aggressive bullshit as he tried to punish me through training. My leg throbbed afterward, but from that moment on, I was acutely aware of my positioning, making sure that I was too far for someone to kick me or so close that even if they tried to kick me, there wasn't the space to build up enough momentum for it to hurt. In the moment, it felt like a valuable lesson, but a decade later, I ask myself, *Was that abuse?*

When I go down that road, the first words that pop into my mind are, "Can't argue with the results." But there's also that pause. A hesitation brought on by uncertainty. I don't know when it teeters from tough love to too tough, from acceptable to abuse. I know it played a key part in making me into such a badass ninja. But I also know it sucked.

Maybe I was drawn to that kind of coaching. Maybe that kind of coaching works, but at a price.

I watched a documentary on sumo wrestlers that explored how a number of the athletes died because the coaches and their methods are crazy. My first thought wasn't shock or disbelief or even horror, but *yeah, I can see that.*

The coach-athlete relationship hinges on a power imbalance within systems that not only enable but reward it. US gymnastics rose to dominance under Romanian coach Béla Károlyi, and it wasn't until recently—after decades—that his controlling coaching methods shifted from being praised to criticized. My entire competitive career I was led to believe this is just the way things are done. You have to choose: a hands-off coach who shows up on the day of a fight to corner and collect their paycheck or Béla Károlyi. Both Big Jim and Edmond loved to quote Russian athletic studies, revering infamous coaches known for abuse and results. But that Soviet-era method of being a controlling asshole is bullshit and people need to give that shit up.

Because if someone tried to pull that with my kid, I would kick their ass.

But instead we allow coaches to create environments where this behavior thrives. They build clubs and gyms where athletes are forced to vie for limited attention and time. Teammates compete against each other instead of supporting each other, fostering cultures of acceptance and silence that allow this kind of coaching to persist. In my lowest moments, I would look around the gym at people whom I considered my closest friends, people whom I would call to help me hide a body, hoping that for once someone might come to my defense, but no one would say anything.

I still waiver between, "That was really fucked up" and "But it worked." Sometimes, life is about reconciling how two things can be in conflict but still true. Of course, this reflection and analysis is only possible with years of experience and even more years of distance.

When I first met Edmond, no one was even willing to give an aspiring female MMA fighter a second look, let alone train me. I was appreciative to have finally found a decent coach. GFC took me in when I was a nobody. I'll never forget it.

Putting all of the bullshit aside, Edmond and I were the perfect fit as a fighter and a coach. Everything he had is what I needed. Everything he didn't have, I was already a master of. Running a small gym in the Valley with mostly Armenian fighters, Edmond wasn't necessarily the greatest, most in-demand boxing trainer on the planet, but his style of striking worked for me.

When it came to grappling and transitions, I could put everything together myself. But I have really upright posture as a judoka. I don't change levels like a wrestler. My knees are bad, so I can't really throw kicks or move backward. What I needed was amateur boxing, where you focus on distance, precision— not getting hit—and to learn knees and elbows. With Edmond's Muay Thai background, he taught me how to incorporate them in the judo/amateur boxing/knee-and-elbow-incorporating hybrid style I was trying to create.

As time went on and my status within the sport grew, so did my training circle. I worked with Renner and Ryron Gracie to learn their system because Gracie Jiu Jitsu is at the foundation of almost everyone in MMA's grappling.

After winning the Strikeforce title and putting women's MMA in the spotlight, I went to train with Nick and Nate Diaz. The Diaz brothers are two incredibly talented UFC fighters who shared my love for both training hard and smoking a shit ton of weed. Their place in Stockton, a five-hour drive north of LA, could not have been any more different from Edmond's. The Diaz method is the furthest thing from Eastern European–inspired coaching.

Every morning, we'd wake up, smoke a bowl, and just hang around the house until Nick would randomly say, "OK, I'm gonna go train now." Off we'd go. Afterward, we'd come back, smoke more, and I'd eat chocolate out of the Easter basket his mom had bought me to make me feel more at home since I was there over the holiday. Then we'd train again. After, we'd either smoke weed and go to bed or smoke weed, go out to the bars, smoke more weed, then go to bed.

It was a blast, although not sustainable for me. One day, halfway through practice, I looked down to see that I'd been grappling with my Lululemon workout shirt inside out, the built-in bra flapping around. I was so high that I hadn't noticed. For an hour.

Even when I came down—both figuratively from the massive amount of marijuana consumed and literally back home to LA—the trip was a transformative experience. The Diaz brothers were known for striking, and while there, I was working with their boxing coach Richard Perez. I was given the opportunity to have more freedom and creativity in my striking style. To tie the end of every combination to the beginning of the next to create a never-ending flow of strikes.

I returned to the gym excited about expanding my skills. I had struggled with combinations, where you string together a series of punches. I could manage a sequence of three, maybe four, but after I got back from Stockton, it was like I could punch with power and balance with every step I took. I didn't need anyone to call the combinations for me, I was finally flowing—bam, bam, bam, bam, bam, bam BAM, bam, bambambam, bam bam bam BAM—and so on.

Edmond did not share my enthusiasm. I needed to be perfect, and Edmond demanded perfection. That's part of why we were such a great fit, even if we spent far too much time arguing and debating the right way to achieve that.

"This is sloppy," he said, holding mitts for me shortly after I got back.

"This is gonna have to go."

"Not good."

"Fucking awful."

No matter what I did, it wasn't good enough.

"Fine," I said, exasperated, and aware that perhaps after two weeks fueled by weed and chocolate I wasn't in peak physical condition. "Fine tune me then, that's your job."

It was clear he was insecure that I had been training elsewhere. It would only get worse. Any time I trained with anyone else or anywhere else, he would tell me I was regressing. Whatever I thought had improved Edmond told me was "shit" and that now we had to work harder than ever before.

But it was that relentless quest for perfection that pushed me. He was demanding in the ways that a trainer needs to be. He would see the tiniest details. Areas where I was not the absolute best were dissected and debated. When you're trying to learn from wins, like I was, instead of losses, you *need* that attention to detail. While I loved training with the Diaz brothers, I couldn't go out there in the cage and bang it out like they could. I didn't have the hardware for it.

No one could get down to the tiniest details and speak my language to make me understand those striking nuances the way Edmond could. Our relationship wasn't perfect, but as my ever-climbing undefeated streak could attest, the outcomes were.

I found I was reciting my mother's momisms to myself.

"If it ain't broke, don't fix it."

"If it works, then it's right."

"Dance with the one that brung ya."

By the time I fought Holly Holm, there wasn't a gym out there that didn't want me. And though it was never spoken, Edmond's insecurity had started to fester. His value became attached to me. He became anxious about me not paying attention to him, so he created conflict. That way I had to focus on him.

But I never even thought about change. Even though having Edmond as my coach was draining and exhausting and a lot of bullshit, things were working. And how the hell would I even have time to change camps?

From the day I signed with the UFC, there was never a moment where I was able to sit down and address what I personally needed to work on next as a fighter. A year after my first Strikeforce win and five months after Dana told me he was adding women to the UFC, I stepped into the Octagon and defeated Liz Carmouche by armbar at four minutes and forty-nine seconds into my—and women's—debut in the UFC (dislocating my jaw again in the process—thanks, little Jimmy!), claiming the title just before the end of the first round.

Not only was the fight exciting, but as importantly in a sport that's also a business, my fight sold. Dana was happy. My agent was ecstatic. Everyone around me was thrilled at what I had achieved. Everyone it seemed except for Edmond.

That night after my win in front of over 15,000 people at the Honda Center in Anaheim, I went back to the hotel and slipped away from the chaos to my then-boyfriend's room. I was exhausted post-fight with my mouth all cut up from Carmouche's cross-face nearly imploding my skull. I lay down on the bed and fell asleep. An hour later, I walked back into my room. Edmond was waiting in the living room of my suite. Marina was sleeping on the couch.

"Where were you?" he shouted.

I was confused.

"We didn't know where you were!" He was pissed. "You go and don't tell anyone where you are. It's dangerous. You leave your best friend. Marina was worried for you."

Marina, who was staying in my room with me, groggily shook her head behind him, raising her eyebrows as if to say, "Don't bring me into this. I'm fine."

"We couldn't find you, and we thought that you died," Edmond said.

"You thought I died?" I asked, incredulous. I couldn't help but laugh.

"How can you just disappear without telling us?" Edmond wasn't backing down. "Something could have happened to you. All these people. It's not safe."

"I just won the fucking UFC championship," I said. "Now I'm arguing with you about safety. I can obviously keep myself safe. I can fucking beat people up."

After six weeks of preparation, I had been looking forward to letting my guard down. To step outside of fight mode and catch my breath. But now, arguing with Edmond, he was keeping me on reactive defense mode. Why, on the biggest night of my career, was he raining on my parade with this bullshit?

There's a lot of emotions after a fight, I rationalized. *I'll deal with it later when things calm down a bit.*

In the narrated version of my life, it's at this point that the Morgan Freeman voice would read, "But things would not be calming down."

For almost half a decade, I was going from fight to fight. I would walk out of a win and be told, "You got to fight again." I never had time to work on myself. To recover. The only thing I had time to spend on learning was how to fight the person I was fighting next. It's the kind of thing that you can't understand unless you've lived it.

I was constantly bruised, banged up, and sore. Always completely mentally and physically exhausted. Arguing with Edmond was a contributing factor, and it felt like maybe that was designed as a feature, not a bug. But I was too depleted to even think about wading into the logistical and perceptual clusterfuck that changing camps would bring.

The issue with Edmond was when it was good, it was great. It just so happened that the times when it wasn't good seemed to come at the worst possible moment. If we were at a point where it would be convenient for me to jump ship, everything was fantastic.

"Ronda, let's go out," Edmond would say. "Let's get you hookah."

"We'll throw you a party and have a barbecue."

He and his team of coaches would take me to the Russian spa with the steam rooms where they hit you with branches. (If you haven't experienced that, it's way more relaxing and way less weird than it sounds.) They'd get all my favorite foods, like borscht and watermelon with feta cheese. We'd drink Russian beer. They would peel me the fish jerky that I loved so much. They knew all the little things that would make me happy.

Once we were in training camp, when it would take the end of the fucking world to change camps, everything would shift. Two weeks before a fight, it was arguing nonstop about nothing. He'd be picking a fight with me sometimes even in the days leading up to the match. I'd be up until after midnight, trying to defend and explain myself.

Every coach I ever had was kind of an asshole. I had come to accept that. They weren't supposed to be your friends; they were supposed to tell you what you needed to hear and do whatever necessary to help you prepare for fighting a person with your bare hands. Fights in combat sports are rough. Training for them is tough. But the further I get away from competing, the more I've started to see just how terrible of a standard that is, and how so much of what we find acceptable in the name of coaching is unacceptable.

The more successful I became, the more controlling Edmond became. Signing with the UFC not only took my career to the next level, but also Edmond's demands. He wanted to know where I was and what I was doing at all times. He said this was about my well-being as a fighter. He started to FaceTime me randomly. I pushed back, saying it was an invasion of my privacy. But instead of that resolving the issue, it just led to us constantly arguing about it. It was, he assured me, so he wouldn't worry. I reluctantly offered a compromise that if I was busy, I would answer the phone and say,

"I'm busy, I'll call you later." His rationale seemed rational at the time, but in retrospect, it was over the line. It was a line he was constantly testing, and I was constantly on the defensive trying to push him back.

I could see his insecurity. He worried about someone getting in my ear, convincing me I could do better, that I didn't need him. To prevent that, he did everything possible to monopolize my time. Soon, every training session was followed by getting a meal. I had learned there was a lower probability of him starting an argument about nothing if we already had plans to go somewhere together after practice. Plus, I would tell myself, I had to eat anyway.

I'm spending too much energy arguing with my coach, I thought, realizing the constant bickering was more draining than workouts themselves. But, unlike at the Pedros, where it was their way or the highway, with Edmond I felt like I had a voice. I could argue, press my point, and sometimes, even get my way in the end. When you have come up through a dysfunctional system, you don't realize "less dysfunctional" is still dysfunctional. Driving to practice each morning in my beat-up Honda Accord, I'd try to think of ways to diffuse arguments. I never knew what would start one, but I knew once Edmond got going it would never end. Whatever I said to defend myself would lead to another perceived offense, then another. The stress of setting him off put me on edge constantly. I was dodging punches in the ring and Edmond's emotional land mines outside of it.

I thought back to my days with Big Jim and my carefully crafted replies to avoid his wrath. How the way to win the Pedros over had been based on how much you kissed their ass more than how well you did. I found myself adopting that approach with Edmond. If I could constantly butter him up and make sure that he was in a great mood, I could probably avoid an argument. If I could avoid an argument, we could just focus on the training.

———

The Carmouche fight generated headlines because it was historic. But there's only one first. The future of my career—and women in the UFC—balanced on my next fight.

The morning after going one round with Liz Carmouche and a round with Edmond, Dana mentioned tying my next fight to the upcoming season of *The Ultimate Fighter*. TUF is a reality competition where participants—coached by current UFC fighters—compete for a shot at a UFC contract. After the series finale airs, the two coaches fight each other. This was the first time the show would have female contenders. It would play, Dana explained, a major role in shaping the future of the UFC's women's division.

"Of course," I told Dana. "Anything." I had meant what I said that night at Mr. Chow.

Last minute, Miesha Tate was swapped in for an injured Cat Zingano as my opposing coach. A change of plans that the producers decided to spring on me by sending a smirking Miesha through the door as cameras rolled. From the moment I arrived on set, it was clear the producers were on a mission to create drama beyond the competitive tension between the UFC hopefuls.

The responsibility of my team's career futures weighed on me. The unscripted-programming-let's-start-some-shit antics of the production crew and their delight in Miesha's willingness to indulge them grated on me. But it was the ongoing tension with Edmond that pushed me toward the brink.

I try to look back to the good times between Edmond and me, but there was no extended time where everything was going well. While I worked to hide our conflicts from the world, it wasn't like the rest of the team was unaware. That night, after Miesha and I had each selected four women and four men, I thought it would be a nice gesture to take my coaches to dinner at Morton's Steakhouse.

"First, we need to talk," Edmond said, after the camera crew had packed up for the night. He called together the entire coaching staff I had assembled: Marina, Manny, MMA fighter Andy Dermenjian from GFC, and former world wrestling champion Leo Frincu.

Edmond didn't like my attitude or my tone or I can't even remember the grievance because it was never actually about the interpreted slight. For almost an hour, he ripped into me. He told me how I knew nothing. That I was nothing. He threatened to leave.

I kept apologizing even though I didn't know what for. Everyone else stood there in awkward silence.

That night, I got back to my room and collapsed on the bed. What a fucking nightmare. My phone buzzed on the nightstand. It was a text from Leo, who had been my strength and conditioning coach since my amateur career.

"I can't stand here and watch you take this verbal abuse," he wrote. "I can't be a part of this anymore."

I typed out my reply. "Then why don't you fucking say something? Why are you sitting there silent when I'm getting my ass chewed out?" I deleted it before sending. I typed again, "I understand." I hit send.

The next day, Leo left the show.

With each day of filming, it became more unbearable. Every time a fighter was eliminated, was a punch to the gut. And that was the highlight.

During the day, I juggled Miesha and the producers' attempts to antagonize me. She'd walk by me and blow kisses. She accused me of standing too close to her coach/boyfriend, who had previously tweeted about knocking out my teeth. If he and I were the last two people on earth, the human race would die out. They constantly baited Edmond, which inevitably rolled downhill onto me.

After dealing with Miesha's bullshit as the cameras rolled, I dealt with Edmond's bullshit after the cameras were off. He ranted about the things I did wrong and how everything was my fault. He picked fights with anyone he could. He threatened to leave every single night. I pleaded with him to stay. I'd already had one coach leave (because of Edmond), having our only striking coach walk off would expose how dysfunctional my camp really was to the world, my upcoming opponent, and a bunch of producers who would love to see that drama play out. I felt trapped. But I couldn't leave my team of fighters whom I'd grown to love and feel responsible for. I couldn't disappoint Dana.

So I gritted my teeth, promoted the show I couldn't stand, and promoted the fight I couldn't wait to be past, on top of filming roles in two of the biggest action franchise films, *The Expendables 3* and *Furious 7,* all while training like a madwoman.

I submitted Miesha, again by armbar, but without the satisfaction of that ripping-a-chicken-leg-off-the-bird pop, as she tapped the second I locked her arm early in the third round. It was the first time in my MMA career that I had a fight go past the first round, and the only one to go three deep.

At the post-fight press conference, as I sat between two of the night's other winners, Dana made an announcement. Something he had asked me about a few weeks earlier.

"Rousey versus McMann, February," he told the reporters. My next fight would take place just eight weeks later. "That's the headliner."

"That's a fast turnaround," one of the reporters said.

Dana nodded. "She goes right back into camp."

"Your thoughts on that, Ronda?" the reporter asked.

"I've taken such a long time off that I feel like I want to fight again soon," I said. "I don't want to sit on the shelf."

It was what I felt like I was supposed to say, an answer that wouldn't portray weakness. But the truth was I was beyond exhausted.

When you're the champion, your sole job is to defend your title. My win over Miesha had upped my pro record to 8-0. I intended to someday leave the sport unquestionably undefeated. And when that day came, I didn't want to walk away like undefeated boxer Floyd Mayweather, who spent a lot of time talking about how great he was but was defined by only picking opponents at their weakest during the legacy-making years of his career. I believed it was my duty as champion to take on all comers, whether challenged by your opponent or promoter.

When I think of a true championship reign, it calls to mind this documentary I watched on polar bears. It talked about how a male polar bear will find a female and guard her for the entire breeding season. In the footage at the beginning of the season, he is shown fresh, strong, white as snow. Then, it cut to the end of the season. The male was now stained red and brown from fresh and old blood, both his own and that of his many challengers. He is skinny, bleeding, limping, but still the champion. There's no taking time off to recover from the last fight, the champion *defends,* meaning you wait to be challenged. The challengers don't wait for you. The contender's luxury is to come in fresh, to pick and choose the best times to fight, while the champ is worn and bloody. As the first and only champion in my division since its UFC inception, the contender's luxury was an advantage I never had.

A lot of people run from their limits. If you're the champion, you're supposed to be chasing your limits with a vengeance.

I would spend my entire UFC career chasing those limits.

I beat my next challenger, undefeated Olympic wrestling silver medalist Sara McMann, in just over a minute. Five months later, in July, I was back in the cage, delivering a blink-and-you'll-miss-it sixteen-second knockout to Alexis Davis. That next February (delayed because she got injured again), I topped that by submitting Cat Zingano in fourteen seconds in our overdue title fight.

At that point I was such a lopsided favorite that I had to fight to sell my opponent in order to get people to buy in. I was dominating almost to my detriment. The feeling for a lot of fight fans was trending toward "Ronda's gonna win in a couple seconds. I don't need to spend $60 to buy a fight that will fit in an Instagram clip."

To sell the event, I had to find a way to handicap myself. To put myself at a disadvantage against a girl who did not otherwise stand a chance. I had to work to get people to think, *This could be the time she loses.* I had to promote my opponent in a way that didn't portray weakness. And all the while, I had to hide the fact that if I got hit, I was probably fucked. Not even Dana knew that.

After the Zingano fight, I went straight into my book tour, hitting ten cities in three weeks. Somewhere along the way, I got a cold that I just couldn't shake. When I got home, I was coughing up blood. My mom dragged me to urgent care, and I was too exhausted to protest.

"You have pneumonia," the doctor said, showing me my chest X-ray. I stared at it, my only thought being that nothing could impact my upcoming training camp ahead of my fight.

I'd already been scheduled to defend my title against Bethe Correia in her home country, the UFC-crazy Brazil.

———

We were just over a month out from the Bethe Correia fight. It was Tuesday, the third week of camp. Camp was, as fight camp always is, grueling. I felt drained, both physically and emotionally. My younger sister, Julia, had come to the gym with me. Despite always being surrounded by coaches and training partners, training camp could feel lonely. Having her was a diversion, but not a distraction. Plus, she was a buffer. Edmond was on his best behavior when she was around.

As a fighter, all of your focus has to be on beating your opponent. As I came up in MMA and had the resources to do so, I outsourced everything that distracted from that singular focus. Meals, I got a nutritionist to handle. I booked a hotel room near the gym during the week where I could nap between practices and avoid driving the gauntlet of LA traffic. And when I stepped into the gym, I always deferred to Edmond, especially in camp.

People refer to the pinnacle of greatness in your career as reaching the top of the mountain. What they rarely tell is how slippery of a slope it is, how easy it is to fall if you let your attention drift for just a moment. Even if you know you are the best in the world, you must be aware that someone is out there trying to take that away from you.

You need to have someone who will be the person to tell you to get your ass up and train even when you don't feel like it. To do the drills you don't like doing. And then to do them again. In the gym, Edmond was my someone. He would say do it, and I did. That was our agreement.

That Tuesday we were in the ring, sparring. Julia sat against the wall across the way, just out of earshot, scrolling on her phone.

Edmond told me I couldn't be dating Travis. I didn't even try to argue. I just didn't agree. Edmond, as he always did, kept pushing. This time, I just refused to give.

My relationship with Edmond had never been romantic, but since the start of my MMA training, before it was even a career, Edmond had been the most important male figure in my life. Now we had reached a place where my role in his life was intrinsically tied to how other people viewed and respected him, and the control that he had over me was slipping away. He knew he couldn't keep me captive arguing for hours or call at all hours without Travis having something to say about it. Travis wasn't just another guy I saw when away from the gym. Travis was a 245-pound symbol to Edmond that his time at the reins was up.

We were supposed to be sparring, fighting where the goal is to work on your technique, not injure your partner. But his hits got harder. And harder. They weren't the kind of slaps you throw when you're trying to train someone. They were the kind you throw when you want to hurt them. He was barehanded. I was wearing heavily padded training gloves and swung back.

"Defense," Edmond barked. "Only defense. You're not throwing punches." I was just supposed to take them. I took a deep breath, then slap after slap. The gym had grown quiet. Sparring centers around standing face-to-face with another person and willingly letting them throw punches at you. So when does it become abuse? If you can't even figure out where the line is, it's hard to know if it's being crossed.

I could see other fighters exchange awkward looks, not sure what to do. Julia was looking up from her phone now, eyes wide. Edmond slapped me again. And again.

"No, no, no," he shouted. "Again."

He slapped me in the face, the ferocity of the hit catching me by surprise. Then again. And again. With each blow, I could feel where the bruises would soon appear. As I had been doing with Edmond since the day I first showed up at his gym, I stood there, knowing my resolve would outlast his.

I watched as Julia's expression changed from shock to concern to sadness. But it was more than just sadness. It was helplessness. I knew if I had been the one watching her in that ring, I would have jumped through the ropes and pounded him until someone pulled me off. Everyone else in the gym, even the men that I called my teammates, looked on. No one said anything. They didn't know where the line was either.

Training ended, but the relentless tirade didn't. Edmond followed me into the locker room. Inside, away from the eyes of the gym, but certainly still within earshot, Edmond started yelling. I wasn't supposed to be dating Travis. He had just left his fucking wife, what, two days ago? They were still married. Did I realize how bad that looked for me? Travis was treating me like a rebound, he was disrespecting everyone at the gym. I wasn't focused. I wasn't training hard enough. Was I listening? I wasn't leaving there until we got this resolved.

That is how I found myself, sitting on the floor of the Glendale Fight Club locker room, six hours into what was supposed to be a two-hour practice. I was beyond drained, I was empty. I couldn't take it anymore.

"This is fucking out of hand," I finally said, rising to my feet. "I understand you're trying to watch out for me. But you're not my parent. I'm not your child. I'm a grown woman. Now, get the fuck out of my way."

There are moments in life where you make decisions understanding that, for better or worse, you will pass a point of no return.

As I sat there crying on the GFC locker room floor, I broke. I was tired. I was sore. I was incapable of continuing like this.

Changing camps was not an option. Finding a gym that's a right fit takes months in even the best scenario. And even *if* you find one quickly, it takes time to find that rhythm and for you to get to a place where they know what you need. The one thing that I did not have was time. I was already mid–training camp, and I wasn't going to pull out of a fight on Dana, especially one I asked for. I also didn't want to leave home or my family again. I had spent my whole life in places I didn't want to live for judo, and I didn't want to get trapped in another Buffalo Grove, Illinois, or Methuen, Massachusetts. Not to mention the chaos a move that dramatic would bring in its wake. I already had paparazzi camped outside the gym, my house, the dog park. Anywhere I went, those fuckers were lying in wait. Had I even attempted to look elsewhere, I'd never escape the speculation of "There's something wrong with her camp." My opponents would see a crack, sense a weakness. Edmond knew all this and took full advantage of it.

But that wasn't what I viewed to be the biggest risk. Despite the fact that my face was plastered everywhere in the mainstream, within the fight world my mystery was a big advantage. My fights were so brief that people didn't even have a chance to analyze what I was capable of. Very little video of me grappling or training existed. On purpose. There was so much more that I could do that people never saw in my fights. That's why I was able to drop Sara McMann with a liver shot, then turn around and knock out Alexis Davis with an overhand right. As a fighter, I didn't want anyone to know the extent of my abilities. Shopping different gyms ran the risk of unraveling my mystery—or perhaps even worse, getting rocked in training and revealing my biggest secret of all.

On my way home from Glendale, I made a call that I knew was the equivalent to pushing the red nuclear launch button, but there was nothing else I could think to do.

I called my mom. I told her everything. I told her I needed to stage an intervention. My only experience participating in an intervention had been with a heroin-abusing ex-boyfriend who went on to steal my car and leave me with his dog to score drugs, so I was certainly not an expert.

My mother was never a fan of Edmond. For the first four months that I trained at GFC, Edmond refused to even glance my way. I saw it as paying my dues. My mother saw it as disrespectful to me as an Olympic medalist. Edmond had admitted that he didn't see a value in training female fighters until he met me, and I viewed that as a culturally embedded Armenian norm that I needed to upend. My mom viewed it as sexist bullshit. We were likely both right.

She thought Edmond was arrogant. The oversized mural in the gym seemingly putting himself on the same level as Muhammad Ali certainly didn't contradict that perception.

My mom had never openly told me that I should change gyms, but she encouraged my training at other places with an enthusiasm that said as much.

Beyond her disdain for Edmond, here's what you need to know about my mother: My mom is intense. As a competitor, she said that she would rip her opponent's heart out and eat it in front of the referee if that's what it took to win. She once grabbed an international judo referee by the tie and choked him unconscious on the mat because he made a sexist comment. Her advice to her children in going off to college was, "If you're in a bar fight, grab the nearest stool and use it as a weapon."

If my mother likes you, she likes you. When Mom doesn't like you, she doesn't bother with the formalities. She doesn't fake smile. She doesn't make small talk. She cuts you down with a look that says if it were legal, she'd cut you with a sharp object too.

But nothing compares to the seething rage and mafiaesque desire for revenge that comes from her even perceiving that you have crossed one of her children. She will never forget. She will never forgive. And you will spend the rest of your life looking over your shoulder, wondering if you will end up buried in a shallow grave somewhere in the desert.

That's probably why when Edmond arrived at my mom's house that evening, he brought along Big Dave from the gym. Two bodies would be harder to hide, especially one as big as Dave's.

The Edmond who walked into the house that evening was a shell of the screaming figure from the locker room. His shoulders were slumped, his head hung low. He spoke in almost a whisper, unable to make eye contact. My mom never took her glare off him. He walked down the front hall, through the living room, which opened into the kitchen, and sat down in a black wooden chair. The way he was positioned with his hands on the kitchen table, lit overhead from the hanging lamp, was reminiscent of a police interrogation.

My mom sat down to Edmond's left. To his right, positioned along the L-shaped couch, was the rest of my hastily assembled in a small council: Marina to back me up when Edmond inevitably tried to gaslight me, my sister Maria to make sure my mom didn't actually commit murder, and my massage therapist Diana, to whom had I broken down sobbing during my appointment earlier in the evening. I wanted Edmond to understand that he was alone. To feel what it felt like to be trapped in a room where no one would come to his defense.

Edmond tried to start, "Ronda, I'm so sorry—"

"No," I cut him off. "Shut up. I'm going to talk, and you're going to listen."

Edmond nodded.

"This ends now. You sat there for hours—fucking hours—screaming at me over who I'm dating. It's none of your fucking business."

"It wasn't that," Edmond started to say.

"I'm still fucking talking!" I shouted. "You stood there punching me, trying to hurt me because you were angry at me! Hitting and hitting me, not letting me fight back, in front of my little sister! How does that make me better?! You had someone literally blocking the door, physically preventing me from leaving—for hours! I'm in fucking training camp!"

I was screaming at the top of my lungs. Edmond kept looking down at his hands.

"Today got out of hand," he whispered.

"And it's not just about today," I said. "It's every day. Always something. I'm supposed to be training for a fight, not fighting with my coach. I am the fucking UFC champion. Fucking quit wasting my time and train me."

"What can I do, Ronda?" Edmond asked. "Anything. I'll do it."

"I want it in writing," I said.

My mom produced a pen and paper, and I dictated the terms to Edmond. Our interaction was to be strictly professional. He was not to call me outside of training. He was not to discuss anything outside of the scope of training with me, including my dating life. He was not to be alone in my presence at all. By the end, it was almost a full page front and back, and the boundaries that for so long had been blurred were clearly defined, scribbled out in his poor penmanship.

"Now, sign it," I said.

He signed it and stood up to leave.

"I swear to you, Ronda, I'm sorry."

He waited for me to accept his apology. To show that things were going to be OK. I said nothing.

My mom took the paper and folded it up. She walked into her office, filing it in the black three-drawer filing cabinet where she keeps records on her enemies.

"This is fucked up," she said.

I was a month out from my next fight.

"I know," I said. "But just let me get through this fight, and then I'll deal with it."

"I'll give you through this fight," my mom said.

The next day, I went back to the gym. My mom came and sat by the side of the mat, making sure she was in Edmond's sight line. It was tense and awkward, but Edmond and I got in the ring. We didn't address what had happened, we just trained.

As camp progressed, things got better. Edmond trained me with the same ferocity that had drawn me to him as a coach, but without the bullshit that had pushed me to the brink. When we were on, we could communicate to each other with a look, a motion, a word. It felt like we were making magic together, like we were one mind. *This* is what our fighter/coach relationship always should have been. He felt more like a dear friend than a feared dictator. The intervention had actually intervened.

And not since I had again destroyed Miesha Tate in our rematch had I wanted to beat someone to a pulp as much as I did Bethe Correia.

In the two years since *The Ultimate Fighter*, two of the women I had picked for my team had become two of my best friends. Shayna Baszler had been my first pick. Bottom heavy with shoulder-length jet-black hair, Shayna had the look of a fourteen-year-old but the laugh of an old man. She moved like a grappler of a much different lineage than mine and could throw down like a brawler. She was technical on the ground and all heart on her feet. With unmistakable charisma about her, Shayna was the one person you'd be sure to notice and remember in a room full of bitches trying to act tough.

Jessamyn Duke had the frame of a supermodel laced with sinewy muscle and a strong Kentucky accent that gave "girl next door" vibes. We bonded over our love of gaming and science fiction/fantasy books. The two of them along with Marina and me lived together in an early twentieth-century three-story house I rented just off the Venice Boardwalk. Constantly together, fans had started calling us the Four Horsewomen, a throwback to a legendary stable (team) in professional wrestling. We'd embraced the moniker and the Horsemen's four-finger hand sign.

In Bethe's second UFC fight, she beat Jessamyn by unanimous decision. Afterward, she held up her four-fingers, then pulled one down, sending a message that she was coming for us. Shayna was livid and demanded a fight with Bethe. When the ref declared Bethe the winner by TKO, she held up her four fingers, then dropped to two as if to say, "Two down."

I met up with Dana and demanded her next fight. Not only that, but I wanted to beat her in Brazil, make her suffer the embarrassment of her own people turning on her in her home country.

It was a perfect fight for me to promote. Not only had she come for me, but her name is pronounced "Betch" which made for such easy wordplay. That was the only thing that came easy.

The weeks of juggling training camp with intercontinental promotion were grueling.

Why do I keep doing this to myself? I'd ask myself during the thralls of fight camp. When I'd lie awake, heart pounding, envisioning every possible way the fight could go. When I was sitting on planes to, from, and around Brazil doing an insane amount of press and promotion while my opponent was resting at home. Every time I woke up struggling to unlock my knee. Every time I saw stars during training. *Why do I keep doing this to myself?*

When I touched down in Rio for fight week, I had to push all those thoughts aside. The only thing that mattered was stepping into the cage in top physical form ready to fight.

While my mind felt at times as if it was working against me, approaching the final days in the lead-up to the fight, my body had never felt better.

There was an unforgettable sense of inhabiting the absolute greatest athletic form I could possibly achieve. I was faster, sharper, stronger, more explosive, more innovative, more anything than any fighter has ever been. On the mat, it was as if I could see every movement in slow motion when the rest of the world could only see it at normal speed.

Even my weight cut was going well.

The only thing keeping me from declaring pre-fight perfection was that I missed Travis. The fight hotel was tucked away on a small, relatively secluded stretch of beachfront. There was only one spot in my room that had enough service to FaceTime, so I sat in that spot with my arm in one position talking hours every night before the fight. It actually got to the point that my right shoulder was sore from holding the phone. I dubbed the ailment "FaceTime arm" and promised Travis I'd deliver a knockout with it.

I was falling deeply in love. I was in the best shape ever. Edmond was on his best behavior. I felt ready to kill a bitch with my bare hands. It was as if this is what I was born to do.

At the weigh-ins, Bethe screamed in my face as I stood, unflinching, staring daggers, and, in my mind, promising her pain.

The next night, keeping my word to Travis, I knocked her out in thirty-four seconds.

Walking out of HSBC Arena—the same venue where eight years prior I left the World Judo Championships with a silver medal instead of gold like my mother—I was wrapped in the arms of my family, being cheered by a country that wasn't mine. I handed out high fives to fans with tears in their eyes.

This is why I do this, I thought.

My fight game was never tighter. More important, Edmond and I had turned a corner.

I felt like I had dodged a bullet. What I didn't realize is that I had lit the fuse of a cannon.

5

I came back from Rio looking forward to the future. Despite being held in August (one of the worst times of year for audiences) and broadcasting in the US in the middle of the night, the fight sold more than any other pay-per-view that year, approaching 1 million buys and exceeding my previous numbers by 50 percent. It outperformed Connor McGregor vs. Nate Diaz's July 4th weekend bout, held during the UFC's heavily publicized Fight Week, without a fraction of the promotion machine behind it.

I was planning to request a break following the Correia fight. I didn't need forever, all I wanted was to not have to turn right around and go back into camp. When the UFC proposed that Holly Holm and I would face off after the New Year, it meant I would have a full three months between fights. For anyone else, that'd be a concerningly quick turnaround, but for me it was the respite I desperately needed.

My mom and all three of my sisters had come to Brazil for the fight. Afterward, we stayed and tried to play tourists. However, any effort to stay under the radar in Rio was a losing battle. We visited the 125-foot Christ the Redeemer statue that looks out over the city, taking the obligatory outstretched-arms photos. But our visit was cut short by my security team quickly ushering us into the trolley down the mountain to quell the growing mob of hundreds of people that amassed once word of my being there spread. Attending a professional soccer game in Rio's Maracanã Stadium, we were rushed from our seats to a private box because my presence was creating too much of a scene. We admired the wavy patterned sidewalks of Copacabana Beach and went in search of Brazil's best acai bowls, doing our best to ignore the paparazzi zipping in and out of traffic on scooters.

"If we run them over, it's their fault," my bodyguard Luis said with a shrug.

We were heading down to dinner at the hotel and had just turned the hall corner, when there was rustling and suddenly a blur of motion.

"Ronda!" a small middle-aged woman from housekeeping screamed, popping out from behind the small potted tree.

"Jesus Christ!" I shouted, throwing up my hands as if ready to fight, instinctively pushing my family behind me. My mom tensed, ready to throw down with me.

"Selfie?" she asked sheepishly.

I looked around the empty hallway.

"OK," I said.

Suddenly, three other hotel staff members spilled out from a tiny broom closet, holding out phones.

"Selfie." "Selfie." "Selfie."

After that, we stuck to ordering large amounts of room service and eating on the balcony overlooking the Atlantic to the sound of the waves and occasional shouts of fans gathered several stories below who had stationed themselves outside the lobby doors day and night. Despite it all, I enjoyed the leisure. I couldn't remember the last time I'd taken days off and not felt overwhelming guilt.

Back home, after the fight, Edmond accepted the power shift between him and me as a condition of going forward. The same went when it came to respecting my relationship with Travis, whom Edmond and the guys at the gym really did love. But it was still slightly awkward.

When we officially came out as a couple at the gym after coming back from Brazil, a couple of guys were critical.

"I hope you're ready to get your ass kicked," they told him.

"I'll show up and get my ass kicked by fifty of you every day just to look at her face for a minute," Travis said. I could tell he was staying in the gym after that just to keep an eye on me.

Outside perception had become an obsession of Edmond's over time, though he wouldn't admit it. As Edmond saw it, our relationship had the makings of a PR disaster on the horizon. His concerns weren't unfounded. Days before I left for Rio, Travis's soon-to-be ex-wife accused him of domestic abuse, opting to try it in the court of public opinion via Instagram. He had my support. Even his first ex-wife, with whom there was no love lost, came to his defense.

"If you want to end this now, I completely understand," Travis said. "I won't hold it against you."

The UFC had suspended him pending investigation. Travis was certain he would be vindicated, but the media, public opinion and even people he had once considered friends turned on him assuming the worst. He was giving me an out from the inevitable controversy this would bring, especially given the clickbait boost any headline with my name would bring.

But now, a few weeks after my fight in Brazil, the final report showed there was no proof for the accusations. That same day, the UFC announced that the date for my next fight against Holly Holm was being moved up by six weeks. It would be my seventh UFC title fight since I'd joined just over two-and-a-half years ago. But I was their goose that laid the golden eggs, and they couldn't stop pressuring me to produce more.

Dana had called me just days earlier.

"Hey babe, I need your help." Somewhere around the time he became a billionaire, Dana picked up the Hollywood "babe" vernacular.

"Yes is the answer," I said without even knowing the ask.

"I fucking love you," he said, laughing. "Lawler is out. He hurt his fucking hand or his thumb, some shit like that. Anyway, he's out so the fight with Condit is postponed. I need you to fight Holly Holm in Melbourne in November. It's going to be the biggest fucking crowd in the history of UFC. No one can fill it but you."

While media or movies or maybe the way it's typically done might lead you to believe that these kinds of things are brokered through agents, Dana and I always had a direct line of communication. There was no buffer, and as I saw it, no way to say no.

I had promised Dana to fight whenever, wherever. I meant that as if it were a blood oath, Knights of the Round Table (except for the one who slept with King Arthur's wife)–level loyalty. But that was only part of it.

I was pursuing perfection. And with every win, the expectations of what perfection meant became harder to achieve. It wasn't enough to be undefeated. It wasn't enough to deliver faster wins in faster turnarounds than anyone ever had before. It meant overcoming anything that could possibly go wrong. It meant proving I was capable of winning even under the worst, most impossible circumstances.

It wasn't just that I couldn't say no to Dana. It was that—to me—saying, "No, I need to rest" was like saying, "No, I can't do it." It would mean admitting to myself I had a limit, and to be—and believe you are—the best in the world you just can't think like that.

"November? Like in two months?" I asked.

"Yeah, second weekend in November," Dana said.

I groaned inwardly. I desperately needed this break. *Guess training camp starts tomorrow,* I thought.

"Dana, I promised that if you gave me this opportunity, I'd be the one that steps up when these other guys don't. Move it to November."

"Great!" Dana said. "We'll get started on promoting it."

"Fuck," I sighed as I hung up the phone from Dana. For the first time since my MMA career started, I didn't feel raring to fight. I just felt tired.

As a fighter, you have to have tunnel vision. You can think about nothing but the moment that you step into the cage. You learn to ignore everything. Some of it is irrelevant noise: the media hype, the trolls on social media. Some of it is useful information: pain signals your body sends you, symptoms of exhaustion, signs from the universe.

In the weeks leading up to the Holm fight, the stress was starting to express itself in weird ways. I've always had trouble with intrusive thoughts, like if you say, "Try not to think of a blue duck," I will keep thinking of a blue duck constantly to remind myself not to think of the blue duck. The harder I tried to push a thought out, the more I'd be consumed by it. Only it wasn't blue ducks, it was self-destructive thoughts. I was living a bucket-list life, and yet, I constantly found myself thinking about dwelling on horrible things that happened years before or ways that everything I had worked for could all be taken away—and then I just couldn't stop thinking of them. Outside I exuded confidence, but inside I constantly battled these fears.

As a young athlete, I had turned to superstition. My first major senior tournament was the US Open—and I was determined to shock the American judo scene by winning the whole damn thing. I should have believed I was capable based on skill alone, but I didn't know if that—if I—was good enough. I thought I needed luck on my side. So I packed a lucky shirt, a lucky pair of socks, a lucky rock, a lucky belt, a lucky pair of gi pants, talismans that I thought would give me an edge.

I lost in the finals.

The next tournament—the Rendezvous in Montreal, Canada—everything that could go wrong went wrong. It was one of those days where, to the surprise of no one who knew me, I lost my gi pants, my undershirt, and the belt that I borrowed from someone else a month ago after losing my previous belt. (I am many things, but well-organized is not one of them.) Yet, without my luck tokens, I ended up crushing everyone in the tournament. I came away with the No. 1 national senior ranking for the first time in my life and vowed to stay away from keeping or doing things for "luck."

But, as years passed, I started to find myself falling back into my old ways. By the time I was on top in the UFC, I had my "lucky" battle boots. Cheap, faux-suede boots that were falling apart but that I had worn for every professional title win. I had my little ritual for when I entered the cage: Stomp my left foot twice. Then my right. Jump and stomp both. Walk to my corner. Shake my arms. Slap my right shoulder, then my left, then my thighs. Touch the ground. Bounce from foot to foot. Squat and pop back up. Stomp my feet once more. Stop. If it felt good, I knew the fight would go great. If it felt slightly off, it became one more thing I'd had to overcome. One more "what if" in the back of my mind to combat.

These little superstitious tics were my way of feeling like I had control of a future that scared the shit out of me. Much later, I would come to realize that my preoccupation with superstition was only providing opportunities for me to dwell on things that could possibly go wrong and how I could have prevented them—but we're not yet at the "much later" part of the book. I didn't have the mental bandwidth to think that reflectively. I was so exhausted that if I printed an entire book just repeating the words "beyond exhausted," that wouldn't begin to convey how tired I was.

One day, in the lead-up to the Holm fight, my hairdresser Abe innocently mentioned that an itchy left palm is bad luck. One day his left palm was itchy, and all these bad things had happened to him. After that, my left palm itched incessantly, accompanied by a feeling of foreboding.

I started making signs of the cross discreetly with my thumb anytime I had an intrusive thought or itchy palm or otherwise self-interpreted sign that something negative was going to happen. It got to a point where I was making hundreds of little thumb crosses a day. I lived in a constant state of dread I couldn't shake myself out of and was too embarrassed to mention.

I'm the baddest bitch on the planet, why is an itchy palm fucking me up so much? I'd ask myself, but I didn't have an answer.

I started burning incense in the gym. I lit candles at the church down the street. I tried to wear bright colors to bring up my mood. But nothing stopped the increasingly consuming feeling of impending doom. It was as if I was running on a receded beach, constantly looking behind me for the tsunami that would overtake me.

"Just get through it," I told myself, part pep talk, part reassurance. "Just get to the fucking ring and do your job, so you can go home and get some fucking rest."

It was the first time I was looking forward to the fight just being over. But that didn't matter, I had to be "the best on my worst day."

It was a philosophy I had learned from my mom. My mom said that on any given day there were a number of elite athletes capable of winning. The differentiating factor between *good* and *undeniably great* was the ability to be the best in the world on your worst day. You have to train so hard that your worst is better than anyone else's best. The Olympics only come around every four years; you can't guarantee it will land on a good day.

It became a mantra that I repeated to myself in the moments when I wanted to give up, when anxiety and doubt crept in: "You gotta be the best on your worst day."

Little did I know this constant mantra was convincing me the worst day was coming.

———

Training for a fight in Australia was one thing. Promoting a fight in Australia was another completely. I had proved capable of drawing a live international crowd in Brazil, but having an opponent from that country had helped, even if the fans had come with the hopes of seeing me beat her. We weren't just talking about filling an arena's worth of spectators in Melbourne; Etihad Stadium—capable of holding 56,000 fans—had more seats than the UFC had ever filled.

If selling the most in-person tickets in the history of the UFC wasn't tough enough, we needed that record for a fight that was taking place on a Sunday morning so that it could sync up time zone-wise with a Saturday night broadcast in the United States. And even if we accomplished that, the fight would only be considered a commercial success if I sold more pay-per-view than ever before in the UFC's PPV desert month of November. I'd need to get over 55,000 people in the seats and over 1 million people purchasing the broadcast.

"We need you to fly to Melbourne for media," I was told as I was preparing to enter camp. There was a press conference, then pre-fight promotional requests that never stopped without any regard for the fact that I also needed to actually prepare for a fight. I was sitting in a dressing room after a gauntlet of appearances when the UFC PR lady handed me my media schedule for the next week. Starring down at the pages-long printout, I burst into tears.

"I'm not a fucking robot," I pleaded. "This isn't a Britney Spears concert we're promoting here. I can't just go out and go through some rehearsed motions. I have to fucking fight. Please make this easier on me."

Media never took time away from my training, just my rest and recovery. But I was starting to crack. It was the first time I had ever asked to lighten my media schedule. The PR lady returned a little bit later with a printout. It was the same amount of appearances, just condensed into fewer days.

"That's the best I could do, honey," she said sympathetically. "Hope this helps."

I forced a smile and thanked her. I looked down at the paper in my hands.

You have to be the best on your worst day, I thought to myself.

There would be two of us in this fight, but it was up to me to get people to care. My underdog opponent was able to fly under the radar, doing radio call-ins from her gym in New Mexico. When I asked about this, UFC's media relations' explanation was that no one else was interested in talking to her. But my back was hurting from carrying yet another fight. Every second I spent traveling and doing media was an opportunity that my opponent got to rest or train that I didn't. I referred to it as the "contender's luxury," where they take the fight only when they are 100 percent and carry none of the responsibility for selling it.

I understood the role that the media played in my rapid ascent within the sport. My success was not solely because I was an amazing athlete. Other talented athletes had come before me. I had succeeded not just because I won, but because I got people to care. The media provided me a platform to connect with audiences, and in return I provided them with quotes that weren't the same boring bullshit and stories that sold. I was under no illusion that any of my media relationships were anything more than mutually beneficial, but I wanted to believe there was a level of mutual respect.

But the more visible I became, the more my relationship with the media became strained. Because I had struggled with social anxiety, my mom had put me in judo as a way to force me to interact and socialize with other kids. Now, instead of being forced to socialize with a couple of other kids, I was being forced to engage with the viewing/reading/scrolling public. Once the media was tired of telling my inspiring origin story, there was a noticeable shift. It felt like they saw me more as a headline than a human. And for the first time since I had come into the spotlight, I had something that I wanted to keep out of it: my relationship with Travis.

Did I think I had found the love of my life? Yes. Did I need to have it reported and analyzed all over the internet to drum up clicks? Fuck, no. Dating is hard enough when you don't have people trying to secretly snap pictures of you during your mom's birthday dinner at Benihana.

As for my mom, things had been strained since Rio. Edmond and I might have decided that we could move forward, but my mom could not. Her dislike for Edmond had always been at best thinly veiled, but since I had asked her to intervene, it had become outright contempt. One day before the Correia fight, Edmond made the mistake of acknowledging her presence in the gym.

"Hi, AnnMaria," he said. "How are you?"

Her eyes narrowed. My mom is barely over five feet, but when she looks at you that way, it doesn't matter if you tower over her, you feel tiny. Though there was some poetic justice to Edmond being the focus of the same stare he'd weaponized for so long.

"How the fuck do you think I am?" she asked. "I'm in your fucking gym and fucking hate you, so not very fucking well."

True to her word, she had let me get through the Correia fight, but as soon as I stepped out of the cage post-win, it was open season discussing Edmond. She had tried to bring up the subject of changing coaches several times since then. I did what I had always done, which was deflect and avoid.

I hadn't yet said the words out loud, but with my fight against Holly Holm on the horizon, I wasn't looking for a new coach. I was looking for a way out. I was 6-0 in the UFC, 12-0 in my professional MMA career (15-0 if you counted my amateur fights). Holm was only 2-0 in the UFC, having made her debut just six months prior, but was 9-0 in her professional MMA career.

After I beat Holly Holm, I'll have defeated everyone who is undefeated in the UFC, I thought to myself. I could walk away without any lingering doubt.

When the timeline for the fight was moved up, forcing me right back into camp, I knew my mom would disapprove of my decision to stay with Edmond. But I felt I had no other choice.

"I'm not asking you to respect my decision, just to accept it," I said. Knowing I couldn't avoid her forever, I had stopped by her house to see if she wanted to get coffee. We hadn't made it out the front door.

"I think he's a terrible person and a terrible coach," Mom said. "I'll never accept that."

"You don't have to like him," I said.

"Good because we are way past that point."

"This is my career," I tried to explain. "I don't go to your office and tell you how to run your company. I respect that you know what you're doing. That's all I'm asking from you. This is my career and my decision."

"Well, it's a stupid fucking decision," she said.

I thought that we had left it at that as I entered into a compressed training camp. The difference between training camp and training is best described as the difference between preparation and practice. Training is about staying in shape and developing your skills. Camp is when you shift your focus toward putting those skills into action. It's about preparing yourself to be at your absolute peak at the absolute right moment to face a single person who will occupy every waking moment of your thoughts until they are standing across the cage from you.

Training camp is different for every fight. While I started training for my next opponent the minute I found out who it would be, my official camp started six weeks out from a fight. We structured it as a countdown to the cage. The first week at elevation was for bulking up muscle and getting ready for the most grueling weeks of my life. In Week 5, I'd start my weight cut program preordained by my nutritionist. Usually, the first few pounds would slide off, but for the first time in my career, that didn't happen. Every day, I would step on the scale and the number wouldn't move.

In the UFC, I was fighting at 135 pounds. My body is not a body that should ever weigh 135 pounds. I had initially fought at 63 kg (138.6 pounds) in judo because I could not make weight consistently any lighter than that, especially with only a few hours to recover the morning of the competition. Even then, fighting and making weight up to twenty times a year in judo started my battle with eating disorders. The strain that weight cut put on my body is why I moved up to the 70 kg (154 pounds)—and I still had to cut weight to hit that number. In MMA, I had been able to make 135 *only* because it was a few times a year with many months to recover. Until I stopped giving myself time to recover.

When you don't take care of your body, it rebels against you. Stress hormones release other hormones that make you inflamed and hold on to weight. The weight cut was getting harder on me. I was training all out, twice a day, every bit of food measured and monitored down to the ounce and hour eaten, and still could not get below 155. I viewed those twenty pounds as one more challenge to overcome. Bad weight cut? "Best on your worst day," I whispered to myself.

Week 4 we honed in on the game plan. Holm was a former boxer with a decent boxing record of 33-2. Her striking ability was a threat. I had always been aware of the risk posed by a strong striker, even more so especially since I had been concussed fighting Sara McMann.

There was one significant difference between that fight and this upcoming one. Sara McMann had been a grappler who got off a couple of lucky shots. Holly Holm could strike. She knew how to keep distance. I knew that and planned for it.

What I had not planned for was my mother. I was driving to practice when the text alerts started buzzing. The entire hour drive to Glendale, they didn't stop. When I parked, I figured out why.

There, at a conference table in her office, sat my mother. She was doing an interview with some random media site that I had never heard of. As the reporter broached the subject of my coaching, she sat, chin resting on her folded hands. The reporter seemed nervous, stumbling over his question. My mom seemed calm, thoughtful, anticipating.

"If you don't mind, you don't have to, you know, we were talking about it when we started the interview." He hesitated. "Uh, specifically, Edmond, her coach now, who I believe is her striking coach, but he's the head coach, are you at issues with the way that he's kind of corralling her?"

At the mention of Edmond's name, my mom's eyes narrowed, her mouth becoming a straight line. Her expression was nothing short of pure hatred. She had been waiting for this moment. My mom looked straight at the camera.

"I think Edmond is a terrible coach, and I will say it publicly," she said, jumping in before the reporter had even finished. It was as if she knew exactly what he was going to ask. "He hit the lottery when Ronda walked in there.

"I think she stays there out of superstition. It's like somebody who, you know, pitches a no-hitter when they're wearing red underwear and they wear that red underwear every day. And I think it's superstition, and I would caution anybody from going there. I think he uses her to lure people in.

"I told Ronda I'm not going to be quiet about this anymore. He's a bad person, and people should not go there."

She shrugged. "And if he wants to sue me, that's my honest opinion.

"By the way," she added as if trying to put a Band-Aid over a missing limb. "I think Ronda is wonderful, and I love her. He's a horrible person, and she wins despite him."

I sat there staring at my phone in disbelief. The site had also released the "we were talking about it when we started the interview" part of the interview. In it my mom said, "I would run over him with my car if there wasn't a law against it," with a crazy look in her eyes that left no doubt that she meant it and was still considering it despite the legal consequences.

By the end of practice, media had descended upon the gym.

I couldn't even speak to my mother because I had no words. For the first time in my life, I understood what someone meant when they said, "I'm not angry, I'm just disappointed." I was also furious, but more than rage, I felt let down, betrayed. Our relationship wasn't perfect, but I could not believe she would create a fucking spectacle in the media. She knew the distraction this would cause. She knew it would hurt me. That it would give my opponent confidence. And she did it anyway.

"You gotta be the best on your worst day." I repeated the maxim I'd learned from her. "Gotta be able to block out all the bullshit."

A few days later, Dana called me. He wanted to have a security detail follow me from now on.

"Really?" I asked.

"It's just about protecting some of the top champions," Dana said.

I was used to having security at events or when I traveled but having someone assigned to watch me as I just went through my daily life seemed unnecessary and somewhat out of the blue.

"OK, I guess," I reluctantly agreed.

A few hours later, a bodyguard knocked at my door, and from then until the fight, top-flight security followed me from home to practice. It would later slip that my mom had called Dana, convinced him Edmond was a threat to my safety, and that I needed to be guarded constantly for my own protection.

As Week 3 of training camp rolled around, I realized that in all the media I was doing, I wasn't just trying to sell other people on the fight, I was trying to sell myself. During breaks in training, sitting against the wall of the gym, or at home sprawled out on my couch in the evenings, I would catch my mind drifting, daydreaming of a life after fighting. Then, I would pull my focus in, telling myself the same thing I had told myself just a few months before: "Just get through this fight, then you can rest." Having made myself that same promise for several training camps in a row, even I wasn't sure I believed me this time. I had been going nonstop for five years, and I just felt so tired. My left palm would itch, and I'd make a cross with my thumb. "You gotta be the best on your worst day," I kept repeating, but this time I added something. "Can't stop just because you're tired."

My mom called me and told me she wasn't going to come to Australia for the Holm fight.

When I started out in MMA, she had told me that it was "the stupidest fucking idea she had ever heard," but she had attended every single one of the amateur fights and all but one of my professional fights. (It was in a random casino next to the airport in Calgary in Canada.) The night before fights, after I had weighed in, she would come to my room and lie next to me in the bed and tell me all the reasons why I was going to beat the other girl. That I had trained harder. That I wanted it more. That I had sacrificed so much. That this bitch didn't deserve to even breathe the same air as me, let alone be in the cage against me. The night before a fight, my opponent was my mother's mortal enemy.

She would run her fingers through my hair as I lay there, drifting off to sleep, my stomach full and my pre-fight nerves gone.

"You got this, Bean," she would tell me before leaving my room for the night. Kissing me on the cheek on her way out.

"I don't understand what control it is that he has over you, but I can't support your decision to stay with him as your coach," she said.

"What about supporting me?" I wanted to say. But I was too tired to argue, so I just said, "OK."

"You gotta be the best on your worst day," I repeated. "Can't just win when your mom is there."

It was two weeks out from the Holm fight and five days before I was set to fly to Melbourne. I had just gotten home from two-a-day training. Training camp serves to push you physically and mentally to the brink, to a point where you think you can't go on, only for you to find that you can. All I wanted was to eat dinner and go to bed. I was starving. By this point in camp, I should have been shifting all of my focus on to fine tuning for the fight, but I had been struggling with my weight. I wanted to weigh myself before I ate. But the scale was in my car.

"I can get it, babe," Travis said, but he was in the middle of cooking, and I could not wait another second.

"I'll get it," I said.

I ran out the back door and down my back steps, something I did twenty times a day. But when I reached the concrete at the bottom of the eighth stair, my foot just went out from under me. I tried to steady myself, but wearing socks, I had no friction to leverage. There was nothing I could do to stop myself, no railing to grab.

I blacked out when I fell, landing awkwardly on my knee and hitting the back of my head on the corner of the step. A few seconds later, I came to. *I just knocked myself out*, I thought in total disbelief.

My knee throbbed. I'd already undergone six knee surgeries since my first torn ACL at sixteen and was almost able to self-diagnose the difference between ice it and operate on it. Something was definitely torn, but—I bent my knee—manageable. I had created my entire fighting style around an unstable right knee. I could get through this. I pushed the pain out of my mind, walked to the car, grabbed the scale, and went back in the house. I wiggled my knee. It was immediately evident that my surgically replaced ligament—which is basically responsible for holding your knee in place—had snapped. I tried to blink away the tears and the photo vision spots dancing in front of my eyes. Travis kissed my head and brought me ice.

"You gotta be the best on your worst day," I told myself. "Not going to let slipping on the stairs stop me."

I boarded the flight to Melbourne hoping that when I stepped off the plane in Australia it would be like when Dorothy walks out of the house in *The Wizard of Oz* and suddenly everything goes from black and white to Technicolor. It didn't.

We were whisked away to the fight's host hotel, the Crown Metropol. It was part of a large casino complex with restaurants, gaming floors, food courts, and shops connected by a maze of escalators, atriums, and glass-encased walkways. Save for the jet lag and the accents, it felt like I had traveled halfway around the world just to end up in a slightly alternate version of Las Vegas.

My room was the standard globally nondescript modern design, white with dark accent walls and a muted palette of gray furniture atop almost pumpkin orange wall-to-wall carpet. A wall of glass windows looked over a bustling city and river twenty-four floors below.

We pushed the furniture up against the suite's walls and put down mats so I could train as much as possible without having to leave my room.

The bathroom was painted black with two walls covered in mirrors. A large white marble counter with sinks ran across one side of the room. Against the other wall was a large white bathtub. Typically, as part of my weight cut, I would do two or three twenty-minute sessions in a hot tub to sweat off the final pounds. The night before weigh-ins, I sat in the tub for two hours straight, submerged in hot water while trying to force my body to sweat out fluids that I hadn't been drinking. I was so dehydrated that I could feel the pain in my kidneys as I pushed them to the limit.

To account for being able to broadcast at a reasonable hour to a US audience, the time between weigh-in to fight was going to be my shortest yet. "Best on your worst day," I reminded myself. "Can't be just one good weigh-in better, can't just be a few hours of recovery better."

Fight weigh-ins are a public event, in front of a live crowd. They are also the last time you will see your opponent before the referee says "Fight." You are feeling at your physical worst and weakest yet have to portray absolute strength and dominance.

I stared at myself in the mirror that morning. My face was so sunken in it looked like I was making a fish face.

"Can you make me look as full faced as possible?" I asked the makeup artist.

She looked at me like I had set her an impossible task. "Let's see what we can do," she said in a tone that was both upbeat and unconvincing. Despite her best attempts and a significant amount of blush, I still looked skeletal.

At the arena, I walked out on the stage and stripped down to my underwear. My mouth was dry, not from nerves but because it had been a day since I'd had anything to drink. I approached the scale. I paused before stepping on it and exhaled deeply. I was trying to squeeze every last possible fraction of an ounce from my body. I held my breath as I stepped on the scale.

"One-thirty-four for the champion," event announcer Joe Rogan's voice boomed around the arena. I stormed over to where Holly Holm stood for the obligatory pre-fight face-off pose. I walked straight at her. Dana grabbed me, pulling me back slightly. I assumed the ready-to-throw-punches position. She came toward me, but instead of setting up to pose, tried to force her fist between my outside arm and my face. She punched me in my sunken cheek. Dana jumped between us as we were pulled apart.

Since the fight had been announced, I had been trying to sell it. Trying to get people to care, while she had been doing an "aww, shucks, I'm just a nice gal" routine, playing up that she was a preacher's daughter. She talked about how she had nothing but respect for me while letting me do all the heavy lifting. And now, here in front of everyone, she tried to take a cheap shot.

"That fake sweet act, I see right through you," I said, pointing at her. "You're going to get it on Sunday."

The crowd roared.

I went backstage, chugged two bottles of water, and headed back to the hotel. My kidneys ached. Painful lumps caused by dehydration and lack of electrolytes formed on the roof of my mouth, I ate my post-weigh-in snacks, looking forward to a full meal for the first time in days. Holly's attempts to try to get into my head were laughable. All I cared about was that I was less than twenty-four hours from getting through this fight.

My standard post-weigh-in/pre-fight evening followed a loosely structured schedule of eat, drink, sleep for the night, wake up, eat, drink, and sleep/hibernate until late afternoon. However, in Melbourne, we were slated to step into the cage at around 2:00 p.m. There would be no hibernation or recovery time. I tossed and turned all night in a restless sleep. In the morning, I got up and ate, but as soon as I went back to sleep, the security escort knocked on my door.

"You ready?" Edmond asked.

I reminded myself "best on your worst day," scratched my left palm and made a thumb cross. I thought of my dad and how whenever my mom asked him that question, he said, "I was born ready."

I was dressed head-to-toe in black. In the Reebok era of the UFC, only champions can wear black, with your name in gold letters. My hair was pulled tight into three small ponytails that met and wrapped together in a tight bun. I put on my "battle boots," those cheap, gray falling-apart knee-high boots that I wore into every fight.

The members of my coaching team were assembled in the living room. Edmond. My judo coach and childhood friend Justin Flores. My grappling coach Renner Gracie. My wrestling coach Martin. My nutritionist Mike Dolce.

Travis, who had come to Australia with me and would be watching me fight for the first time, gave me a kiss as I headed out the door. He was more nervous than I was.

"You got this," he said.

I smiled and nodded. I knew I had this. Just like I'd had it the last dozen times. But there was something about hearing him say it that made it mean more. I walked out into the hallway and headed out for the stadium.

We were led through the fluorescent-lit, concrete corridors that are woven under every major arena and stadium to my locker room. The warm-up room typically consisted of a room full of near wall-to-wall mats, but before me lay just a single strip of mats in a line.

"I can't practice lateral movement like this," I said, looking at the space. This fight was all about moving laterally to herd Holm up against the cage. "I can't really do anything…"

In the background, I could hear someone being ordered to go get more mats. The strip widened by just a few feet. It wasn't much of an improvement.

"Best on your worst day," I told myself. "Can't be just one warm-up room better."

I went through my warm-up, a series of drills and stretches, grappling on the ground with Justin, then throwing punches with Edmond. Edmond wrapped my hands as an official watched, then signed off on the wraps to indicate they weren't hiding weights or anything else illegal that could give me an advantage over my opponent. It was getting close to fight time.

Edmond reached into his bag and pulled out my mouth guard. It was the one that was blue inside. My left palm itched. I scratched it and made a thumb cross.

"This isn't the right one," I said. "This is the bad one."

I had several mouth guards, which are made by taking a mold of your teeth and then creating a mouth guard from that mold. In order to take that mold, you have to hold the guard in your mouth for ten minutes while it solidifies. In this case, my previously injured jaw had spasmed while the mold was being cast for the mouth guard Edmond had pulled out of the bag. As a result, the bottom row of teeth didn't have any support behind them.

Edmond looked back in his canvas duffle, unzipping every compartment. He looked back at me. "It's the only one I have."

I shook my head. It would have to do.

"Best on your worst day," I reassured myself. "Can't be just a mouth guard better than the other person."

As an elite athlete, you train yourself to ignore anything that could distract from your goal. Pain. Crowd reactions. The media circus. Shitty weight cut. A fucked-up mouth guard. None of it mattered when I walked out into that arena. The only thing that mattered was winning.

There was a knock at my locker room door. It was time.

The size of the stadium meant that the distance from when you emerged to the crowd and got to the cage was longer than usual. The challenger always goes first, and I could hear muted sounds through the walls of Holly Holm entering to some kind of jig.

If you've never competed at the highest levels, you might expect that in the moments before a competition you might feel nervous. That your hands might sweat. That you might breathe just a little bit heavier. That you might anxiously shift from foot to foot. But that is not the case.

When you have trained your entire life for something, when you are standing on the precipice of that, you feel an overwhelming sense of calm despite your pounding heart. When I closed my eyes, I could almost feel my synapses firing, my muscles preparing for action. My breath was relaxed. I stood up straight and waited for the opening chords of Joan Jett's "Bad Reputation." For the thunder from the crowd when my face appeared on the huge screens in the stadium.

In the final moments before a fight, my senses heightened. As if the world was slowing down, but I was still moving at full speed. I would hear the roar of the crowd, but as I got closer to the cage, it became background noise. Once the door to the cage closed, I would step under the bright spotlights, and it would be as if nothing else existed outside of the chain link.

I stood backstage waiting for the producer to signal it was my cue to go. Four large security men in black polo shirts surrounded me, my coaches trailing behind as I made my way toward the cage. We were just about to exit the tunnel when I tripped. It was barely noticeable, happening as the cameras transitioned from the backstage shots to the in-arena angle.

In fifteen previous fights, I had never stumbled.

Did that just happen? I asked myself, but before I had time to answer I was forced to push the thought from my mind.

"Best on your worst day," I reminded myself one last time.

Looking back, there was all this foreboding. But I convinced myself, "No, there's no doubt in your mind. You're fine. You can do this." I just needed to focus. So, I did and kept walking.

I reached the Octagon. I kicked off my battle boots and took off my sweats. I hugged each of my coaches. My cutman rubbed Vaseline on my face. This was applied before a fight in an attempt to reduce the friction on the skin and lower the likelihood of a blow causing a cut, especially as head wounds bleed a lot. I held my arms out for the pre-fight inspection for anything that might injure my opponent or give me an edge. And then I was pointed into the cage.

I walked up the four stairs, bowed slightly in a nod to my judo days, and stepped onto the canvas. I stomped my left foot twice. Then my right. Jumped and stomped both. I headed toward my corner, shaking out my arms. I slapped my right shoulder, then left, then thighs. I touched the ground, squatted, then popped back up. I stomped my feet one last time, trying to get the blood back into my toes. I was performing a dance I had done a million times. I bounced on the balls of my feet, staring across the cage at my opponent as she paced back and forth on her side.

Legendary UFC in-ring announcer Bruce Buffer started in. "This is the main event," he said, dragging out each possible vowel for as long as possible. Out of the blue corner, the challenger. Out of the red corner, the champion. Referee Herb Dean called us to the middle of the cage to start the fight.

Holly Holm reached out her hands as if to touch gloves.

Fuck that, I thought. Touching gloves before a fight is a sign of respect for your opponent. Holly had thrown away any respect I had for her when she punched me at the weigh-in. Nothing grates me like performative sportsmanship.

I dropped my hands and walked backward to my corner.

"Ready. Ready. Fight." Herb clapped his hands.

Let's get this over with, I thought.

The first hit that she connected knocked me out on my feet. I don't remember what it was, probably just a jab, but it wasn't even that hard. Without the part of my mouth guard protecting the back of my teeth, all my teeth got knocked loose. My entire lip was cut open down to the muscle.

I was barely able to think, barely able to see. The lights hurt my eyes, I couldn't judge the distance between us. I just told myself, *You're fine*. I couldn't let her know I was hurt. The second she knew I was vulnerable and swarmed in, I wouldn't be able to stop her. I kept coming forward to hide that I was hurt, trying to give myself time to recover. My vision kept narrowing in tighter and tighter. Spots became borders that were slowly closing in. My own internal dialogue was fragmented. I had only a tenuous hold on consciousness. *Don't let it show*, I thought. *Just keep coming forward or they'll know. Just make it to the bell, you'll recover.* I can recount in detail every second of every previous fight. I can hardly remember anything from the Holm fight.

People rewatching the fight will say that my game plan didn't make sense. That I didn't react and respond correctly. But from that first second that I got touched, I wasn't there. The information that my brain was so used to rapidly processing during a fight kept coming, but I couldn't process the data.

There was a moment where I had her against the cage, but I didn't even try to take her down because I was trying so hard to get my bearings. I was trying to shake myself out of it. My brain had switched over from "I" to "you," as if I was weirdly separated from myself, and I wasn't cognitively present. Like my body was just reacting to the situation, while my brain was trying to get back to the steering wheel.

At another point in the first round, she was trying to take me down to the mat. My body was fighting it. But I was thinking, *Oh, that would be good if I sat down. I need to rest. I need to try and get my bearings again.* At the very least, I'd finally know how far away she was.

I wasn't sure if it had been only seconds or if the round was almost over. For a split second, I saw an opening. *Oh, I can get an armbar from here*, I thought. But there was no sense of urgency. It was like I saw the armbar but was too busy lying on my back watching it pass me by like a cloud to act on it.

At some point, for only the second time in my career, the first round ended.

My mouth was filled with blood. I walked to my corner, biting my lip like you would if you have a piece of chapped skin, but it was a chunk of flesh that I bit off and spit out. Like it was nothing. Then I bit off another chunk, ripping my teeth into my own lip like you would an apple. I can still feel where the inside of my lip is missing today. It didn't even faze me; I wasn't there.

I went to my stool and sat down. Edmond stood in front of me. He was talking, but it was as if I was hearing him from underwater. I couldn't make out any of his words. I couldn't take in any information. I focused on the only thing that made sense in that moment, hiding that I was hurt. I had one minute to recover. I just needed to shake it off. I sat there, nodded, and went back out for the second round.

And then I don't remember anything.

6

After the fight, a decision was made to take me to the hospital. I don't know who made it, only that it wasn't me.

I was loaded into an Australian ambulance that took me from the arena to a hospital a little farther away where it would be less expected that I'd turn up. The UFC medical staff had called ahead to have me admitted under an alias.

I was wheeled in through an admitting door and ushered into a small exam room with a curtain in front of the door. The lights were dimmed. Travis stood by my side, holding my hand as medical personnel slipped in and out with clipboards, asking me questions and jotting down notes. I could feel my bottom teeth were loose, but their bigger concern was the gaping hole in my inside lip.

The emergency room doctor was kind and quiet. He spoke with the compassion of someone who was used to dealing with people on the worst days of their life. He called for a surgical consult, and they both agreed that my lip should be addressed immediately. As he started to walk out of the room, one of the nurses stopped him on the other side of the privacy curtain. "They can't stay here," she whispered loudly and frustratedly. "They're taking up the whole waiting room."

The doctor stepped back into view.

"It appears you have quite a number of people in the waiting room," he said.

Panic must have flashed across my face.

"The whole team," Travis said quickly. "They're here. They just wanted to be sure you were OK."

"The issue is," the doctor said delicately, "there's probably a dozen of them, and we can't really have that many people out there."

"Maybe they can just come in and see you're OK?" Travis suggested.

One-by-one, each of the members of my team came in, but I couldn't look them in the eye. The pain. The disappointment. The shame. It was overwhelming. I just cried.

"I'm sorry," I said, over and over. "I'm so sorry."

It felt like I was at my own funeral. Where mourners file by, tears in their eyes, not sure what to say in the face of the loss. At least when you're dead you don't have to feel how much it hurts.

I had been in shock immediately after the fight, not just the disbelief kind, but the clinical physiological response kind that releases a massive spike of adrenaline to mask pain as a direct result of a physical trauma. It had started to wane. The painkillers the doctors were administering were dulling the throbbing in my lip, but as the pain ebbed, it laid bare the crushing reality of losing. Physical pain I could deal with but the entire world I had created for myself crashing around me was too much to bear.

After the steady stream of people had exited, Dana slipped into the room. He spoke in a whisper, which was a volume that I didn't know he was capable of. He was dressed all in black, a standard Dana look, but it seemed fitting.

"I'm sorry," I said, tears pouring down my face.

"Don't be sorry," Dana said. "You have nothing to be sorry for."

"I ruined everything. Everything we worked to build."

"You didn't ruin anything," Dana said. "None of this would have existed without you."

I wished that I could believe him.

The nurse entered the room. I was wheeled through a series of empty hospital corridors and up to the OR. The surgeon came in and introduced himself, giving an overview of my injury and the operation he would be doing.

"We'll fix up your lip," he said. "But the teeth, you'll have to see the dentist when you get home."

I didn't even try to pretend I was listening. I couldn't. I had nothing left. I waited for the anesthesiologist to come in and usher me into total darkness.

———

The next morning, I lay with my closed eyes. I knew if I opened them, it would make everything real. That the night before had happened. This would be the first day I woke up in a world where I had lost.

In the hospital, the night before, Dana told me with complete confidence, "I have seen fighters go down before. You'll come back from this."

But what he didn't understand—what no one could—was that coming back would be impossible. I had been pursuing perfection. And when I hit the canvas, that ended. When I opened my eyes, it would be in a world where everything I had been working toward was gone.

For the first time in my life, I had no option but to set my expectations for myself lower.

It is hard to articulate the unrelenting feeling of failure when you realize that everything you have worked for, everything you gave and sacrificed wasn't enough. To realize that the one thing that you have built your life around is no longer possible. It is an inescapable emptiness that hurts so much you want to scream endlessly into an abyss and then throw yourself into it.

I know that I'm not the only person on the planet to have ever felt that depth of devastation—whatever the cause—although it's odd how we try to console people by assuring them that others have felt agony as well. Although, for most people, this moment of their life does not play out in front of millions of people who have paid to watch it, followed by an endless stream of social media memes and stalking paparazzi. No matter the circumstance, I would never wish the pain I felt on anyone, not even my worst enemies.

I finally blinked, and the sterile hospital room came into focus. Travis sat in an uncomfortable-looking standard-issue hospital chair that was dwarfed by his large frame. A small vase of orange and yellow flowers from the hospital gift shop on the side table stood out as the only pop of color, a misplaced sign of joy. Despite my use of a pseudonym, an orderly had recognized me and dropped it off as a quiet gesture. When Travis told me this, I could only cry harder. It represented one more fan that had been pulling for me, who'd believed in me. One more person I had let down.

I was discharged from the hospital that morning, slipping into the back of a darkened SUV. A decision had been made that we would go not to the Crown Metropol where I had spent the last two weeks and where fans and paparazzi were staking out my return, but to the Grand Hyatt where no one would be expecting me. I wanted to literally flee the country. I could not put enough distance between myself and the fight, be that physical or mental, but I had to wait twenty-four hours post-surgery before taking a fifteen-hour flight home.

I sat in my new room and waited. This room was an array of muted darks. It seemed oddly fitting. I drew the shades, took painkillers, and when I wasn't sleeping, cried. Travis tried to get me to eat, but between my lip, my loose teeth, and my depression, it felt like too much. So, he just sat there, holding me. Edmond stopped by, sobbing hysterically.

"I'm so sorry," he said. "I failed you."

It felt like he was hoping I would absolve him of his guilt. That I would tell him it was OK. That it wasn't his fault. But I didn't have space in my own grief to comfort anyone else.

Less than forty-eight hours after the fight, I boarded the flight back home. I slept the entire way, dreading what I knew awaited me when we touched down.

I was tired. My face was bruised from the bout, my lip swollen from the surgery. My eyes were puffy and red from having cried for three days straight. I'd barely eaten in that stretch, and I was jet-lagged from flying halfway around the world. I was physically and mentally broken.

I climbed down the steps to deplane, knowing that at the other end of the terminal was a throng of dudes with cameras slung around their necks salivating over the chance to be "the one" who got a picture of me at my lowest point. There was nothing that I wanted to do less in that moment than walk a gauntlet of camera clicks and screamed questions.

By this point in my career, I had become skilled at cutting through the crowd chaos. Move and just keep moving. Only look forward. Travis, by virtue of his size, tried his best to block for me as airline staff and security ushered us out of the airport, past the paparazzi who followed me, demanding to know.

Until this moment, I had always tried to please the media. I put up with the "Hey, Ronda!" ambushes at dinner, at the gym, at the airport, getting coffee, walking my dog, at every turn. I answered countless questions. I smiled and gave quote after quote. But I had nothing left to give.

For the first time, I ignored them. I said nothing. I looked down, hiding my face in my travel pillow. I didn't want to give them the satisfaction of owning a picture of my fucked-up face that would outlive me.

———

My house looked exactly like it had when I had left. The black leather L-shaped couch draped in fleece throw blankets. Mochi's dog bed in the corner of the living room. Clothes strewn wherever I had tossed them before heading to Australia. The jumble of mismatched dishes stacked precariously on my open kitchen shelves. My black Kit-Cat Klock with the tail and eyes that moved back and forth marking the seconds. A pile of unopened mail from before I had left. These eight hundred square feet had always been comforting and cozy, but now with a gaggle of paparazzi outside trying to peer into my windows, it suddenly felt like a fishbowl.

"I can't be here," I told Travis.

"OK," he said matter-of-factly. "Then let's go."

We loaded his diesel pickup with some clothes and camping gear, resolving to buy anything else we needed on the way. And we got in the truck and drove. For sixteen hours, we drove, stopping only for gas and fast food. The world started to recede. I stared out the window as the California greenery gave way to the deserts of Arizona and New Mexico to the chill of late November in Central Texas. Travis mostly let me sit in the silence of my own thoughts, holding my hand. I found myself nodding off, the exhaustion of the last five years catching up to me.

We arrived at the place we were going to be camping. Campsite would be too formal a description for what was really just a clearing in the woods. Travis set the tent up next to the truck. It was cold in the way that stings your face and stiffens your hands. We pulled out our sleeping bags. There wasn't an inch of space for anything else. The wind blew so hard it shook the small nylon tent. It sounded almost like the world was ending. At another time, it might have felt ominous, but lying there, it felt fitting.

I mostly stayed in the tent. Sometimes, I sat outside in the cold. My physical state mirrored my mental one. My muscles ached. I shivered. I had days of diarrhea, which is even worse when you're in the woods in the middle of nowhere. The skin on my face peeled and started to flake off. It was like my body was trying to expel the failure, to shed itself inside and out.

If this was a classic inspirational memoir, this is the part where I write about how after that week in the woods, I started to find myself again. To find small moments of joy. How I would crack a smile and think things would maybe be OK. But none of that happened. I cried a lot, from body-wracking, snot-rolling-down-my-face sobbing to silent tears sliding down my cheeks. I had yet to turn my phone back on, but sometimes in the darkness, I imagined what the world was saying about me, divided into camps of celebrating my loss and pitying me in defeat.

After a week, I returned to LA as dejected as when I left. I had accepted that I wasn't going to kill myself, but I was all but walking dead. People want to rush grief. They want to tell you to buck up. To get over it. That it'll be OK. But grief is overwhelming. It suffocates you to the point where you are doing all you can just to breathe.

"You're so much more than a fighter," Travis would tell me as we lay zipped up in the tiny tent and as we drove along the empty stretches of freeway. He was convinced. I was not. I *was* more than a fighter. I was a champion, *the* champion. But now, without that, I was nothing.

When we stepped back into my house, my former sanctuary now seemed like a self-imposed prison.

"You can't just drop off the face of the earth," my mom said. She had come to my house, bearing coffee, the day we had returned from Texas. We did not address our falling out, but in the face of everything that had happened since, that animosity fell away. There were few people on the earth who could understand at even a fractional level the pain I was feeling. My mom, who had once cried the entire ten-hour flight from London to Los Angeles after failing to place in the British Open, was one of them.

"I'm pretty sure I can," I said.

"Fuck all those people," my mom said. "You are amazing. And I know you don't believe it, but you are."

My mom pursed her lips. "And there are still people here who care about you. I'm not even asking you to leave the house. Just start by answering your phone."

"I don't know where my phone is," I said.

She pulled a plastic-encased prepaid mobile flip phone out of her bag. "I got you a burner phone. This way we can reach you, and if you decide in this next phase of your life to turn to crime and rob a bank, they won't be able to track you."

"I'd have to leave the house to rob a bank," I pointed out.

I somehow reluctantly agreed to go to my sister Jennifer's house for Thanksgiving the following week.

"We need ice," Jennifer said from the kitchen.

Travis volunteered to make the run, and me and my seven-year-old niece jumped in the truck too. I was not only already high—as I would be for most of the next year—but also at least two glasses of wine in. We were miles away from LA's Westside where the paparazzi lurked on every corner, yet before the turkey was out of the oven, the photos of us running into the market were splashed all over the internet. I never even saw the cameraman who took them.

The next morning, Travis convinced me that it was time to intentionally venture back into the world. It had been almost two weeks since the Holm fight.

"You gotta get out," he half-pleaded. I reluctantly agreed to walk to my regular coffee shop a block from my house. I showered and got dressed with actual intent for the first time since Australia.

We hadn't made it to the corner of my block before the human buzzards circling the corpse of my success came scurrying out, running toward me with cameras. I hated that I gave them something to take a picture of. I closed the door and went straight to the kitchen. Tears fell into my kitchen bong's water as I lit it up. I took a hit, pulling the smoke through, and resolved more than ever to become a hermit.

However, before I could abandon society forever, I needed to see the dentist to resolve the front four bottom teeth that had not settled back into place. My dentist agreed to see me before hours so I could avoid overlapping with any other patients, but when he realized the damage went into the root, he sent me to a specialist nearby.

"You're sure you want to do all four root canals at once?" the new dentist asked.

"It's fine," I said. What were a handful of root canals on top of everything else?

I sat there in the chair as they numbed my lower chin. The TV was playing daytime programming on the wall in front of me.

"Let me know if it gets too intense," the dentist said, repositioning the paper bib around my neck.

"Agghwillgh," I said, with my mouth held open.

I mindlessly stared at the TV, reading the closed captioning of a talk show. The dentist drill whirred. I winced. The assistant sucked the little vacuum up against my cheek to keep me from choking on my own spit. The TMZ intro appeared across the screen. The drill whirred again.

The brightly colored TMZ Sports logo flashed. "Ronda Rousey—Out of Hiding!" The auto-captioned text ticked across the bottom of the screen. "For the first time since her loss, Ronda Rousey has been spotted!" Pictures of my loss, of me covering my face at the airport, of me and my niece getting ice, of me and Travis grabbing coffee, ran across the screen as TMZ staffers made their trademark snarky comments.

The hygienist sucked the gathering saliva out of my mouth. The dentist hammered on my teeth. I sat there, mouth agape, watching it.

"Doing all right?" the dentist asked.

I made an unintelligible noise. How could I even answer that? *Well, I'm sitting here getting four root canals while watching a TV segment recapping the worst moment of my life.*

I'm in the darkest timeline, I thought to myself. *This is my hell. I'm literally in hell.*

I closed my eyes, trying to focus on the dentist scraping out the pulp inside my tooth. I opened my eyes slowly, as if hoping I would wake up from this nightmare. My own face flashed back at me on the screen.

I'm gonna get so fucking high when I get home, I promised myself.

And for the next year, that's pretty much all I did.

It was some time around the holidays when my agent, Brad, stopped by my house.

"I've been trying to reach you," he said.

I still hadn't turned my phone back on since Australia. I wasn't avoiding him, I explained. I was just avoiding everything.

He was grinning from ear to ear. He had big news.

"*SNL* called," he said. "They want you to host."

I did a double take. Was I that high?

"I'm serious. Lorne called me up," Brad said, referring to *Saturday Night Live*'s legendary creator and producer Lorne Michaels. "He said times like this is what this show is for, to showcase and repackage people going through crisis like Ronda is."

If they were looking for someone in crisis, they'd come to the right place. But he also had a point. Hosting *Saturday Night Live* seemed like the kind of opportunity I couldn't pass up, regardless of how miserable I was.

"I'll do it," I said.

"Awesome," Brad said, then slowly added, "One more thing, while I have you…"

In that moment, I wished the conversation was a phone call so I could pretend I had to hang up. I knew what he was going to say, and he knew I disagreed.

"*SNL* is a great way to get you back out there, but I really think you need to talk about the loss," he said.

In true Hollywood agent form—and Brad was one of the best—he felt it was important I address the loss publicly instead of avoiding it forever. Once we did that, everyone would move on.

"I'll do it," I said, much less enthusiastic than I had been in committing to *SNL*. We settled on a sit-down with Ellen DeGeneres on her talk show.

A couple weeks later, I sat in an oversize white chair on the center of *The Ellen Show* stage on a Burbank studio lot and bared my soul. I talked about the loss. What it had felt like standing in the ring unable to orient myself in space. How afterward I had felt like I was nothing. I admitted my suicidal thoughts. Between sympathetic looks, Ellen passed me tissues and told me I was so brave. The audience clapped.

But I wasn't there for the applause. I was done trying to impress anyone pretending to be invincible. Both my dad and my grandfather committed suicide. Once you know it's an option, it lingers in the back of your mind.

I hoped Brad was right that now that I had finally addressed everything, everyone would move on so I could too.

I took the much-needed time I'd been long promising myself. I laid low and smoked a lot of weed. I didn't set foot in the gym. I rarely left the house. Travis ensured that I had a steady stream of chocolate, crepes, and a shoulder to cry on.

I had stopped crying about the fight eventually. I wasn't over it. I would never be over it. But it slowly stopped consuming me, giving way to a constant feeling of shame.

Travis came into the kitchen one morning to see me crying over a half-cooked pan of eggs. Breaking the egg yolk had sent me over the edge.

"I can't even do breakfast right," I sobbed.

"Hey, they're just eggs," Travis said, pulling me into his arms. But it wasn't just eggs.

"It's all right," he assured me. "It's going to be all right." I wasn't sure if I believed him, but I wanted to. He pulled me into his chest, the one place in this world I felt safe, where the outside world didn't matter.

In the evenings, Marina would come home from work, and we'd take bong rips and watch *The Last Alaskans,* a reality show about people living in the most remote wilderness. I envied their near hermetic existence and dreamed of leaving everything behind. I watched as they struggled to uproot dead trees in beat-up bulldozers, worrying about whether they'd kill a moose in time to get them through the impending brutal winter, and think, "That looks like the life."

Travis refused to let me completely drop out of the world.

Since the Holm fight, I had adopted a habit of looking down or away every time someone looked in my direction. I was too ashamed to face the world. Travis would call me out on it every time.

"Stop that," he'd tell me whenever he caught me dropping my gaze and trying to let my hair fall in front of my face. "Don't hide your face. Hold your head high,"

I promised I'd try.

I wasn't fighting, but Travis still was. Now that he didn't have to keep an eye out for me, he had left GFC and was training out of a gym in Vegas. While Travis trained, I'd drive forty-five minutes up into the nearby mountains where it was thirty degrees cooler and hike trails with my dog Mochi. I liked it up there. Being in nature made me feel like none of my problems mattered. The looming rock formations made me feel small. It was the perfect place to try and shrink into nothing.

During the week, I could walk miles without running into another person. I appreciated Travis's optimism for the outside world, but that place is also filled with a lot of total assholes.

A few months after the Holm fight, I was in an elevator at a hotel in Vegas. The doors opened and a normal-looking couple got in. I didn't make eye contact, but I tried to keep my head up, mindful of Travis's words. The guy had a look I knew well—it's the brief double take people do when they're not sure if they recognize you.

"You look like Ronda Rousey," he said.

"Yeah, I get that a lot," I said with a half-laugh, because, well, I do.

"Only you look a lot prettier," he added. "Not like you got your face kicked in."

I stood there for a second with my mouth in the shape of an O, unable to fully comprehend how someone could say that to another person, until the elevator dinged and the doors opened.

"Well, I am Ronda Rousey," I said, overcome with shock and rage. "And you can go fuck yourself."

"No, you're not!" he laughed.

I walked out only to realize it wasn't even my floor.

The woman with him looked mortified.

"You got yourself a real keeper there, ma'am," Trav said, dipping his head cordially at her, and followed me out.

The middle of nowhere Alaska was looking better and better every day.

Not only content to avoid the real world, but committed to it, I immersed myself in World of Warcraft. In fact, I owe a lot of getting through that period of my life to that game, Vin Diesel, and a lumberjack I met online.

I had started playing WoW in the summer of 2013 while filming *Expendables 3*. Because *The Expendables* is an action franchise around some of Hollywood's biggest names (we're talking Sylvester Stallone, Jason Statham, Harrison Ford, Arnold Schwarzenegger), the filming revolved around their schedules. I would film a day or two, then have up to five days off until I was needed again. It left a lot of downtime, which I spent in the digital battlegrounds of Azeroth.

I went from the *Expendables* to film *Furious 7*. One day on set, I mentioned my new obsession to Samantha Vincent, one of the film's executive producers, who also happened to be Vin Diesel's sister.

"What?!" she said, shocked and excited. "Have you met Vin yet?"

I had not.

"Vin loves World of Warcraft," she told me. "You have to meet."

A few hours later, he was picking me up off the ground in a giant hug, spinning me around. We didn't even need words. Bonded over our shared love of WoW, we were basically immediate best friends.

"Do you want to come over and play Warcraft?" Vin asked me. "After shooting today."

"Uh, yes!" I exclaimed.

I was living out of a hotel room during the shoot, but Vin had a giant southern-style mansion he was renting while filming. It had one of those elaborate gates and driveways you see in the movies. I walked up to the door, half expecting to be met by a gloved butler.

"Come in, come in," Vin said, excitedly. The house was like something you'd see in one of those interior design magazines or at least what I assume you would see in one of those interior design magazines as I've never actually read one.

He led me into a giant room that could have fit my entire Venice house. There was an ornate desk setup with a large monitor.

"There it is," he gestured, to a smaller table with a monitor across the room. My mouth dropped.

"I got you a battle station," he said, proudly. "You're going to run dungeons with me. Just follow me while I kill everything to level up so we can get you a flying mount."

I put my hand up to my heart. I had never been so touched. I'd been walking my ass everywhere in the world of World of Warcraft up to that point. We sat down and logged in.

"Are you using the arrow keys?" I heard him yell from across the room as I moved my character through the fictional battle lands.

"Um, yes," I said, hesitantly.

"Oh, you dear sweet, sweet child," he said, shaking his head as if he just found an orphaned puppy in the rain. "I'm going to teach you the way."

He showed the intricacies of how to play, like how to move with my mouse. He plugged in a bunch of code called "add-ons" unlocking features I never knew existed. He showed me all the little details that you can figure out for yourself eventually, but that come way faster if someone experienced is guiding you.

After filming ended, we would FaceTime and run dungeons. World of Warcraft was a place you could go and not be a celebrity, but just you, unknown to everyone else. We bonded over that.

Before the Holm fight, he had come to visit me at my house in Venice.

"Wow, you really live out in the world like this?" he said, gesturing outside my front door. "Like people are right there."

My house was on a small side street, just off Venice Beach, among a dense stretch of tiny beach bungalows next to a dog park. There was always a constant stream of people outside my front door. Tourists. Trendy moms pushing expensive baby strollers. Surfers. Skaters. People walking dogs. Homeless people camping out. Venice has a reputation for being unimpressed. When I first moved into the house, I could slip out into the crowds of the boardwalk and just be one of the people. But as my public profile had grown, I began to see what he meant. At any given time, two or three photographers would be posted up on my corner waiting for me to emerge. My house wasn't on Star Maps, but knocks at my door from fans who'd heard I lived there had become increasingly common.

Over time, as happens in life, we both got busy—me training for another stretch of title fights, him embodying a tree-like creature tasked with guarding the galaxy—and over time, our dungeon raids slowly fell off. But I like to think that Vin is still riding around on a flying mount through the Shadowlands, the wind running through his Draenei tentacles. I really hope he is.

After Australia, I abandoned a life among the people to reside instead in virtual battlefields. That's how I met Omatrya. He was running around the game doing the Headless Horsemen Halloween special, when he passed by to wish me a "Good morrow." I appreciated that he was unwilling to break character unlike other players. He would crack jokes, and we'd group up and quest together. He never asked me about my life. It was just "What are you working on?" within the game, I'd tell him, and he'd reply, "Let's rage!" and off we'd go.

Over time, I learned bits and pieces about his offline life. He was a logger in the Northwest who lived in the middle of nowhere. But mostly we just talked about the game, spending hours on strategy, immersing ourselves in little-known facts. He had no idea who I was—I was just a random person who lived in California. Strangely, he became one of my closest friends during that year. I had found friendship and a place of solace in the virtual world.

It's safe to say that I was depressed. Not just down, but chemically, clinically depressed. I had been edging toward it—or maybe already there—before the Holm fight, but the loss shoved me over the edge. Not a delicate push, but like a 300-Spartan-style kick in the stomach into a pit, and I accepted that I was just going to live there, probably forever.

Losing is not—as many people will tell you when you lose—the best way to learn. I have learned just as much, if not more, from winning. But losing does force you to reassess in ways that winning does not. You don't want to get complacent, but as long as you're winning, it's working. As my mom says, "Can't argue with results." It might not be functional, but it's working.

Until it's not.

After I lost, I had to take a look at what wasn't working.

I had carefully cultivated a "fuck-the-world" image with me stomping toward the cage to the blare of "I don't give a damn 'bout my bad reputation." It was ironic because I gave lots of damns. Before my loss, I would wake up in the morning, grab my phone, check if I had been tagged in any new photos, and scroll to see the stories that had been written about me. I would do the thing my mother always told me not to and read the comments, popping little hits of positivity before the self-esteem gained from reading twenty adoring comments was obliterated by one negative. I would lie in bed consumed by anxiety over what people thought. I would replay interviews over and over in my head, terrified I had said something wrong.

But obsessing over myself worked. I anticipated every curveball question. I would adjust, cultivate, and trim my answers until they were undeniably entertaining, witty, concise, and quotable. I was everyone's favorite interview. But the stress it caused continued to build over time. I lay awake thinking about things I had stupidly tweeted years before that forever lived on the internet. I would literally cry myself to sleep over it, then wake up puffy-eyed to look at what new pictures I had been tagged in like it was the morning's newspaper.

I hadn't truly begun to realize how self-obsessed fame was making me until the day Robin Williams died.

It was August 11, 2014, nineteen years to the day after my dad died. I would like to pretend that Williams's death resonated with me because like my father he had committed suicide, but that's the kind of revisionist bullshit people come up with later on.

As a small child living in the middle of nowhere North Dakota where broadcast TV signals did not reach, I had watched the VHS of *Hook* more times than any person should. That is where my connection to Robin Williams began and ended. And yet, when I saw the breaking news alert pop up on my phone at the gym, my first thought was, *Oh my god, what am I going to post about it?*

"Get the fuck over yourself." I said it so forcefully out loud that I caught myself off guard. I put my phone down on the bench and felt myself recoil in embarrassment.

Are you kidding me? I asked myself, this time rhetorically and silently. *Who cares what you think? No one is asking for your take on a death. This isn't about you, Ronda. Sit the fuck down.*

Since then, I had been attempting to extract myself from my reliance on social media and the constant outside validation of the internet. Following the Holm fight, I put it away completely.

I disconnected myself from everything. It helped that I didn't have any idea where my actual phone was and that my drug-dealer flip phone wasn't compatible with surfing the web. But I also just didn't care anymore. Without the bandwidth to get myself dressed half the time, I certainly didn't have the energy to be beholden to other people's perception of me. The less I worried about what other people thought about me, the better I felt about myself.

I didn't set out for the year after my loss to be one of rediscovery, where I pulled back from the world, but in doing so, I began to reclaim some sense of myself. It's just kind of what happened.

However, looming over everything was one big question that I couldn't escape: When would I return to fight?

7

Every few weeks Dana would check in on me. In the beginning, it was the standard, "Just wanted to see how you're doing." If I was healing up. How I was feeling. How deep in the dark place I was. After a few months had passed, he asked the question that I knew was coming. "Are you ready to come back?"

The answer was no.

On a physical recovery level, it took six months for my loose teeth to heal to the point where I could bite an apple. I also underwent my seventh knee surgery, attempting to repair ligament damage with my own stem cells. (It turned out I had torn the last shreds of my ACL when I knocked myself out on the stairs.) Beyond all that, my body had spent over five years taking relentless beatings in training. I had lost any sense of what it felt like to wake up in the morning and not ache.

But I knew that anything physical I could push through. It was "everything else" that made the idea of returning to fighting feel unbearable.

It had been almost a year since I'd last stepped in the cage. Dana and I were out to dinner in LA and inevitably the subject of my return hung over the conversation.

"Where are you at?" he asked me, referring to my mental state obviously, as I was physically sitting across the table from him.

I sighed. "I don't know." A lot of that post-fight year had been defined by

"I don't know." I knew I had to come back, but I didn't know if I wanted to. I felt like I owed it to Dana. I felt like I owed it to the fans. I felt like I owed it to the world to fight again and be an example of coming back from adversity. How could I face the gauntlet of press and daily demands to discuss my last loss without telling the truth? My brain had taken too much trauma to fight at the top level anymore. I could barely take a jab without being dazed.

"What do you need?" Dana asked. "What can we do?"

I thought for a moment.

"Listen, any bitch on earth walks in this front door, I'll beat the shit out of her right now," I said, gesturing to the entrance to the restaurant. "But I can't go through weeks of interrogations about my last match under the guise of promoting the next one. I just can't go through that right now. I don't know if I ever can."

Dana leaned forward, nodding. He's a businessman and promoter, so the wheels were always turning.

My title run as the UFC women's bantamweight champion had spanned nearly three years and six UFC title fights. But in the months following, it had ping-ponged around the division, first to Holm, who turned around and lost it to Miesha. Pulling off an upset is one thing, establishing a title reign is another.

Dana had approached me about a possible Miesha rematch, but I was still healing at that point, and the last thing I wanted was to jump into a months-long media blitz with Miesha smugly holding a belt that she'd never have been able to take from me.

"You can have the winner of Miesha and Amanda Nunes if you want it," he now offered.

It would be the New Year's card, he said. And yes, he promised, it would be New Year's this time, not moved up on short notice like the Holm fight.

I was still hesitant. I didn't want to have to sit through press event after press event, interview after interview, and be dissected and cross-examined, especially when the true answers were ones I couldn't give if I still wanted to be a fighting athlete. I couldn't get up there and lie. But I also couldn't go out there and tell the truth.

After my loss, I saw how quickly the media turned on me. Running to them and crying about my concussion history would be seen as excuses by people who didn't understand the actual impact that kind of damage can have. And for any future opponent, that information would be the equivalent of pointing a flashing "Hit Here" arrow right at my head. The Holm loss, almost everyone believed (as the betting odds for my next fight would prove), was a fluke.

What I saw as one of the worst moments of my life, the media saw as a ratings opportunity. There was giddiness around witnessing my failure. To see them flip from "Ronda is unbeatable" to "We saw these cracks" faster than it takes to change a channel. I used to laugh about how people chalked up my success to being a one-trick pony (that trick being the armbar) until I started knocking people out to end fights. But in losing, they talked about me as if I was a racehorse. Actually, if I'd been a favored horse, the media gallery would have said things like, "Oh, this is tragic. I hope she's OK."

For my entire career in the UFC, I felt indebted. To Dana for believing in me. To the fans for watching me. To the media for covering me. And while I felt that I had an obligation to fight one more time for Dana and the fans, I didn't feel like I owed the media shit.

They had no real incentive to help me convey the cumulative weight of the last years. I'd spent a year either high or reevaluating, and during that time I reflected on how unhappy dealing with the media made me. I couldn't help but ask myself, *Why am I taking part in this cycle that is sucking so much of my time, energy, and mental bandwidth yet pays me nothing while making millions of dollars for the people who twist my words to talk shit about me?*

"I can fight," I explained. "I just don't want to go through the fucking circus of everything before."

"Then skip it," Dana said. "You don't have to do any of it. You don't have to do any media. You don't have to do any press conferences. You don't have to fucking do anything. You just show up and fight."

I bit my bottom lip, unconsciously poking my tongue into the fleshy indent. Knowing the promotional expectations of top-of-the-card fighters, I had been all but certain Dana would never agree to my terms. He had previously pulled Nick Diaz from a fight card when Nick failed to show up to do media.

"OK," I said, reluctantly. "I'll think about it." It was the first time I didn't say yes to Dana immediately.

A huge grin spread across Dana's face. He knew before I did that I meant yes. After we finished eating and stood up to leave, he gave me a hug.

"Just give me a call when you're ready," he said.

I got in the car and stared out the windshield. I didn't think I'd ever really be ready to fight again. For an entire year, "When will Ronda return?" had been hanging over my head, following me like Eeyore's rain cloud. I just wanted to get it over with. And the longer I was away, I was just going to get rustier.

I watched the fight. Miesha lost, bloodied and tapping to Nunes in the first round. Her title run coming to an end before it ever truly began. Just like Holm. Nunes was 13-4 as a professional fighter, but three of her four losses were to chicks I'd beat in a combined total of 55 seconds.

But a champion's one advantage over the contender lies in their confidence. Nunes's confidence skyrocketed after winning the title, and I knew every win she racked up would make her even tougher to beat. She was only going to get better. It was now or never.

Right after the Nunes-Tate fight, I called Dana.

"Go ahead," I said. "Book the fight."

The truth is if I hadn't felt like I still owed a comeback to Dana and the fans, I easily could have walked away after the Holm fight. My goal of perfection destroyed, there was nothing left in the fight game for me. But I viewed being a champion as almost a public service. The first time around I had been chasing perfection, but maybe greater lessons could be learned from overcoming adversity, I told myself. Maybe this was the role I was called upon to play.

In October, the UFC announced Nunes and I would be headlining the New Year's Eve fight card. She was the reigning champion, but the promotional posters blared the words "She's Back."

Save for the occasional hike, it had been almost a year since I'd last worked out. I don't mean that in an "Oh, this old thing"-gestures-to-self-wearing-a-ballgown type of way. I mean in a lying-on-the-couch-playing-World of Warcraft-cuddling-with-my-dog-and-eating-crepes-for-a-year type of way. Well, sometimes I'd get high and go in the garage to do Pilates, but I don't think that counts.

When I finally got back into the gym, I was amazed by how much that year off helped my body. I bounced back into shape almost immediately. For the first time in as long as I could remember, the end of practice wasn't marked by constant pain and exhaustion. Soreness, sure, but not pain.

True to his word, Dana didn't ask me to talk to anyone. Which only made people talk about me more.

And yet, as I went through camp, it felt like I was just going through the motions. The process just wasn't fun anymore. I called the weeks in the lead-up to a fight "montage time," because if life were a movie, this time-frame would be condensed down to a series of quick clips set to motivational music building up to a dramatic showdown. During training, I would envision it as a montage in my mind. But instead of hearing "Eye of the Tiger," the music in my head was a lot of sad Simon & Garfunkel.

I didn't dare say it out loud, but I was dreading the entire thing. I was coming back for Dana. I was coming back for the fans. But I wasn't coming back for me.

Once again, I found myself repeating, "Best on your worst day." Until I realized that at some point during camp, I was now saying, "Every day is my worst day, and I just got to be the best anyway."

From a technical perspective, camp was going flawlessly. But I was self-conscious about my ability to operate under the risk of getting hit. I wanted to put as much real risk in my sparring as possible. I treated every single hit like it could knock me out, because it could. Fighting is a brutal sport, and because of this, when you're training, the risk of injury is too high if you do things exactly like you would in competition. Instead, training is more of a simulation where you stop before you fully execute. You don't throw a punch as hard as you plan to in the cage unless you're wearing bigger gloves. You don't take hits unless you're wearing headgear. You don't crank an armbar as much as you will on fight night. You have to find the sweet spot where you're trying not to hurt the other person and not letting that restraint become a habit.

That balance between skill and holding back is even more important when it comes to your sparring partners. For high-level fighters, training partners are some of the unsung heroes. They are typically elite fighters themselves who are brought in (and paid) to help prepare a fighter. They come to work with the understanding that—despite protective measures—their job is, in part, to take a beating. Training partners can vary from camp to camp, depending on what your opponent's strengths might be. In MMA, they can also vary from discipline to discipline, such as kickboxing or grappling.

In my previous camps, we would practice in parts and protection. I would do stand-up boxing sparring, but with bigger gloves that didn't make it possible to go directly from standing into grappling. Then I'd do grappling training with smaller gloves that made it possible to do takedowns. I'd "show" my strikes (basically tap the other person) instead of delivering full blows. It was the same thing on the ground, where I'd mime blows rather than deliver them. The protective gear felt bulky, but it was the best we could do to avoid injury and having to postpone the fight or fight injured.

This time around, the gloves semi-literally came off. I trained solely with fight gloves. One of the main reasons you don't train with actual fight gloves is an increased risk of getting cut. With less padding and more exposure, there's also a greater chance that you can injure your hand. Considering I had to have surgery for breaking my thumb after knocking out Alexis Davis in my fourth UFC fight, I was well aware of how real that risk was.

But the biggest threat in this fight with Nunes was being caught again. Training is structured around not having to worry about being dealt a knockout blow—which is the exact thing I needed to be worried about heading into the fight. She had a headhunting style where she constantly swung for the fences at your face. It'd backfired on her before in her losses, but I didn't have the capacity to stand in the pocket with her the way someone like Alexis Davis or Cat Zingano could.

We brought in sparring partners who were ranked UFC fighters, like Raquel Pennington (who had been on Miesha's team in *The Ultimate Fighter* and had since made a career for herself). We brought in guys who were about my size but who could throw harder punches than any female opponent would. I wore MMA practice gloves (which at six ounces are two ounces heavier than fight gloves, but they protected my thumbs and were still about half the weight of boxing sparring gloves). I went without headgear. I needed to have the confidence that when I stepped into the cage, I was truly ready for whatever was coming at me. I needed the reps of keeping my hands closer to my face than headgear would allow, I needed to prepare as if a single punch could be the end of the world. I couldn't afford to take any more hits, even in the gym. I needed to know I could still be in there with the best and not let them touch me.

It was a big risk, but I did extremely well in those sparring sessions. I was going in and dropping people to the ground. My transitions were quicker and tighter than ever, tapping everyone out with ease. People would later question my training camp, but it was technically one of the best. But mentally, I wasn't fighting to win; I was fighting not to lose. Although imperceptible to anyone watching, the physical dominance I was showing in the cage was powered and driven by fear of losing my legacy instead of pursuing greatness.

The day of the weigh-ins, I walked out to the roar of the crowd in Vegas. It was the first time I had stood before that many people since Australia. As the challenger, I stepped on the scale first. I made weight and smiled. Cutting weight for the Nunes fight was one of the easiest weight cuts I ever had. I walked over to the side of the stage to redress. I pulled my jeans back on and bent down to put on my shoes when I heard them announce words that I had only ever heard attributed to me in-person.

Joe Rogan's voice echoed from the arena speakers. "And now, the reigning, defending, undisputed UFC women's bantamweight champion of the World."

I looked up to see my opponent climbing the stairs. Or I assumed it was her. I couldn't be certain given that the woman walking up to the stage was wearing a cheap lion mask that looked like she'd grabbed it at a post-Halloween clearance sale. She stepped on the scale. She turned and, I guess, looked at me. At least, the little plastic eyes of her lion mask were pointed in my direction, the pink painted tongue hanging from the mouth.

We squared up for the requisite pre-showdown face-off, until Dana said, "You're good," signaling we could break. I turned and walked offstage to a cheering arena, leaving the faux feline fighter to handle the interviews.

That night, my mom came by my room. We lay on the bed of my suite, and she told me all of the reasons why I was going to win, for the first time adding "And because you're not so ugly that you need to hide behind a stupid lion mask" to the list.

The next day, the warm-up was great. I had the right mouth guard. The walkout was great. Everything that had gone wrong leading up to the fight before was flawless.

But I got hit once, and that was it. The world swayed. Herb Dean, the same referee who had called my fight in Australia, jumped in, this time quickly. It was the end of the fight, and my UFC career.

I don't remember anything in the cage except that I never left my feet. I didn't want the fight to end. I was certain that I could still fight, but I have to admit that hours later I was still out of it.

My brain was done fighting.

I was done fighting.

I was ushered out of the cage, no less devastated than a year before, but slightly more aware of the moment. We passed through a black curtain into a cement, fluorescent-lit corridor with floors lined by taped-down electrical cables. The space was filled with the frenetic motion of a UFC pay-per-view fight-night. Intimidating security staff checking credentials, black-clad cameramen and sound guys running back and forth, men and women in their thirties, clad in business attire, talking into headsets and carrying clipboards. As I emerged, everything halted. Conversations stopped mid-sentence, heads lowered and voices hushed like a funeral procession was passing through.

We walked into the locker room, and I just stood there, sobbing. Travis held my hands. My mom wrapped her arm around me, my sister Maria standing next to her. My coaches, except for Edmond, who was keeping his distance from my mom, lined the walls of the small space. Dana knocked on the door.

"Is it OK if I come in?" he asked softly.

I nodded.

He gave me a hug, and I wrapped my arms around him, burying my face in his neck, ugly crying.

"I'm done," I said. "That's it."

"Well, at least you'll have a lot to write in your next book," my mom said, attempting sympathetic reassurance.

"There isn't gonna be another book!" I yelled into Dana's neck.

For the first time since I had met him, Dana was quiet. He hugged me for another second, then turned and slipped out the door.

I looked around the room. I just could not be there. I needed to leave. Now.

"I want to go," I said.

"OK," Travis said. "Then let's go." However, he swayed ever so slightly.

"Go," my mom said. "I'll take care of anything that needs to be done tomorrow."

We were led out of the arena, back the quarter mile to the MGM where Travis's supersized diesel truck, which he called Queen Elizabeth (the most powerful woman he could think of), was waiting for us at the door. We ran to the truck with nothing save the clothes on our backs. Travis and I jumped into the back. Maria pulled the seat all the way forward. She looked like a child sitting at the massive steering wheel. The truck roared to life. My mom stood on the curb, watching as we drove off. The truck squealed as Maria turned the wheel.

Travis held me as I cried.

"Fuck this, let go have some babies," I said.

He nodded.

"Babe, I want nothing more than to have babies with you, but I don't want to use them as a Band-Aid," he said. "You get yourself right first."

By the time the post-fight press conference would have ended, the lights of the Vegas strip had already receded from view.

Halfway through the four-hour drive home, Travis leaned over and asked Maria if she could stop at the upcoming In-N-Out. He ran in and came out bearing two bags of burgers, fries, and milkshakes. I ate, then fell asleep with Travis's arms wrapped around me.

I didn't feel better or less empty or less emotion over the loss, but there was a finality that came from that fight.

The first time I lost, I spent hours spiraling and second-guessing everything that had gone wrong. Maybe it was because I was really dehydrated from cutting weight, and my brain didn't have the same fluid cushion. Maybe it was the mouth guard, the way it didn't line up with my lower jaw. Maybe it was the stress of the weight cut, the lack of an appropriate warm-up room, the family/coach conflict, Trav's ex drama, the travel, knocking myself out and tearing my ACL falling down the stairs, the media and the other exhaustion colliding. Maybe my brain just needed time to rest, and if I took enough time, I'd heal. Maybe. Maybe. Maybe.

But this time, I had eliminated every possible distraction. I was rested and healthy. I had felt fantastic all of camp. Everything had been perfect.

And even then, the first time I got touched, I was out. That's how I knew I would never fight again. I just couldn't take the hits anymore. I didn't need to consult anyone or think it over. I just knew.

I ushered MMA into a new era, where it was understood that women not only deserved a spot on the fight card, but atop it. I wanted to be remembered for what I had accomplished in the sport, not as one of those fighters who didn't know when to say when.

Losing was being shown the door. Losing was unspeakably hard. Walking away wasn't.

For some people, their whole identity is tied up in being a fighter. My whole identity was tied up in being a champion. I couldn't be just a fighter that's in the mix. For me, there was nothing left to fight for.

I remember reading about the Battle of Marathon, from which the race derives its name, the story of how a messenger ran 26.2 miles to deliver a message, then collapsed dead. I always wondered how someone could just push themselves until they fell over and died. I didn't wonder anymore. I had run my MMA marathon to the end, and that part of my life had just fallen over and died.

About a month later, Dana called.

"Hey, so you want to fight?" he asked. "Nunes in Brazil. Another shot at the title."

I had to appreciate his optimism.

"No. I'm really done," I told him.

It was the first time I ever told him no when he called.

8

I find it fitting that "experiencing a loss" is used to describe death. To me, that's what losing feels like. Like an overwhelming grief that shakes you from sleep at three in the morning, leaving you staring into the darkness. A loneliness that makes you feel all by yourself even in a crowded room. A scar that fades but never fully disappears. A part of your soul has died.

From the outside, it probably looked like I took the second loss better. But it was equally devastating. I just better knew what to expect. I let the numbness wash over me. I wasn't going to be an example of overcoming adversity for anyone, but I no longer wanted to be everything to everyone. I wanted to be nothing to no one. I wanted to disappear.

My entire MMA career, I gave and I gave. I never said no. I pushed aside what I wanted. I had returned to fight again, not for myself, but for everyone else to whom I felt so indebted.

When I walked out of the Octagon the final time, I knew that I had given everything I had. I didn't owe anyone a fucking thing. As time went on and I started to find my way back to the land of the living and on the other side of mourning my loss, I realized how liberating not giving a fuck was.

I was not, as headlines declared, hiding out from the world, I just didn't want to be around people. As hard as it may be to believe, given the fact that I spent so much time and effort trying to get millions of people to pay money to watch events where I was center stage, I don't like being the center of attention. I'm good at it, but it feeds off me. It made me a lot of money. But it's not my happy place.

LA no longer felt like my happy place either. It's not a place where you can easily hide out if your name has ever been in the headlines. I found myself retreating more and more behind drawn blinds. But even then, I couldn't escape.

A few weeks after the Nunes fight, photos of me standing in my bathrobe, barefoot at my kitchen door feeding my dog on the back porch—taken over my eight-foot fence with a telephoto lens—were splashed across the internet. I had always been under the impression that there was a line that couldn't be crossed. That as long as I stayed within the confines of my property line, if I literally did not step foot outside of the house, I would be left alone. I was wrong.

As the champion, I felt like anyone who stopped me to ask for a picture was a person that I had to be there for. That in exchange for my good fortune. I owed them.

Now, it felt like everyone who stared at or approached me was rubbernecking at the train wreck of my life. Even when I ran into a genuine fan who wanted nothing anything more than just to say "hi," they would say something like "I was so devastated when you lost." Well-intended comments that were constant reminders how I had let so many people down.

There was no "just don't think about it" because the world around me wouldn't let me forget.

A few weeks after my fight, Travis and I took a road trip. I was in desperate need of a change of scenery. No one was ever expecting us in the small rural towns we passed through. We didn't even know where we were going to stop along the way. We had checked into a two-star motel, just off the interstate, for the night after driving all day. Flipping channels, we had landed on *Tosh.0* as we lay in bed. I cuddled into the nook of Travis's arm, my happy place, watching as host Daniel Tosh offered witty commentary on videos pulled from the Web.

"That was more depressing than a Ronda Rousey comeback," he quipped.

The studio audience didn't even laugh. They groaned.

I turned off the TV and cried on Trav's chest. I was literally a fucking joke now. One that didn't even land with the audience. And I couldn't get away, not even in the middle of nowhere.

The sting started to dull after a while. Then it callused over with resentment. I resented the fans, resented the media. I was determined to outwait my infamy, and in a way it worked. The news cycles ran on without me. I gave them nothing new to talk about.

Travis and I already spent every day together, but we officially moved in together when I left Venice and we bought a place in Riverside, seventy miles outside of LA, well beyond the boundaries of its Thirty Mile Zone of stationed paparazzi.

Travis's first ex-wife (with whom we shared custody of the boys) had remarried and moved there, so we got a place almost walking distance from her new house, so the boys could move freely between our homes. Travis had started fighting to support his sons, but I could tell it pained him spending months away from them training for fights. We decided to retire and be full-time parents for the boys together while they went through some of their most formative years.

I never pursued fame as a goal. It was a tool I leveraged to make my goals happen. And fame wasn't something that just happened to me, I worked for it. Coming up in MMA, I did every single interview, took every opportunity, every big commercial deal, every magazine cover, every red carpet possible. It didn't matter if it was in the middle of training camp, I did absolutely all of it. To be the fighting people's champion, and hopefully the next big action hero, I had to hustle my ass off every day. I made sure my face was constantly plastered everywhere to the point it was almost impossible to escape.

I had benefited from fame, but I fucking hated it. The stress of being under constant scrutiny for every word I said and angle I was filmed from every second of the day was crushing me. I was constantly being snuck in a back door, kept in a private room. It was isolating even when I wasn't alone. I wanted to do normal things with my family. To stand in line without being asked for a photo. To go to a public bathroom without feeling like I was walking a red carpet. To be able to just exist in the world and not be on display in it.

I couldn't just turn off the frenzy I created around myself. So instead, I wore it down by dropping out of the public eye altogether. And to an extent, it worked.

A week after we closed on the house in Riverside, under a waterfall in New Zealand, Travis asked me to marry him. I accepted before he could even fully get the words out.

———

I did not realize it at the time, but losing set me on a path to happiness. It forced me to step back, to reassess and reprioritize. To ask myself: What do I want to do? For the first time in a long time, I was presented with a question where I didn't have a rehearsed, witty reply.

Failure forced me to realize I was living my life not for me but as a "fuck you" to anyone who had ever doubted me. Spite had been such a huge motivator for me in the beginning, and I accomplished so much because of it, but it had begun to fester. I became so obsessed with proving my doubters and detractors wrong that I was doing things I didn't even want to do just to show them how successful and happy I was. To make it so they couldn't escape my face.

When I lost, knowing the pleasure those people derived from my failure consumed me more than the failures themselves.

One day after venting my frustrations, Trav looked me directly in the eye and told me, "Fuck them. They don't deserve a second thought. Living life out of spite to them is still allowing them to dictate your life."

He was right. I decided it was time to change and picked up a shovel.

I set to work making the house in Riverside, a small 2.4-acre farm built in 1979 and in desperate need of updating that we affectionately called "Browsey Acres," into a home and trying to figure out what I was going to do with my life now that I wasn't a fighter. For so long, my life revolved around pursuing perfection. Now, I wanted to spend it pursuing happiness.

I started with a garden. Well, actually I started by smoking a lot of weed, playing a lot of video games, and ordering a lot of food delivery, then moved into gardening. Emboldened by shows about life off the grid, gardening seemed like the perfect entry point when it came to self-sufficiency skills that would allow me to exit society entirely. Plus, it was something I could do without having to leave the yard. "Yard" being a euphemistic description of the concrete-bordered dry dirt squares in front of our farmhouse.

According to the internet, the first step was working the dirt. I found an old hoe in the barn, bought some seeds off Amazon, and went to work. Like an amateur, I took my hoe out into the midafternoon ninety-plus-degree heat and hacked at the ground for hours.

Following a week's worth of labor and some time and labor-saving suggestions from the local nursery, I got to the point where I could plant some seeds. I walked around the house and grabbed the hose, pulling it behind me ready to get this garden growing. In a scene straight out of a silent comedy, I found the hose was ten feet too short to reach my seeds. I dug through the garage until I found two old watering cans. I drizzled each little seed plot with water.

Against all odds, one bud began to emerge. I was elated.

The next morning, it was gone, eaten by a squirrel before it ever had a chance.

Undeterred, every morning, before the sun started fully baking, I put on my large straw hat and gloves, grabbed my watering can, and set back out to tend my nonexistent garden. Then it happened. I saw a single seedling had sprouted from where I planted dozens of sunflowers.

"Hey there, little guy," I said, lovingly.

This time, I was ready. I built a small makeshift fence around the tiny plant. I fortified the fence as the flower grew, the lone result of a month's worth of work tilling the dirt and seventeen packets of seeds. There it stood, surrounded by the floral equivalent of Fort Knox.

It would have been easy to view my entry into gardening as unsuccessful given the hard work and time I had put in, not to mention a lack of sufficient water, but as my little flower climbed toward the sky, I viewed it as a testament to what was possible. It was the first time that I didn't focus on where I had failed, but where I had succeeded. All the failed seeds didn't matter if even just one grew. Not only that, but I had to recognize that sometimes, the speed of progress is beyond your control. I was being forced to stop and smell the sunflower.

Not long after, Trav surprised me with four little chicks, in what began our regenerative ranching journey. Two days later, our brood was reduced to three when a hawk swooped down and stole little Moa right in front of me as I ate breakfast.

"Moooooa," I tearfully cried out toward the sky as the hawk flapped away, my helpless chick struggling in its talons.

We built a little fortress around their henhouse, then added ducks to our flock. The more the farm grew, the happier I became. I started to discover the difference between outward validation and things that were validating in themselves. I was much happier scrubbing algae from the walls of our duck pond with no one to appreciate it other than the ducks pushing each other to get to the water than I ever was being photographed leaving a fancy restaurant to a crowd of people pushing each other to get my autograph.

For my entire fight career, I was living in a world that was go-go-go. Life consisted of endorphin-fueled training or serotonin overload, bucket-list-level shit. Jetting off to the Cannes Film Festival promoting a movie I'm costarring in with fucking Rocky himself. Flying in an F-16 with the US Air Force Thunderbirds. Surfing in Malibu with Red Hot Chili Peppers' lead singer Anthony Kiedis—who mentions he's bringing his friend Ed, and Ed turns out to be actor Edward Norton—just to happen upon surf legend Laird Hamilton paddle-boarding by. I was having unforgettable experiences that most people would remember their entire lives, but instead of enjoying it, I was ticking off boxes and not taking it in.

I had just fought Zingano in 2015 when I got a call from my agent, Brad. "Hey, do you want to do a spot at WrestleMania with the Rock?"

Which is how, a few weeks later, I found myself front row at Wrestle-Mania 31 in San Francisco along with the other Four Horsewomen, Marina,

Shayna, and Jessamyn. We watched as Dwayne "The Rock" Johnson walked down the ramp to confront the "WWE's Authority," Triple H and Stephanie McMahon, real-world executives who also played fictionalized versions of themselves in the ring.

"We can create a WrestleMania moment, right here, right now," the Rock said, launching into one of his trademark rhyming taunts.

Triple H dismissed the idea. Stephanie, who despite being one of the nicest people I have ever met, played one of the best heels—or a villain in pro wrestling terminology—in WWE, sneered, slapped him in the face, and ordered him out of the ring, mockingly waving him off.

The Rock turned, looking as if he was going to leave, walked out of the ring and circled around until he stood in front of me. A chant of my name started to circle around the stadium, like an audible version of "the wave." Seventy-seven thousand fans, the most in WrestleMania history, roared as my face appeared on the jumbotron above the ring. The Rock and I exchanged looks of disdain for Steph and Triple H as if to say, "We *totally* did not rehearse this, but fortunately I happen to be here and if you want me to join you in kicking some ass, I'm in." The WWE relies a lot on exaggerated unsaid looks. The Rock gestured to me to join him.

As I jumped over the barricade, one thought went through my mind: *Don't look stupid.* The Rock and I did a few more "We gonna do this?" "Yes, we're gonna do this" glances. A fist bump later, we entered the ring.

I stood in the ring with three of the biggest names in WWE history at its largest-ever event, the crowd screaming *my* name. Steph, in full character, declared me the most dangerous unarmed woman on the planet, dominant in the Octagon, but not the ring.

"You need to understand something, Steph," I said, trying to act as if it was authentically happening in the moment, not the scripted down-to-the-sentence work of WWE. "Any ring I step into is mine." The crowd was locked in on us.

The Rock took the mic, then lunged at Triple H, backing him up against the ropes in a series of choreographed blows and chopping him across the chest before throwing him my way for a hip toss. The crowd erupted. Steph came at me, yelling, then raised her hand as if to slap me. When I grabbed her arm as if to rip it off, the crowd went wild.

"And that is the biggest WrestleMania moment of the night!" the Rock had declared as Steph and Triple H retreated up the ramp.

He wasn't the only one to think so. At the year-end Slammy Awards (never one to miss a chance at self-promotion, WWE had its own award show to give awards to itself), it was declared the "This Is Awesome!" Moment of the Year.

I wish I could say stepping into the ring for the first time was a transformative moment, but honestly it is one of those vague memories you only think about when someone brings it up.

WrestleMania was still going on as I boarded the private flight that WWE had chartered so that I could get back to LA for training. My mind was only focused on: "I've got my next fight coming up." And nothing mattered more than that.

"How was the WrestleMania thing?" my mom asked me that night on the phone, not really knowing what WrestleMania was but just that it was a big deal.

"It was good," I said.

"Did you have fun?" she asked.

"Sure, it wasn't a life altering event or anything, but fun," I said.

I shrugged. "I mean, it's a cool thing that I got to do, but it's not like this is going to be my future."

———

Now, nearly two years later, I had a newfound appreciation for living in the moment, but found I was having a hard time remembering things from one minute to the next. I'd forget countries I'd been to, events I attended, things I scheduled, where I had put my phone, seemingly 1,000 times a day. I was starting to worry about the lasting effects decades of head trauma had left me with. Did I have CTE? Was I deteriorating? One of my greatest fears is to end up a shell of myself, old and broken in mind and body, unable to move or experience new things, unable to remember what I'd done. Every time I forgot something I wanted to cry. Sometimes I would.

"You're getting in your head," Trav told me. "You're not becoming more forgetful. You've always been like this, except before you'd just shrug and say, 'At least I'm cute!' And move on."

I did so many things not for the enjoyment they gave me at the time, but for the satisfaction of remembering I'd done them. But those memories were fleeting, I couldn't hoard them. I'd forget them. Collecting enviable experiences didn't equate to happiness the way I had hoped. The present was all I had. I found my phone for the twentieth time in an hour, wiped my eyes, smoked a bowl, and went outside to check on my prized sunflower and chickens.

Between that WrestleMania spot and my new life as an amnesiac horti-culturist, a few things happened in succession.

Shayna left MMA behind for pro wrestling. Toward the end of her fight career, she'd started dabbling in wrestling "just for fun." She made her first unofficial wrestling debut just a few weeks before her last UFC fight. Watching her train for the ring and hearing her talk about wrestling was like watching one of those romantic comedies, when everyone else knows the main character is madly in love, even if they haven't realized it yet. When she told me she was going to pursue it as a career, the first word out of my mouth was, "Finally."

She worked her way up the independent circuit, toured in Japan, and was having the time of her life. I saw her happier in the ring than I had ever seen her in the Octagon. She trained in LA at first with her mentor, former UFC fighter and pro wrestler Josh Barnett, but when it became clear that she had the potential to pursue wrestling as an actual career, she moved to Flor-ida, the unofficial mecca of professional wrestling. Aspiring wrestlers flock to Central Florida the way Hollywood draws aspiring actors. Shayna had caught the attention of the WWE and was training out of their Performance Center where the organization develops wrestlers through its NXT brand.

Think of NXT as WWE's minor league system with the weekly Raw and SmackDown shows being the "Big Leagues."

Jessamyn was also transitioning out of MMA and looking at pro wrestling as a possible next step.

Marina—much to my delight—had ditched the loser boyfriend and fallen in love with Chris, an up-and-coming wrestler known in the ring as Roderick Strong, whom she'd met through the pro wrestling circle that was taking the place of MMA in all my best friends' lives. When she found out she was pregnant, she took a leap and moved with him to Florida.

With my social circle now centering around pro wrestling, it was never far from my thoughts. Travis and I had set a wedding date for August. I looked ahead to our life together, to the family we were building with the boys, to a future that I hoped would sooner rather than later center around the needs of a very tiny person. As I thought about that next phase of my life, I asked myself, *Is there anything I feel like I haven't done yet before I close this chapter?*

My favorite part of moviemaking was fight choreography. Acting was fun, but scripting fights was my passion. However, post my UFC losses, the movie offers stopped coming. I never aspired to be the next Meryl Streep, I'd die to be the next Bruce Lee. Pro wrestling provided an opportunity to do what I loved most about cinema: stunts. But where films can get away with telling the story, breaking for a fight scene, then cutting back to the story, WWE offered almost the purest, most difficult way to use fight choreography as a form of storytelling. It was done live in front of an audience, sometimes even improvised on the spot. After working on films where we rehearsed for weeks to shoot fights one beat at a time, the skill it took to perform an entire fight live while making every move believable from every angle blew my mind. Travis was right: In my heart I am more than just a fighter. I am also an entertainer, a storyteller. This felt like the perfect way to combine them all.

Once I considered the possibility of pro wrestling, I found that pursuing it was all I was thinking about. My style of fighting was always about following concepts, not memorizing techniques. I just had to learn how to use them to tell a story with a fight.

I had spent so many years sacrificing any kind of enjoyment in the pursuit of perfection, that it had been a long time since I'd been able to just have fun in the gym without this nagging feeling that I should be doing more. Since my WrestleMania appearance with the Rock, I'd done a little bit of wrestling training, but just playing around, not in pursuit of a career. My friends had been doing it, so I tagged along.

In the ring, I could just enjoy myself. I liked running the ropes. I liked taking bumps (the term for where you fall to the mat in wrestling). I just liked learning new shit, the challenge of how to create the most entertaining fight possible. I would lose track of time and train for four, five hours straight without even pushing myself, lost in trying to piece this new art form together in my mind. I didn't even feel tired.

I still hadn't figured out what I was going to do with my life now that I had left the UFC behind, but I was having so much fun learning to wrestle that it didn't matter. I asked Chris, Marina's to-be-husband, for names of people to train with in LA. He referred me to former WWE champion Brian Kendrick.

"He's good?" I asked.

"We aren't really friends," Chris said, in a tone that alluded to some past disagreement without providing details. "But if you're looking for someone to train with, I respect his knowledge so much that I'd highly recommend him anyway."

It was the most backhanded glowing referral I'd ever heard.

Kendrick trained wrestlers out of a gym called Santino Bros. in LA's greater urban sprawl. The gym was in an industrial part of town in one of those neighborhoods that can elicit a raised eyebrow when you mention going there. It wasn't actually a gym, but a wrestling ring set up in a converted garage among a row of garages, each a different blue-collar business. To one side of Santino's was an auto repair shop, on the other side, a paint shop. It was small and had a level of grime that can only come from a combination of nearby exhaust fumes, smoke, and the sweat of people grappling with each other in a poorly ventilated space.

A substantial revenue generator for the gym came not from training aspiring wrestlers but from producing custom matches. Custom matches are well-known in the wrestling world, but less so to the general public. For a couple hundred/thousand bucks a pop (depending on the talent), fans script out private matches. For some wrestlers, custom matches are almost a rite of passage. These types of matches are how a number of women in the industry make most of their money. It's a lot of scissoring the head, groin shots, and weird kinky shit. At Santino's—just like many other gyms—it was a standard part of the business model. We'd practice in the ring between shoots. On more than one occasion, the ring was a little damp. I never asked from what.

In contrast to GFC, which had walls of windows, here I didn't have to see anyone nor could anyone see me. It was a perfect little hidey-hole to get away from the world.

We'd train, then smoke weed and hang around and shoot the shit. No one expected me to be this finely tuned athletic machine. It was like a lax sort of excellence.

With no expectations, I found myself training with the focus and intensity I used to put into preparing for a title fight. I also found myself starting to wonder, "What if..." What if I wanted to do this as a career? What if I wanted to make a run at the WWE? What if it actually happened?

I called my agent.

"Hey, Brad," I said, casually.

"What's up?" he asked.

"I had this idea. What if...?" I paused.

"If...?" Brad met my drawn-out question with one of his own.

"OK," I said, restarting. "You know I'm getting married, and you know the girls are all in Florida. Marina just had a baby."

I could envision Brad on the other end of the call, waiting for me to get to the point.

The words rushed out. "So, I was thinking instead of a bachelorette party, I wanna do an RV trip with the girls. Only since Marina can't come with a baby, what if we could all train together at the Performance Center for like a week before the road trip? You know, for fun. What do you think WWE would think of that?"

Brad didn't even hesitate. "They'd fucking love it!"

It hadn't been spoken aloud, but WWE and I had been flirting. We were interested in each other. We thought there might be something there. We wanted to see where it might go. But neither of us wanted to say anything and scare the other one off in case the feeling wasn't mutual. Someone had to make the first move.

The Performance Center, known among wrestlers as the PC, is a giant warehouse-type training facility. It's probably half the size of a football field, crammed with a half-dozen wrestling rings. There's the weight room, cardio machines, and athletic training staff that you'd expect from a sleek, state-of-the-art sports training facility. But it has the production resources and capabilities you'd expect from a film set.

It smells like rubber, sweat, and hope.

Seventy or so NXT wrestlers train out of the PC at a given time. They come from all places and all backgrounds. Some wrestlers like Shayna have had success as a professional or college athlete before transitioning to "sports entertainment." Others, like Marina's then-fiancé/now-husband Chris, work their way up wrestling's independent circuit to get their WWE shot. Wrestlers like Solo Sikoa come from legacy wrestling families, meaning they were literally born into this world. And there are wild card stories like Liv Morgan. Liv (whose actual name—Gionna Daddio—is an even better ring name than Liv) was a gorgeous former cheerleader working at Hooters when the trainer at her gym passed along her info to a WWE contact who set her up for a tryout despite her having no real wrestling background.

Wrestlers range from near giants, the size of linebackers and sumo wrestlers, known for their power and strength but who move with impressive agility for their size, to petite gymnasts who can do crazy flips off the top rope, and every size and build in between.

NXT was founded by and under the control of Triple H, real name Paul Levesque. In addition to being my in-ring WrestleMania nemesis, he is arguably one of the best professional wrestlers in history and one of the better people on the business side. He is married to Stephanie McMahon, who is the daughter of WWE's Emperor Palpatine, Vince McMahon. Vince took over the company from his father in the early 1980s and spent the better part of forty years playing a real-world pro-wrestling version of Monopoly, buying up and absorbing smaller promotions until he basically owned them all. It's hard sometimes to know where the evil, unethical, slimeball character of Vince McMahon played out for the cameras ends and the actual questionably ethical, many times sued, and multiple times accused of sexual misconduct Vince McMahon begins. That blurred line between character and reality is a recurring theme within the WWE universe.

But in both versions, Vince alone sits atop the WWE hierarchy. His two children, Steph and her older brother Shane, have both appeared as wrestlers in the ring, but Steph was more engaged on the actual corporate side. She was born into the business, but put in the effort to more than earn her place there. Together, she and Triple H were the heirs apparent of WWE. If NXT's ascent was any indicator, the future looked bright. It was creating an early fanbase for up-and-coming talent and helping move female wrestlers further from eye candy to equals.

WWE loves to do well-produced video segments about the legacy of women within the organization, but the truth is women have largely been footnotes. For the longest time, they were relegated to serving male characters in a valet role, an overly sexualized supporting character that takes cheap shots when the ref isn't looking. Over time, as the level of female talent grew and society as a whole started to shift, the organization gradually expanded the role of female wrestlers. WWE bills itself as a sports entertainment organization, and just like in the mainstream entertainment industry, there was, by all accounts, a casting couch culture where men backstage in powerful positions pressured female talent for sexual favors in return for airtime. There were so many public accusations and scandals it's hard to keep track, and more that I'm sure the WWE managed to sweep under the ring.

Women weren't just being demeaned backstage, but center stage. Up until 2007, "Bra & Panties Matches," where female wrestlers won the match by stripping their opponent down to her underwear, were an actual fucking thing. Even after that gimmick was retired by WWE executives—I'm sure very reluctantly and with a lot of lamenting about political correctness—it was still clear that the organization placed more value on a woman's physical appearance than her physical ability.

The Divas Era with its pink rhinestone butterfly title belt dawned around the same time. Women, while now portrayed as wrestlers, were still expected to look a certain way—think lots of makeup, little clothing, and huge boobs. It would take almost another decade, years after I proved women could be a huge combat sports attraction, before women truly started to get time in the squared circle (what diehards call a pro wrestling ring). And it was only after WWE was basically armbarred into it, following a global social media backlash to #givedivasachance after Divas were given a total of thirty seconds—less time than it takes most people to read this paragraph—for a nationally televised tag match. Four women were given less time to collectively wrestle than every single man on the roster got for his intro music alone.

Presented this information as a person outside of the wrestling world you might draw the conclusion that there is a troubling foundational sexist, patriarchal culture within the WWE. You would be right. I have nothing but respect for the female wrestlers who paved the way for women wrestlers today. And nothing but disgust for the amount of sexist, degrading bullshit they were put through.

NXT seemed to be making inroads into changing that. Sure, there were still a lot of pretty girls with enhanced tits among the mix of WWE hopefuls, but it was no longer a requirement. Not only that, but women were getting more opportunities to prove themselves as stars. It was a movement Triple H was leading and one that diverged greatly from what I heard about Vince's vision.

Contrary to the catfighting that WWE loved to play out in story lines featuring its female wrestlers, there was a real sense of camaraderie among them. In part, because professional wrestling isn't a competition but a team performance. Unlike MMA or judo, your success doesn't hinge on executing a move against the person on the mat with you, but on doing it together. I liked that.

In July 2017, the Four Horsewomen arrived at the home of the WWE's next

generation. For the better part of a week, we trained nonstop. I was able to practice without the pressure of a tryout, but I knew that the WWE higher-ups were
watching. Bumps are made out to be this big deal in wrestling, whereas in judo,
they're no big deal at all. We literally do falls as our warm-up. Marina and I
jumped in the ring, taking falls to the canvas over and over like it was nothing.

Afterward, Shayna, Jessamyn, and I got into our rented RV and road-
tripped back to LA. We drove across the country along endless stretches of
freeway, stopping at truck stop gas stations and middle-of-nowhere diners
that started to feel vaguely familiar until I was absolutely convinced I was
retracing a route I had taken before.

"Where are we?" I asked.

"We just left Texas," Shayna said. "So, I guess somewhere in New Mexico?"

My mind flashed back like in a movie, where suddenly the pieces fall into
place. The last time I had been on this stretch of road was when Travis and
I had driven out to Texas after my first UFC loss. I had been sitting in the
passenger side of Travis's truck, tears were streaming down my face. It was
late November. It was cold and gray. I had been convinced my life was over.

Now, less than two years later, I stared out at the same stretch of highway. The sun was so bright it almost hurt my eyes. I had just had one of the
most fun weeks of my life. I was surrounded by my friends. I was pretty sure
I was on the verge of an incredible new career opportunity. I was about to
marry the love of my life.

My life was far from over. In so many ways, it was just beginning.

———

Travis and I were married on a remote Hawaiian mountainside overlooking the ocean, just before the sun set into the Pacific.

As I walked barefoot down the grass path, toward the man who would
be my husband, the beaded train of my long white gown trailing behind me,
I realized that everything that I had been through, everything that I had
experienced, every loss, every disappointment, every heartbreak, had been
worth it because it had led me here.

9

Less than two weeks after our wedding, I kissed Trav goodbye and headed to Las Vegas. Shayna was in the finals of the first WWE Mae Young Classic, an all-women's professional wrestling tournament put on by NXT featuring its own up-and-coming talent as well as indie wrestlers not signed to the brand.

Shayna had advanced to the finals, and I was committed to being ringside to see her live. It was one of the first times I was stepping back into a crowd since I had left MMA. It seemed somewhat fitting, considering that one of the first times I had left my house at all was to support Shayna at an indie show in a tiny gym where Marina and I jumped out at the very end to help pull her out of the ring. Shayna had come a long way since then. As I braced myself to walk out into the crowd, I reminded myself so had I.

The fans cheered when they saw me. A chant of "We want Ronda!" went round the arena. It was a nice reminder that everybody in the world didn't hate my guts. Shayna went out and killed it. I could not have been happier for her as I watched her live her dream.

I knew that if I made the jump to WWE a lot of people would doubt that I had earned my place, but I also knew a lot of people would want to see me. A lot of people would doubt I earned my place *and* want to see me.

The evolution of women in WWE had caught my attention, and I wanted to do what I could to help move that forward. In the UFC, I had proven that giving women a shot wasn't a charity case, it was a business case.

Getting the UFC to add a women's division felt like breaking down a locked door. In the WWE, women at least seemed to have a foot in the door. But despite all of their skill and talent, they were still fighting to get the respect they deserved. I knew that I could use the spotlight that followed me and all of that mixed emotion that people had toward me to help change how women in WWE were viewed. I had spent my entire MMA career focused on creating opportunities for myself, which also happened to blaze a trail for other girls to follow. Now I had the opportunity to be a part of consciously building something to benefit us all.

Not only that, but I could do it with my friends. The Four Horsewomen together again. Training with them at the PC, even just for those few days, reminded me how much I had missed our crew. We had converged in MMA, then gone on to our own orbits, getting married, having babies, starting new careers. And now, we had somehow all come back together in the world of WWE. At the Mae Young Classic, I could see all of the pieces falling into place.

It felt like pro wrestling wasn't as much a decision as it was a calling. I didn't choose WWE. It wasn't something that I trained on the indie circuit for years trying to do. It wasn't something that I set out to do. It was something that I just couldn't get away from. It was like the universe kept tapping me on the shoulder and being like, "Hey, pro wrestling." And I'd go, "Now's not the time." Now it felt like the universe was hitting me upside the head with a folding chair.

By the time I left Vegas, I had made up my mind. I was going to go for it.

———

A few months later and a year since I had walked out of the UFC cage for the last time, I found myself sitting down across from Triple H to discuss getting into the WWE ring. My agent, Brad, sat to my right. We were in a private dining area at République, one of those fancy LA restaurants that I had never heard of where entertainment industry folks were always doing dinners and asking you when you sat down, "Have you been here?"

With its central location, wall of windows, high glass ceiling, brick interior, and gothic arches, it's not the kind of place you choose if you're hoping to slip in and out unnoticed by paparazzi. Considering how many times I had met Triple H before, I was surprisingly nervous.

You got this. I gave myself an internal pep talk.

The server brought over a bottle of wine, poured a small amount in a glass, and handed it to me. I swirled it and took a sip. I nodded my approval. There was no way I was going to send it back like some kind of prima donna asshole. This part of the dinner, like the meeting itself, was just a formality.

There was no point in pretending this meeting was about anything other than me joining the WWE, but what would that look like? My plan, as I laid it out, was to make a run in the WWE, not a career out of it. I would go from WrestleMania, WWE's equivalent of the Super Bowl, in early April to its Survivor Series pay-per-view in November. Pro wrestling is a skill that takes a lifetime to master, and I didn't have that kind of time. I figured I'd dip in, be a helpful accessory to the other women for a few months, then dip out and start having babies. Up until this point, Triple H was sitting there nodding.

"What about until April?" he asked.

WWE runs year-round on the creative side, he explained, setting up story lines and developing character arcs. They look at it as a whole season from one WrestleMania to the next. Would I be willing to commit to the entire year?

"I can do until April," I said. "But I want to start by wrapping up my story line with Steph before moving on to anything else."

Triple H nodded in approval. Brad beamed. The server asked to take my plate. I had barely touched my food because I had spent most of the time talking. I nodded and excused myself to go to the bathroom. Standing, I felt the world spin. I stood in front of the bathroom mirror, my face flushed, and did a little happy dance. Then straightened my posture, trying to look as serious and professional as possible. I started laughing. I walked back to the table trying not to look like I was trying to steady my balance on a boat in choppy waters.

I slid back into my seat and leaned over to Brad.

"We've got to go," I whispered. "When I just stood up, I realized that I drank too much while we were sitting down. I can't be drunk in front of Triple H in our first business meeting."

"Wow, will you look at the time," Brad announced.

I tried to say as little as possible amid the flurry of goodbyes, "so excited" and "we'll get you something this week." In one of the most obvious "we were not here together" moves that scream "we were definitely here together" moves, Triple H slipped out first. We waited a few minutes before Brad and I stood, and he guided me to the door where TMZ was waiting outside.

"I thought I just saw Triple H leaving," the cameraman said in a comment that was really a question.

"We were just hanging out," Brad interjected quickly.

"I just really enjoy fine dining," I said, as Brad ushered me into the car. I ducked too late and slammed my head on the door. Fortunately, the camera missed it, but certainly wouldn't help the headache I was sure to wake up with in the morning. I didn't care. In that moment, the only thing I felt was elation. I was going to be in the WWE.

By the end of the week, the contract had been drawn up. I was set to make my first appearance at the Royal Rumble—the WWE's annual kickoff event to build up to WrestleMania—in Philadelphia less than three weeks later.

I had one commitment that I had to fulfill before that could happen, so a few days later, I boarded a flight to Colombia to shoot *Mile 22*. Hollywood hadn't completely forsaken me since my loss—or at least the film's director Pete Berg hadn't. I was determined to prove him right for still believing in me as an actor. Now with the WWE deal in place, weeks of filming abroad was the perfect cover to deflect speculation that I would make a surprise appearance at the Rumble. The challenge was pulling it off. I made a point of posting a picture of myself on set to social media. An elaborate plan had been put in place to fly me from Bogotá to Miami, then catch a private flight from Miami to Philly where I would jump into a car with blacked-out windows and be driven to the loading dock of a hotel. There, I would go through the back door and up the service elevators so that no one would know I was there. Everyone at every step was well-versed on the need for secrecy.

The day came and security knocked on my door in Bogotá. I emerged, hat on, sunglasses on indoors, ready to go. We slipped out a back door to the waiting SUV. I shifted nervously on the ride to the airport. The first phase of the trip was the most exposed.

The SUV slowed. I looked out the window, directly face-to-face with the airport greeter standing on the curb holding a large sign saying "Ronda Rousey."

The driver hadn't even unbuckled his seat belt when I leapt out of the car, grabbing the sign from her hands. I crumpled the paper and threw it into the car, as she blinked in disbelief. I looked around at the other passengers unloading and saying airport goodbyes, but no one seemed to have noticed.

I tipped my hat down farther over my face, pulled up my hood, and headed into the airport. I boarded the flight to Miami, kept my face to the window, and somehow landed undetected. From there, in a scene that could only have been interpreted as a cartel drug bust, I was led, head down, hat tipped, sunglasses on, hoodie up, surrounded by airport law enforcement, off a plane from Colombia to a waiting car on the tarmac.

But it wasn't until the chartered flight from Miami touched down in Philly that it started to feel real. The morning of the Rumble, I was led through a series of cleared hotel hallways and service elevators to a car in an underground parking lot that drove me to a bus that then headed to the back entrance of the venue. For six hours, I waited on the bus, the anticipation building. I had received no guidance or direction on what was actually supposed to happen now that I was here.

Suddenly, there was a knock on the door. I looked around uncertain if I should answer it, when I heard the door open.

"Can I come in?" a familiar voice asked. It was Colt, "Rowdy" Roddy Piper's son. His dad had been a WWE legend and my fight name namesake. When a mutual friend introduced us early in my MMA career, I had asked Roddy for his permission to use the Rowdy name.

"Sure, kid," he said. "No problem. Do the name proud." I promised to do my best.

As I prepared to move into WWE, Roddy was never far from my mind. He had passed away suddenly from a heart attack at just sixty-one in 2015, and I dedicated my win over Bethe in Brazil to him. Now, stepping into his world, I was more committed than ever to honoring him. With his family's blessing, I had modeled my first WWE shirt after his signature red-and-white tee. Now his son stood before me, smiling.

"I wanted to give you something to wear for your debut," Colt said. "This was my dad's."

He was holding one of Roddy's trademark leather jackets. Colt helped me put it on. It was oversized but perfect.

"Can't wait to see you out there," Colt said. "Dad would be so proud."

A little while after he left, there was another knock. Triple H's large frame filled the small doorway into the bus. He strode over to the table, picking up a pen and piece of paper, and started drawing.

"This is the ring," he said, pointing to a box he'd sketched out.

"This is the ramp," he said, pointing to lines off the box.

"This is what we call hard cam side." He pointed off to one side of the ring. "This is where the cameras are. This is where the announcers' tables are. This is where the girls will be. Steph will be here."

I watched as he gestured around the paper.

"And here," he said, stopping as if indicating the X on a treasure map, "here is the sign."

The sign being the WrestleMania sign. Ever since John Cena had pointed at the WrestleMania sign a decade earlier, it had become an iconic gesture. It says to the crowd that this moment is a key moment.

"You're going to come down here. You'll walk into the ring. They'll be here," he said, pointing. *They* referred to the predetermined winner of the Rumble, Asuka, and the two current women's title holders, Charlotte Flair and Alexa Bliss, who she would have the right to challenge for a title shot at Mania as a result of her win.

I nodded, waiting for him to go on, but he stopped.

"Then what?" I asked. "What do I do? Should I do anything? Do I shake anybody's hand? What should I do?"

Triple H shrugged as if I should know.

"I don't know. Just feel it. Do whatever you want."

I looked at him. Then down at the paper to see if he had jotted down secret instructions I missed. Then back up at him, my eyes wide.

"Feel it?" I asked, incredulous, searching for more direction. The WWE had orchestrated a multinational effort under a level of secrecy typically reserved for military operations or jewel heists to get me there. He had literally hand drawn me a map. And in the end, I was being sent out there with just "do whatever you want."

"Stand there," he said, completely confident. "Take a minute just to register everything that is happening. Whatever you're feeling, let it show on your face. And then just do whatever you want."

He paused, then added, "Just make sure you point at the sign."

Triple H stood up and gestured that it was time to move. I followed him through the series of Super Mario Brothers–esque tunnels that run under every major sports arena to the backstage area that the WWE calls Gorilla. Inside, a monitor played the feed from the ring. Triple H, Shane McMahon, and Vince sat in the room as wrestlers entered and exited on cue.

Asuka eliminated Nikki Bella, and the crowd went wild. Asuka pointed twice at the WrestleMania sign as Charlotte and Alexa entered the ring to see whose title she wanted to challenge for at WrestleMania.

Gorilla is a space that marks the line between real and fantasy. You walk into Gorilla from a random arena hallway as yourself and emerge out of it a WWE superstar to a sea of thousands of cheering fans. Bouncing from foot to foot, I waited for my cue. Then the opening riffs of Joan Jett's "Bad Reputation" blasted through the stadium. I stomped my feet, steeled myself. And then I heard it. A sound I thought I would never hear again.

It was the noise of an arena full of fans.

Cheering.

For me.

I pushed my way through the thick black curtains that separated me from the world. I stood at the top of the ramp, taking a moment to take it all in. Then I stormed into the ring. The crowd went wild.

I pointed to the WrestleMania sign.

I turned to the girls in the ring.

"I'll see you there."

10

With my in-ring debut set for WrestleMania, WWE put me through a gauntlet of medical tests like a house getting appraised before you buy it.

I knew my body was beaten up, but it was my brain that I was worried about. I couldn't sleep the night before the MRI, terrified of what it might show. I was near tears when the docs not only cleared me, but also said I had a "pristine brain" after looking at the scan. I never cried about losing my phone again.

Officially cleared to make my debut, we had six weeks to build a narrative that people would care about enough to want to watch. The most obvious option—which is what the WWE always opts for—was to leverage my previous WrestleMania confrontation with Steph and Triple H to set up a new dispute. Triple H and Steph in their TV role as villainous WWE brass (not to be confused with their real-life role as non-villainous WWE brass) would face me and Kurt Angle, a former Olympic gold medalist turned pro wrestler, in a tag team match.

For the better part of two months, the kayfabe—acting as if pro wrestling is not scripted and that everything going on is real—lead-up played out weekly on TV. At the Elimination Chamber pay-per-view, I threw Triple H through a table. In retaliation, Steph slapped me in the face. She told me beforehand she's known for having a "helluva" slap.

"Give me your best shot," I said.

She wasn't wrong. When she connected, I saw stars. It immediately confirmed to me that I shouldn't be fighting anymore. I don't care how infamous her slap is, an open hand strike from a woman who's never fought in her life shouldn't stun a UFC champion. Disoriented, I tried my best to hide it and focus on the rest of the televised segment. Kurt demanded Steph and Triple H face us at WrestleMania. They tried to back out, only to find that through a shocking contractual technicality they had to take the match. And the stage was set.

Behind the scenes, we were all working together to create a match that would go down in history. Weeks before WrestleMania, I was invited to the WWE Warehouse to prepare.

Pulling through an unsecured gate and up to the large white building that sits on the edge of a residential neighborhood and industrial strip in a middle-class suburb in Connecticut, I was certain we were lost. What stood in front of me was nothing like the busy, state-of-the-art PC. It was literally a warehouse. I looked around the nearly empty parking lot for signage to indicate that this warehouse was *the* WWE Warehouse but found nothing. GPS address indicated this was the place, so I walked up the ramp, toward the gray metal door next to a set of loading docks.

"Hello?" I said, pulling open the door, more than half expecting to step into a pro wrestling version of *The Wizard of Oz* where the new world is Technicolor. What I found was just a warehouse. Concrete floors, large planks of wood, moving dollies, a small forklift, and rows and rows of shelving stacked twenty feet high with cardboard boxes and plastic bins. The only immediate indicator that I might be in the right place was a large Saturday Night's neon sign hanging from the ceiling, a relic from a WWE show defunct since the early 2000s. I walked in, and there, to my right, tucked into a small corner of the massive warehouse, was a single wrestling ring in a room scarcely bigger than the ring itself. The walls around the ring were painted all black, a stark contrast to the otherwise gray floors, white walls, and exposed aluminum ductwork.

Kurt, Steph, and Triple H were all there as well as producer Sara Amato.

A former wrestler and the PC's first female trainer, Sara was a driving force in NXT's shifting the portrayal of women from side piece to serious performer. Together, we spent hours standing around the ring talking through the match. First, the big picture vision, and then how we'd tell the story through the action to get there. I didn't even have an established moveset yet. Someone would suggest a move, and we'd pause and try it out in the ring to see what it might look like. It was a collaborative back-and-forth.

I felt empowered in a way that I hadn't before in my athletic career. In judo and MMA, training felt more like taking orders. Any attempt to give input during practice had been met with accusatory glares implying that I was only stalling for a few extra minutes of rest before getting back on the mat or that I was too much of a know-it-all to do as I was told. But here, sitting among some of the best minds in the business, they were eager to hear what I thought. My suggestions were met with nodding, followed by "And then what if we ..." or "Let's try it and see ..." and a gesture to jump into the ring and test out if it worked. Triple H literally showed me how to tie my wrestling boots. It was surreal. I loved every second.

During breaks in training, I wandered through the warehouse space. At first glance, it appears to be a regular industrial storage building, stacked with the various set pieces, rigging, signage, cables, crash pads, and broken-down stages you might expect. Blue plastic bins, cardboard boxes with "FRAGILE" stickers, and wooden crates with labels saying things like "new ropes," "breakaway glass," "Hall of Fame podium," and "Banners (Maybe?)" with names of pay-per-view events stretching back twenty years. But as you walk back through the building, it transforms into the WWE's 50,000-square-foot grandma's attic, ending in the pro wrestling equivalent of the contents of the Louvre and of every abandoned locker auctioned off on *Storage Wars* combined, with the movers being told, "Just put it wherever."

A five-foot, banana yellow, fiberglass "Macho Man" Randy Savage cowboy hat sits in front of a wall of the Undertaker's caskets, stacked seven caskets high and six caskets wide. Dozens of aluminum ladders are wedged between the shelves that a life-sized Andre the Giant cardboard cutout leans against.

Boxes cover the floor. There are boxes stacked on tables. Boxes stacked on boxes. Boxes on scattered shelves, wedged in Jenga style. Boxes set down in any open space that could fit a box, inside them containing every pro-wrestling artifact imaginable. Boxes taped shut. Boxes with the flaps folded over. Boxes completely open, overflowing with shirts of wrestlers long retired. White legal boxes with lids, neatly labeled to indicate its contents as decades worth of old, no-longer-published WWE magazine titles. Hard plastic boxes with lids, holding neatly organized manila file folders of black-and-white 8x10 photos. Boxes filled with unopened mail from Japan postmarked 1995. Boxes of lanyards from a wrestling promotion WWE absorbed two decades prior. An oddly shaped box labeled "Gimmick Guitars."

Every surface, most of those surfaces being other boxes, is covered with the contents of what one can only assume also used to be in boxes. A still shrink-wrapped VHS tape featuring bikini-clad women called *Tropical Pleasure WWF Divas*. (WWE used to be called WWF until, in one of the many lawsuits involving Vince McMahon, they were sued by the World Wildlife Fund and lost.) A copy of *Wrestling World* magazine from 1973 asking "Does Bruno Sammartino Want the N.W.A Crown?" *TV Guides* from the 1990s. Ziploc bags filled with yellowed newspaper clippings. A fake puff-puff cigar still in its box. A red lunch cooler slapped with a Stone Cold sticker. A prop dagger with a straw taped to the back of it through which fake blood once must have spewed.

The in-between spaces are filled with things too large to fit in boxes. Vespas, car bumpers, actual cars, more coffins, office chairs, crutches, oversized novelty checks dated 2008, and parts of bronze-painted papier-mâché statues. It is a jumble of near-priceless WWE history and shit your mom would have made you throw out ages ago.

"It's a work in progress." A voice behind me made me jump. I turned to see a guy in a T-shirt emerge from a small office.

I nodded in agreement. "So am I."

In the lead-up to WrestleMania, we spent weeks working to prepare. We spent more days at the warehouse and even when we were apart, there was back-and-forth refining every detail. I was constantly working on my pro wrestling moveset. Two up-and-coming wrestlers from NXT, Lacey Evans and Dakota Kai, were both kind and brave enough to be my crash dummies as we developed moves like my finisher: The Piper's Pit.

We met again at the Performance Center and got the input of pro wrestling Hall of Famers and legends Shawn Michaels and Michael Hayes. This was in addition to Triple H and Kurt, who were also Hall of Famers. I watched masters of the craft gradually weave a masterpiece together. It seemed like tweaks and changes were always coming in, from moves to facials (wrestling speak for emotions shown toward the camera), down to miming pulling Steph's hair from my fingers. But I trusted the process. WWE had been doing this for decades, I told myself. The entire match was finalized a few days before I left for New Orleans, the site of WrestleMania 34. I flew in early, and for almost an entire week, the four of us rehearsed the match over and over until we had it down to the most minute muscle twitch.

There was a learning curve, but it was more of a change than a challenge. My entire athletic career had been built around preparing split-second reactions for a near infinite number of possibilities, that each move could go multiple ways and each of those moves could go multiple ways and each of those moves could go multiple ways. I had to be ready and respond to every single one in a millisecond. Now, instead of needing to simultaneously solve a series of ever-changing complex algebra equations, I just had to follow a series of directions I'd read over a thousand times.

Pacing backstage in Gorilla, wearing a replica of Hot Rod's jacket with the words "Rowdy" emblazoned across my sports bra, I went through the choreography in my head.

A leather-clad Triple H and Steph made an only-at-WrestleMania entrance complete with laser light show and biker motorcade.

Vince pulled me aside.

"Don't forget to smile," he said. "You have an amazing smile. The world smiles with you when you smile."

I flashed my global-grin-inducing smirk at him, then stepped up to the curtain.

"See you out there," Kurt, wearing his trademark star-spangled wrestling singlet, said to me. The "You Suck!" chant Kurt had turned from a taunt to his theme song rose up through the stadium, punctuated by pyro blasts.

"Bad Reputation" blared through the Superdome, and I walked out into the arena, excited to give the world a show. I emerged through a ten-story LED Mardi Gras mask and paused at the top of the ramp, once more taking it in.

Just like they had in the UFC, people tuned in to watch my Wrestle-Mania debut for one of two reasons. They were fans of mine and wanted to see me do well. Or they were hoping to see me fail. Either way, they were watching. Instead of pushing through the crowd at a UFC fight, the stage was elevated just above the fans. Instead of amongst them, I was above them. Their cheers were deafening.

I stepped into the ring, taking off the leather jacket and Piper-inspired kilt. The kilt had been a late addition. In the weeks leading up to joining the WWE, I had tried a number of looks, primarily skintight black bodysuits with various cutouts that undeniably looked cool but weren't really me. As I lay motionless in the MRI tube during my medical exam, listening to its whirs and clicks, it hit me. "It should have a skirt!" By the time the MRI tech pushed the button to slide me out of the machine, I had visualized the entire look that I now stood wearing.

The rest of my WWE gear mirrored my UFC fight gear, just a sports bra and shorts. My padded fight gloves had been replaced by open leather gloves that covered my wrists and knuckles modeled after my gauze fighting hand wraps.

"Ronda Rousey! Ronda Rousey!" For the first time in my life, I didn't block the cheers out so I could focus. I let myself listen to the roar of the crowd.

The ref called us to the center of the ring, and Steph took a cheap shot before he even said start. She is incredibly good at playing bad. The bell rang, but Kurt held me back. We were, we wanted to make sure everyone knew, better than that. What we were really doing was building toward the "hot tag." The crowd wanted to see me in the ring more than anything, so we were going to keep me out until their desire to see me reached a fever pitch.

Kurt and Triple H started pummeling each other in the ring, as the crowd chanted, "We want Ronda!" The two legends continued going back and forth. Kurt threw Triple H over his head. Fans cheered.

As Triple H battled back, some of the most classic scenes in the pro wrestling playbook played out. Steph took cheap shot after cheap shot when the ref conveniently wasn't looking. Kurt was pinned, only to kick out at the last second. Kurt stretched out his arm to tag me in, our fingertips almost touching but just out of reach. Steph tried to help her husband by grabbing Kurt around the neck, but Kurt moved at the last second, resulting in Triple H almost hitting Steph. The close encounter was followed by the requisite overexaggerated "Whoa!" expressions of shock on each of their faces. Kurt reached out again as if to tag me, but Steph pulled me off the apron, I smacked my face on the extended edge of the wrestling ring on the outside of the ropes, and again out of his reach.

Kurt threw Triple H from the ring. It was my turn to tag in, our hands finally connecting. The crowd exploded.

Shouts of "Yes! Yes! Yes!" surrounded me. I charged at Steph and ripped her through the ropes. I slammed her to the ground, again and again. Then, just as I had done before every judo and MMA match, I slapped my shoulders. I stomped my right foot. Then my left. I backed her up against the ropes, throwing the rapid punches, but making sure not to connect with a closed fist. I tossed her around the ring like a rag doll, exactly like we had practiced.

I went for Steph and caught her in an armbar. But she poked me in the eye to escape, a heel move if there ever was one, in fact it was Roddy Piper's signature. Steph kicked me, and I sold it as if I was in pain. In a move that had made me laugh every time we rehearsed it, Steph tapped her shoulders, then stomped her feet, mocking my pre-fight ritual. I met her by grabbing her throat. I lifted her up on my shoulders, slamming her to the canvas. As the referee counted the pin, Triple H pulled the official off, then grabbed me by the leg, pulling me out of the ring. Kurt re-emerged, and the two guys tried to put each other through the announcers' table before Triple H jumped into the ring to check on his writhing wife.

When Triple H turned back to the action, I stood before him, fists raised, gesturing, "Let's go!"

He brushed the protesting referee aside, and we met in the middle.

Eventually I backed Triple H into the corner with a couple of jabs before unloading with both hands, fists closed. The crowd went wild. I turned to hit the ropes. He tried to cut me off with a kick to the stomach. I caught it and tripped his supporting leg, somersaulted and stood, lifting the six-foot-four, 250-pound Triple H over my shoulders as if it were effortless. Seventy-eight thousand one-hundred thirty-three fans—the biggest crowd of my life—lost their fucking minds.

Steph jumped in again, pulled Triple H off my shoulders, then ran from the ring as I followed. Kurt threw Triple H around inside the ropes. Steph intervened to give Triple H the advantage, and finally I leapt into the ring to save the match.

"This is awesome!" The highest praise that notoriously rough pro wrestling fans can give boomed through the Superdome. "This is awesome!"

Triple H lifted me as if to throw me to the ground, which I reversed with a hurricanrana (a head scissors). I pulled him down and caught him in an armbar. The crowd jumped to its feet. He struggled to break free, about to tap, when Steph wrapped her arms around my neck, catching me in a rear naked choke. I fought to my feet. It was almost time to end this. I threw Steph to the ground. I grabbed her arm between my legs. At that exact moment, Kurt pulled Triple H into his signature ankle lock, a move Kurt had adopted from the first ever UFC-WWE crossover star, Ken Shamrock. But just before we were able to put them away, Triple H launched Kurt in my direction, breaking my hold.

We all four lay in the ring, not needing to feign exhaustion after twenty minutes of continuous action. I was out of breath but felt like I could do this forever. Steph and Triple H got to their feet first, taking what looked to be an advantage over Kurt and me. Steph pulled me up for the Pedigree (Triple H's signature move) that I had reversed on her husband moments earlier. I threw her over my head and rolled into the armbar. I grabbed her arm.

"Nooooooo!" she wailed. "Nooooo!"

"Say you're sorry!" I said in an unscripted moment. I was lost in the story. I couldn't help being swept away in it.

"I'm sorry!" she screamed.

"Too late!" I cranked, just enough to make it look good, but not enough to pop her elbow from its socket like you'd tear away the leg of a roast chicken.

She tapped dramatically.

The fight hadn't been real, but the emotion was.

The match would go down as one of the best tag matches in Wrestle-Mania history and in the history of the company. An instant classic.

Steph gave me a huge hug backstage.

"That was amazing," she said. "You're amazing."

It had been weeks of preparation, but it paid off. I had come into the industry worried that I might not be welcome, but WWE had rolled out the red carpet for me.

Little did I know they'd start to slowly retract it.

II

I went from "The Road to WrestleMania" to a wrestler's life on the road.

From the outside, professional wrestling isn't that hard to figure out. It's basically a live soap opera for dudes with lots of fight choreography. I'm not saying it's only for dudes, but it's definitely being scripted by dudes, for dudes. You have good guys and bad guys, good guys who turn bad and bad guys who turn good. I guess the message there is trust no one.

As an actual wrestler, there's the unending and nowhere-recorded list of etiquette that I was constantly unknowingly violating to the point that I was pretty sure people were just making stuff up to fuck with me at that point. There is a shit ton of terminology and a vast amount of institutional knowledge that both publicly and behind the scenes shape how things are done. There are unwritten rules about everything from how hard or soft you should shake someone's hand to wiping your feet on the apron when you enter the ring.

WWE is a year-round operation. Wrestlers spend well over two hundred days a year on the road, traveling or performing. The organization operates three types of shows: pay-per-views, weekly broadcasts, and untelevised house shows.

WrestleMania is WWE's flagship event, part of a series of ten or so annual "pay-per-view" events that are so named because they used to cost $40 or $50 a pop to watch, but now can be accessed via a streaming service subscription. Pay-per-views are spectacles. Everything is magnified. The arena. The crowd. The lighting. The crew. The cameras. The level of security.

The number of wrestlers. The length of the show. The catering spread. The signs backstage pointing you in a hundred different directions.

Wrestling fans mark their calendars by pay-per-view dates: Royal Rumble, where thirty people fight it out in the ring at once; WrestleMania; Money in the Bank, where wrestlers fight it out to grab a suitcase suspended twenty feet in the air that can be "cashed in" at any time for a title shot; Summer-Slam, the biggest event of the year after WrestleMania; Hell in a Cell, where a giant chain link cage is put over the ring to both be used to climb and jump off of as well as prevent escape; and a half-dozen other events with names like Survivor Series, Elimination Chamber, and Crown Jewel. They're held in major cities like New York, Los Angeles, and Philadelphia, as well as now twice a year in Saudi Arabia, a nation that restricts the rights of women in a way that I'm certain Vince McMahon wishes he could.

To build up to those events, WWE produces two live televised shows per week, *Monday Night Raw* and *SmackDown* (currently on Fridays). Each of these shows is considered its own brand, and at least once a year, WWE reshuffles the rosters. These shows cycle through large to midsize cities like Milwaukee, Memphis, Portland, and Pittsburgh. The weekly broadcasts are a combination of scripted storytelling done through "backstage" segments (which are largely pre-taped but occasionally live) as well as in-ring promos and wrestling segments.

Finally, there are house shows, or live shows. Unlike the multimillion-dollar spectacle of pay-per-views and the ever-churning hype machines of Raw and SmackDown, live events are a throwback to the independent circuit days. It's a scaled-down crew responsible for a scaled-down setup, not much more than a couple of jumbo screens, a few sets of lights, and a ring.

Multiple live shows take place almost every week of the year, wedged between the *SmackDown* and *Raw* tapings. They occasionally pass through New York City or Miami, but they're mostly in places that few people outside those towns could find on a map, like Monroe, Louisiana; Peoria, Illinois; Bangor, Maine; and Laval, Quebec. I was unaware of live shows' existence before I found myself regularly performing in them, but they quickly became my favorite stage. They feel like the twenty-first-century version of the old-timey circus, where you roll into a small town, and everyone excitedly comes out to watch the performance. They're not about reading overly dramatic promos, overly produced constantly changing segments, or the glam of hair-and-makeup. They're just about going out, doing cool shit in the ring, and interacting with the crowd.

For the next year, my life was a never-ending cycle of live shows, TV shows, and pay-per-views.

"Hello, and thank you for choosing to fly with us," the flight attendant's voice announced over the intercom. "This flight is heading to McAllen, Texas. If that's not your final destination, please let us know."

Well, my ticket scanned in, so that must be right, I thought to myself. Honestly, it had gotten to a point where I had no idea where I was going beyond the gate number on my ticket. I had long ago stopped trying to keep track of cities or dates. Occasionally, I was home long enough to swap out the clothes in my suitcase before kissing my husband goodbye and heading back out the door.

Now, I was coming off a live show tour in the Southeast, followed by a Raw in New Orleans and a trip to Orlando to train at the PC for a couple of days before flying out to Houston to catch a flight that was apparently heading to McAllen. Three rows behind me, I recognized two other wrestlers, setting my mind at ease.

The tiny plane landed, emptying into a six-gate concourse with nothing more than a Coffee Zone and an airport gift shop. I could hear the crowd before I could see the terminal exit.

"Ronda! Ronda!" my name echoed, punctuated by cell phone camera flashes. I smiled, apologetically, and kept walking. In the beginning of my MMA career, when I never said no, I shook every hand, I took every picture, I signed every autograph. But in the end, I was always disappointing someone. There was always one more selfie to take. One more thing to sign. So, I reached a point where I just kept walking.

As we approached the "No Passengers Beyond This Point" sign separating us from the crowd, I ducked behind a six-foot-four former college football player turned wrestler who went by Mojo.

"I'm going to use you to block for me," I said.

I was taken to the tiny office where people file complaints about lost luggage. My sister Maria, who traveled with me sometimes, and I stood waiting in the small window-walled room as people stared through the glass. I felt like a zoo animal on exhibit.

"It's not usually like this," the police officer helping with crowd control said, half apologetic, half surprised. "People have been waiting for over four hours."

I shrugged.

"It's always like this."

We pulled out of the airport, and I looked to see how far it was to the closest Cracker Barrel, the Americana-themed diner serving twenty-four-hour breakfast with its cluttered country market selling everything from fudge, biscuit mix, and twenty-five flavors of glass-bottled soda to knit shawls and wooden signs painted with words like Blessed and Live, Love, Lake. Cracker Barrel had become a staple of my life on the road. It's not fancy, but it's reliable. Sometimes, there is just something comforting about knowing what you're going to get.

Two wrestlers—known to the world as Elias and Finn Bálor—were waiting to pay their bill as we walked in. Away from the makeup and the hair gel and pleather pants, it can be hard to identify individuals from their in-ring personas, but even in street clothes, they have a certain look. Tall. Fit. Well-moisturized.

"Imagine running into you here," I said, overly dramatic.

"Yeah, me and Ferg just stopped to get some breakfast," Elias said, using Finn's real name. "You know the drill, just trying to kill time."

The waitress held up menus to signal she was ready to seat us.

After my standard breakfast of two eggs over easy, turkey sausage patties and toast, we tried to kill time before the arena opened its doors for rehearsal. When you're trying to fill the hours between an 11:00 a.m. hotel checkout and a 4:00 p.m. call time, the clock seems to slow. We stopped at a Target where I took a picture of myself wearing a hot dog costume and texted Triple H, "Thinking of changing out my walkout look." He vetoed the idea. We sat in the parking lot playing board games until the doors opened.

Based on my singular experience, I had been led to believe that the preparation we'd put into our WrestleMania match was the WWE model. Not only that, but in our first meeting, Triple H had said they structure story lines all year around building toward a finale at Wrestlemania. Nothing could be further from the truth. The WWE model actually was no preparation, and there was no creative or producer input, instead wrestlers were expected to come up with a match on their own in the days leading up to an event (if they even had that luxury), using live shows as a way to flesh it out and rehearse, and then, day of the event, an edict would come down from the top that everything was going to change.

I had requested to face Nia Jax as my first WWE title run story line. At six feet, 270 pounds, Nia, whose cousin is the Rock, was an opponent I could believably battle it out with, leveraging my athleticism and her size to create incredible matches. However, going into Money in the Bank, my first pay-per-view following WrestleMania, I was informed my pairing with Nia would be a one-off to set me up for a rivalry with Alexa Bliss. The word had trickled down from Vince to Triple H to the producers to me.

"Huh?" I did a double take.

"It's a good thing," the producer told me. "Alexa's the biggest star."

"Alexa is ninety pounds, she is the exact opposite of big," I said. "She is tiny."

"She sells the most merch." As the producer spoke, I heard the words in Vince McMahon's gravelly voice.

"OK, if that's what they want," I said, trying to work through the logic. *It's part of the process*, I told myself. *They're putting me up against Alexa because they want to test me. They want to see if I can sell well enough to convince everyone that this little five-foot, ninety-pound chick with blond pigtails could actually hang in a match with me. This is just going to make me better.*

But it became clear I was trying to rationalize completely irrational decisions. Making me better never factored into the thought process, it was about finding a way to thrust me into the cogs of a system, one built on accepting that everything must be last minute because we're all beholden to one nearly eighty-year-old man.

Coming into WWE, I hadn't imagined that I would do a singles match all year, let alone as my second match. I begged for some time to rehearse, and Nia was kind enough to travel to Browsey Acres for a couple of days so we could put together some of the match in the ring that WWE had loaned me. We didn't have the best minds in the business working with us to make it great. It was just me and Nia in my backyard, and a producer to consult with the day of the event. It was a big test, even more difficult than Mania. But we managed to pull out a decent match.

Just as it seemed I had Nia dead to rights in an armbar, Alexa crashed our match, striking me in the back with the metal suitcase she had won four matches earlier. Inside, it contained a "contract," which gave her the right to challenge Nia right then, right there. Alexa stole my win and, in defeating Nia seconds later, took the title for herself. At SummerSlam (the next major event on the WWE calendar), I claimed what was rightfully mine with a vengeance, submitting Alexa with armbar, and became the first woman to have held both a UFC title and WWE title.

SummerSlam was a short match, with even less rehearsal and help than before. I could feel resentment from the fans over my being handed the title so quickly. I had not set out to be a WWE champion. In fact, I had asked to not have the title for my entire run. My idol, Roddy Piper, had gone his entire Hall of Fame career without a belt. He didn't need it, neither did I. But my merch was already selling well, and Vince believed elevating me to the champion would provide an even bigger boost. Merch sales seemed to matter more to him than the product itself.

Now, I had to defend it at Hell in a Cell, where contrary to the name, we would not be fighting in a cage. This lead-up series of Friday and Saturday live shows in smaller Texas towns was so Alexa and I could put together our match for Sunday's pay-per-view. Where I had previously spent two months preparing for WrestleMania, we now had two days to stage Hell in a Cell.

I found Alexa in the women's locker room, and we headed out to the ring. A handful of other wrestlers were already out there. We shared the crowded space, focused on our choreography but with a subconscious awareness that at any moment someone might come flying off the rope behind us.

"Doors open in ninety minutes," an event staffer announced. That meant rehearsals would end soon.

We put together and memorized a sequence of eighty-some moves. For all its scripted brutality to give the appearance of a chaotic fight, pro wrestling is really an intricate choreography. It has to be executed flawlessly—one tiny fuck-up and someone could be significantly hurt. Precision takes time to perfect. Time is one of the many things WWE does not provide its wrestlers.

"Doors open in five!" a voice echoed around the empty arena. We needed to clear the ring.

Lexi (Alexa's actual name) and I headed backstage, still talking and walking through the match. While she got ready, I paced the dimly lit hallway, moving through the match in my mind until I could see it playing out, even with my eyes closed.

"I know we're in Texas, but what's the name of the city tonight?" I asked right before we were set to go out. "Edington? Edingburg?"

"Edinburg," a gray-haired man in a security jacket with a slight Southern drawl informed me.

"Hey, at least I know the state!" I said in my defense.

He looked at me unimpressed.

I wanted to explain that the month before I had yelled to the crowd, "Thank you, Ohio!" only to be told, "Um, you're in Michigan." But "Bad Reputation" started up, and out I went.

The match went well, but not perfect. The crowd seemed to enjoy it, but live show crowds were a lot easier to please. Even with less time to prepare, I felt like I was light-years ahead of where I had been for my WrestleMania debut. I was able to remember more and more complex choreography in less and less time. Despite the unbelievability of our matchup, Alexa was a joy to work with and taught me so much about relying on emotion, creating moments and comedy in addition to my intensity and athletic prowess. My matches weren't getting better, but at least I was.

"Are you heading out tonight?" the WWE security head asked as we walked out of the arena to the parking lot. It was just under 150 miles to the next stop in Corpus Christi. Wrestlers fall into two camps on the road—those who prefer to head out to the next stop directly from the show and those who spend the night and head out in the morning. I was in the late-night camp, still coming down off the adrenaline rush of performing.

"There's flash flood warnings," he cautioned. "Avoid the route along the coast."

It was after 3:00 a.m. when we pulled up to the Holiday Inn. Rain was coming down in sheets. There were buckets in the lobby collecting water dripping through a leak. The carpet squished under our feet as we dragged ourselves to the check-in counter.

The next morning, I made my way down to the tiny workout room. My back ached. A fracture in my spine, first discovered in my initial WWE medical evaluation, combined with taking bumps every week, wasn't doing it any favors. Neither was the rain. I was hoping a half hour on the elliptical might loosen it up before heading to the venue. I looked around the small beige space. A rack of dumbbells was against one mirrored wall, cardio equipment facing another. A few weeks prior in a nearly indistinguishable two-and-a-half-star hotel gym, I had run into Windham Rotunda, better known as Bray Wyatt.

We made small talk, and the space slowly cleared. My workout ended, and I climbed off the machine. He leaned toward me.

"Just so you know, these people aren't your friends," he said. "No matter how nice they are, no matter what they say or how they act, we're always just going to be pieces of meat to them. Get in, make your money, and get out."

"Thanks," I said. "Appreciate the honesty." It was the first time someone said aloud what I had started feeling.

Before joining WWE, I had understood it was a business, but I had been under the impression it was run more like a multibillion-dollar sports franchise or major entertainment studio than like a two-bit circus run by a bunch of carneys. It's fitting that the WWE prides itself on its social media presence and one billion combined followers because its elite, big budget organizational image is about as real as an Instagram filter.

WWE calls its wrestlers "Superstars" to the world. To the IRS, it calls us independent contractors. This distinction lets them off the hook when it comes to providing benefits like health insurance coverage or sick leave to the athletes that it expects to regularly launch themselves off ladders and through tables. WWE will be quick to point out it covers in-ring injuries—meaning medical bankruptcy is something you don't have to worry about when they ask you to jump off the top of a twenty-foot metal cage on to a guy standing two stories below—but when it comes to the daily wear-and-tear injuries that plague the vast majority of wrestlers, you're on your own. It is worth noting, WWE isn't completely soulless when it comes to helping its talent out with non-emergency medical procedures as WWE will cover all boob jobs at 100 percent.

Being an independent contractor also means that wrestlers are responsible for paying their own travel cost as they are ping-ponged around the country. International trips are an exception. The organization also covers stays at the designated TV hotel for the "Big Five" events—Royal Rumble, WrestleMania, Money in the Bank, SummerSlam, and Survivor Series. But only because it's easier when it comes to logistical and security concerns.

Otherwise, WWE assists with flying wrestlers into the first city and out of the last, but everything in between is on the individual's dime. With the exception of a handful of wrestlers with bigger names, bigger contracts, and more clout (myself included) who are able to negotiate travel expenses into their contract, the overwhelming majority of talent pays out-of-pocket for travel to over a hundred different US cities a year.

Wrestlers frequently travel together in pairs or groups of three, even four, often sharing rooms at budget chain hotels with free to-go buffet breakfasts and carpooling to save as much on costs as they can. With the exception of its largest stars, WWE requires that all wrestlers be present for every pay-per-view and their brand-related show, whether or not there is any intention of using them. I watched as wrestlers on the roster came only to sit in catering week after week, unused on air.

In Corpus Christi, I got ready in the makeshift women's locker room with the three other women on the live show tour. I paced back and forth playing out the match in my head. It was the same one we'd done the night before.

Wrestlers drifted in and out of the talent viewing area, two dozen or so folding chairs arranged in a semi-circle around a TV streaming an in-arena broadcast. Here, some of the biggest names in WWE sat around, discussing things like kitchen remodels as they reheated their dinners in a lone micro-wave. They waited for their cue, upon which they instantly transformed from a down-to-earth country guy flipping through photos on his smartphone to an angry giant flipping someone through a table. This is what life on the road is really like. Customized speedos and baby-oiled bodies. Chain restaurants and three-star hotels. Driving through the middle of nowhere in the dark of night.

The next day in San Antonio, the site of Hell in a Cell, I stood in front of the mirror in full glam, a nearly unrecognizable version of my makeup-less self from the past few days. My hair was in intricate braids, a look I'd started building out with my hairdresser. Like my boots before, these were my battle braids. When the braids went in, they meant something was going down.

Brad had negotiated a dressing room into my deal for the small team that traveled with me to TV tapings. The once move-and-be-murdered vibe of my silent coach-filled locker room of my UFC days had been replaced by a dressing room humming with an up-to-seven-person team's day-of-event activity: typing, photo editing, filming, cleaning makeup brushes, punctuated by music, scented candles, and, in the biggest departure from my UFC days, laughter.

I walked over to a corner of the room, moving through a one-sided version of the match, bobbing and kicking, clutching and ducking, in what probably looked like some kind of weird interpretive dance.

"Want to hear me go over it?" I asked Trav, who had flown in the day before.

"Sure," he said.

I walked him through step-by-step for the tenth time.

We're going to come out ... Lock up, to the ropes. And we're going to do the twisty doo. I'm going to come off the ropes and be like, "Oh, no." Then it's going to be like, "Ouch my ribs." Then she's going to come down like er-er-er at me. Then I'm going to throw her back. I'm going to back her up into the corner. It'll be like, "Ooooh." Then she's going to be like, "No!" And I'm going to be like, "Yeah."

I mimicked the motions of an armbar, a huge smile on my face.

"You're going to be great, babe," he offered.

Backstage in Gorilla, I bounced back and forth on my toes. A sold-out AT&T Arena crowd of 15,216 people jumped to their feet. No matter how many times I have walked down the ramp, it's a moment that still gives me goose bumps.

Professional wrestling requires incredible skill and athleticism, but it is not a sport. It's not a real competition. You don't actually win titles. Vince McMahon decides that he's willing to let you play a part for a while in a scripted TV show. My experience as a professional athlete, not just a professional entertainer, helped me not lose sight of reality while living in this fantasyland. But even conscious of it, there was a constant battle to not lose myself to the character. I wasn't alone.

One night during a live show tour in Japan, over drinks, Windham shared a cautionary tale. In portraying Bray Wyatt, he had faked a Louisiana accent for so long he couldn't even talk like he used to anymore. He lost that part of himself to the character he created.

It wasn't long before I felt that pull too. The immersive nature of the world of WWE started to creep up on me. I wanted so badly to succeed in the business that I'd obsess over my character until I started to lose track of when I was thinking as the dramatized Rowdy or real-world Ronda.

It's hard for anyone to stay grounded in a world where people are in character more than they're not. More people call you by your stage name than your actual name. For so many wrestlers, their identity is completely interwoven with this imaginary persona they've created. The line between real and not starts to blur until sometimes I wondered if anyone even knows where the line is anymore.

WWE history is filled with examples of wrestlers sobbing backstage over losing a match for a made-up title, of real-life friendships strained by in-ring rivalries, of actual relationships destroyed by fictional story lines, of imaginary championship reigns going to people's heads.

For so many wrestlers, this is a place where they command respect and have clout. It's where people recognize them. It's all they think they have.

This is not a phenomenon unique to wrestling. I'd seen it in judo. I'd seen it in MMA. I'd seen it in Hollywood. Hell, I'd seen it as a bartender and in high school. These circles that you are led to believe are the whole entire world, and yet, are completely insignificant to everyone outside them. You build your identity around your place in this tiny space, and without *that* thing, outside of *that* realm, you are convinced you are nothing. But, just like everything in WWE, it's not actually true.

Fourteen hours after Hell in a Cell, including a four-hour car ride to Dallas, I walked into yet another arena, for Monday Night Raw.

Every week, wrestlers are given a call-time, usually six to eight hours before the broadcast starts. Weekly shows are held in NBA and NHL arenas or the occasional smaller city minor league venue or event center. You walk through a metal door into a cold, concrete, fluorescent-lit hallway indistinguishable from the city before. Sitting in chairs or standing next to doorways, event site security surround you in yellow jackets dotting the halls. The same white paper makeshift signs are taped throughout, large black arrows pointing you in various directions. Each features big block text and an identifying icon. Catering with a knife, fork, and spoon. Doctor with a medical symbol. Gorilla with a gorilla. Writers Room with an equal parts aspirational and delusional bust of Shakespeare. Production Meeting fittingly indicated by an empty conference table where no one is coming up with any kind of plan. Vince's Office, which, in what seemed like a missed opportunity, is not designated by an inverted pentagram.

The arena is filled with the sounds of clanking metal, drilling, crates being wheeled in various directions, and the unfolding of hundreds of chairs. WWE production staff dressed in suits and wearing headsets roam the halls back and forth.

Wrestlers trickle in. Giant men in hoodies and sweatpants unfold themselves from behind the wheel of compact rental sedans. Fit women in oversized sunglasses, dressed in tight outfits to adhere to guidelines requiring women arrive looking "sexy," pull small rolling suitcases behind them. Everyone walks with the slowness of a constantly aching body toward the arena.

We greet each other in the halls, playing out various exchanges of the same conversation.

"Do you know what you're doing?"

Followed by mutual hysterical laughter.

I bumped into Liv Morgan rushing down the hall.

"It's going to be great, tonight," she said, with a sarcastic smile.

The official rationale WWE gives for requiring everyone to be on hand for every event is that injuries can occur and having all talent there makes it possible to swap someone in if necessary. The truth is WWE wants everyone there because they don't have a fucking clue what they are actually doing until the last minute.

While claiming to be the longest and second-longest weekly episodic programs in the United States (based on the number of shows they've done, not actually the length of time they've been on the air) across its Raw and SmackDown shows, one would think that WWE has had plenty of time to figure out how to plan out a show more than a few hours before the broadcast is set to go live. You would be wrong.

"Wait, what's happening?" I asked. I had been told I was shooting a promo, but now, according to Liv, a decision from "the top" had been made for me to issue an open challenge, taking anyone right here, right now.

A producer knocked on my dressing room door. "Did you hear the change in plans?"

My face indicated that I had. There were never actually plans, just changes in plans.

I was aware WWE was scripted but could have never imagined that those scripts—in some cases full-page monologues—would be delivered on the day of taping, only to be replaced three or four times over the course of a few hours, single word changes highlighted yellow in an ongoing series of completely unnecessary tweaks that "Vince wants." If you deviated from a hastily changed word or two, you'd hear about it later.

Perhaps the biggest kayfabe is that WWE is actually run like a functioning company and not the absolute fiefdom of one man. Nothing gets done at WWE without Vince's approval. Story lines are scrapped at the last minute on his whim, sending writers and segment producers scrambling to come up with something new. Outcomes of matches change at the last second, sometimes during the match itself. Segments are cut. Monologues rewritten. And everyone just accepts it with a shrug.

"Everyone is getting updates before I do," I told the producer.

"We'll find a better process," he assured me. "Now, about rehearsal times…"

"Rehearsal times?" I asked.

"The schedule for the ring."

I was incredulous. "There's a schedule for rehearsals?"

It had been over six months, and this was the first I was hearing of a schedule.

"I thought everyone just kind of showed up," I said. "No one had ever mentioned a schedule. Where do I find it? Is it written down somewhere?"

"Not really," he said.

I looked at him waiting for him to either finish that sentence or realize how ridiculous that sounded.

I headed down the hall, turning left into the women's locker room, a space that a few months earlier I had been nervous to even enter. I worried that they wouldn't feel like I had earned it. Hell, I probably would have felt that way myself. But the other girls, with minor exceptions, could not have been more welcoming to me as I crossed over into their world.

Given the traveling carnival nature of WWE, the women's locker room referred more to a collective of the organization's female wrestlers than it did any kind of physical backstage space where a "Female Talent" sign might be slapped up on a given day. We were a unit, if not a complete utopia. It wasn't uncommon to see chicks bicker over someone not selling (in wrestling, "selling" refers to an appropriately dramatic reaction to make your opponent's moves look believable) or someone being too demanding. There were women who weren't even on speaking terms. But regardless, we'd all have a good time amongst the chaos. As Nattie liked to say, "We're a dysfunctional family, but we're still a family."

That night, I faced off against the Riott Squad—a trio featuring a heavily-tattooed Ruby Riott; Liv Morgan sticking out her trademark blue-dyed tongue; and Sarah Logan, two streaks of Viking-inspired face paint across her left eye.

We had no time to rehearse the last-minute changes in the ring, so Sarah was calling moves to me on the fly—the problem is I didn't know all the terminology yet.

"Backbreaker!" she shouted under her breath.

"What's a back-AHH?!" I found out the hard way.

Thankfully the crowd could almost never tell how much we were struggling to keep up with the mayhem.

If WWE were to be judged as a truly competitive sport, the best scoring system to apply would come from one of the most unlikely places: pairs figure skating. Wrestling isn't about brutality, but about flawlessly coordinating your movements in synchronicity, making sure everyone is hitting their mark, even if that means making on-the-fly adjustments. If the adjustments are on point, no one will ever know.

After the show, I visited with Steph for a few minutes to catch up. I couldn't help but wonder at how different she was from her father. Fans were still trickling out, when a crew of hard-hatted workers began deconstructing everything in the arena and hauling it out to semi-trucks plastered with the supersized faces of the wrestlers walking by.

It was after midnight by the time we got back to the hotel. Three hours later, I was in the lobby leaving for the airport. It was still dark. I rested my head against the car window as we drove.

I had the upcoming weekend off. I could spend a few days feeding my chickens and hanging out with the goats and donkey that we had added to Browsey Acres before a black SUV rolled up my gravel driveway to take me to another plane.

But next time would be different than all the other weeks that rolled into each other. I was very aware of where I'd be going next. WWE had announced its next big show three months prior. It was going to be in Australia. In Melbourne. In the same exact stadium where I had fought Holly Holm.

12

had zero intention of ever returning to Melbourne. "It's fine," I kept repeating, mostly to myself, but also to everyone else who asked how I felt about making the return. "It's fine" sounded better aloud than the truth, which was that just the thought of returning to Melbourne filled me with dread. It had taken me a long time to move forward. I wasn't entirely sure I had it in me to go back.

I squeezed Trav's hand tightly for the entire fifteen-and-a-half-hour flight. Tears slipped down my cheeks. So much had changed, I told myself. I had changed. It was going to be fine.

I stepped out of the airport and onto the WWE bus taking us to the hotel. I stared out the window silently as Melbourne materialized to my left, the suburban sprawl giving way to the city skyline. It had been years, but it still felt familiar. *This is where we went right*, I thought. We turned right.

"We're almost there," someone said. The bus slowed to a stop, I looked up and saw it. The twenty-eight floors of the Crown Metropol. We were at the same fucking hotel.

The last time I had set foot in this hotel, I was Ronda Rousey, undefeated UFC champion. Then, I wasn't. That hotel. That room. It was part of the before. It was the room of a person who no longer existed, from a life that I would never be able to go back to.

"We can book you somewhere else," a concerned-looking Triple H said later after I mentioned having been to this exact hotel before.

"It's fine," I muttered.

We walked inside and were handed our keys. Travis took the paper sleeve with the room number printed neatly on the front. I squeezed his hand as I walked to the elevator. The elevator beeped as we passed each floor going upward until it dinged at twenty-four, and the doors opened. We looked at the small sign on the wall indicating one set of room numbers to the left, another to the right. It looked oddly familiar.

I stared down the long hallway and took a breath, following Trav. We got to the door and stopped. Travis opened the door, and we both stood there for a moment, stunned.

"You gotta be fucking kidding me," I said.

I stared at the same white walls. The same orange carpet. The same view overlooking the river and the aquarium. It wasn't just a familiar room. It was the same fucking room.

I burst out laughing. I had been telling myself and everyone around me "it was fine." It seemed the universe wanted to make me prove it. In that moment, I resolved to do just that—to go out there and prove it to the universe and, as importantly, to myself.

The last time I had been here, the worst thing that could have happened happened. Nothing I could think up was ever going to be as bad as that.

The next afternoon, for the second time in my life, I stormed into what had been renamed Marvel Stadium to the sounds of Joan Jett and an announcer shouting, "Rowdy Ronda Rousey" to the roar of over 50,000 people.

The Bella Twins and I defeated the Riott Squad. A match I won not just by armbar, but by my newly invented double armbar, locking up both Liv Morgan and Sarah Logan at once for a simultaneous tap out. The Bellas raised my arms in victory, my WWE title belt over my shoulder. I looked around the Melbourne stadium cheering my name, tears welling in my eyes. It felt like a weight had been lifted not just off my shoulders, but my soul.

It wasn't redemption, but it was closure.

The week after we got back from Australia, the Bellas turned on me to set up the headline matchup between Nikki and me for WWE's upcoming all-women's pay-per-view, Evolution.

I had joined WWE to help move its women's division forward, but I was hesitant to be the face of that movement. I had no desire to be WWE's big star. Instead, I wanted to help create WWE's next star. Like how Roddy Piper made Hulk Hogan. Hulk Hogan emerged as the first mainstream wrestling star in part because Roddy had made himself so hated by the fans that anyone who beat him became their hero.

In the UFC, I had focused only on my own legacy. I had opened the doors for women, but I built that division just for myself. My goal had been to walk away undefeated and take the title with me, leaving the girls to come forever in my shadow. In pro wrestling, the title isn't something to be taken with you. Your last match is always a loss, so the belt can be passed on. Leaving those who come next in your shadow serves no one but yourself. You lay your legacy down to serve as the step up for the women who follow you.

When I came into WWE, it felt like we were in the middle of important changes. I don't know exactly why Triple H made elevating the women's division his mission. Maybe he wanted to create a more equitable world for his three daughters. Maybe he saw the business opportunity. Maybe it was a way to stick it to Vince. Maybe he just believed it was past time for women to have the same platform and opportunities as male wrestlers because it's the fucking twenty-first century. Whatever the reason, Triple H was our biggest advocate. I was the superstar who was going to help take the women's division from the afterthought to center stage. In wrestling, they talk about "putting someone over," meaning to make them look good, helping them win over the crowd. My goal was to help put the women's division over.

We might have been rivals at WrestleMania, but on this front, Triple H and I were on the same team. He had sold me on the future of women in the industry. It was a vision that I believed in so strongly that I obsessed, worked, performed, and traveled more than ever before. Once WWE made me champion of the division, I felt responsible for it. My pro wrestling journey stopped being about just having fun and became about pushing the women's movement forward. Again, I never said no.

When I was asked to headline Evolution, I was hesitant. Nikki Bella was a sure thing Hall of Famer, but I was just passing through. I asked the higher-ups to slate Charlotte Flair and Becky Lynch as the headliners, as the two future Hall of Famers were in the middle of an epic feud, but my request was denied. The justification was that Nikki Bella and I were the only names recognizable outside the company, meeting in the ring for the first time. Charlotte vs. Becky had already been done what felt like a thousand times. WWE's creative team convinced me that in order to slay a giant, you first have to create one. To make my dropping the belt mean anything, I had to elevate myself within WWE as a once-in-a-generation wrestler, not a one-off champion.

Evolution was the perfect platform. Backstage, it was as if you were walking through the history of women in the organization. They called us all together for a photo before the show. Standing between the women who had come before me dating back to the days of the WWF and the women coming up from NXT, for the first time, I understood my place in this history. Around me were women who, across decades, had been fighting for not only their own place in this industry, but all of ours.

The feeling carried over to the crowd. There was something palpable to the energy, as if they wanted to see us succeed. Often in wrestling, fans try to "hijack" the show, when the crowd loudly voices its displeasure with the match itself and tries to take attention away from the ring. Occasionally, it's in the form of booing or cheering for wrestlers who aren't there. More often it's insults and rude chants. I once watched fans chant, "We want beach balls!" (implying they'd rather be batting around beach balls than watching the match) to Bray Wyatt and Matt Hardy, two wrestlers who gave their everything every time they stepped into the ring. No matter who you were, no matter how much of your life and body you've given to entertain these people, fans won't hesitate to turn on you in an instant.

But at Evolution, they were cheering for each and every match. It was the kind of event that drew dads proudly bringing their daughters, groups of mom friends on a night out, and teenage girls. There were girls bringing their boyfriends to wrestling and not the other way around. The pro wrestling crowd is known for being assholes, jeering as much as cheering. But for just one night, it felt like they wanted to support the women.

Being there, you believed change wasn't just possible, but happening.

Charlotte and Becky went before us. They put on a five-star last-woman-standing match—they must have thrown at least twenty chairs into the ring. Theirs was a hard act to follow, especially a match with no gimmicks between a rookie (me) and a semi-retired Divas Era champion returning to wrestling after having suffered a serious neck injury (Nikki). We were extremely limited in what we could do, and the pressure was on.

Nikki and I had an incredible build-up to our match. I delivered the best promo of my career to that point—with the approval of Nikki—in the lead-up to Evolution. Nikki claimed that it was she who knocked down doors for women in the WWE. My reply was "The only door you ever broke down was the door to John Cena's bedroom!" (A reference to her former fiancé and WWE legend.) There wasn't a jaw in the building that didn't drop. Our match had one thing others didn't: Symbolism. It was the embodiment of the Divas Era vs. its next iteration as Superstars (just like the men were called). The Patriarchy vs. The Women's Revolution.

In the match, Nikki had an early advantage, aided by her identical twin Brie taking the occasional and obviously expected cheap shot. But I battled back to the delight of the crowd and retained the Raw title.

All the women in the show gathered at the top of the ramp after to celebrate the night's achievement.

Backstage Nikki, who had wondered if she'd ever wrestle again after having broken her neck, threw her arms around me.

"The Divas are dead!" she declared proudly.

Those were powerful words coming from her. Under the Divas distinction, despite all women had accomplished in the ring, they were still lauded more for their appearance than their performance. Until now. The titty-shaking era was over. The age of athleticism had begun. Walking out of the arena that night, you could not feel anything but hopeful.

What I hoped to do more than anything was to help bring up the next star, and no one was better positioned for that role than Becky Lynch. Becky had the air of an underdog, a head full of red extensions and a face that looked even prettier when she scowled, a perfect fit for an industry centered around conflict and appearances. Her thick Irish brogue made you want to listen to her talk. She had passion on the mic that could make even WWE's rehashed, overly dramatized writing captivating. After Evolution, the plan was that we would build toward the two of us intersecting the following month at Survivor Series in the Staples Center, the very arena where I had first caught the eye of WWE brass.

Days before our match, the women of SmackDown invaded the ring, led by Becky. Nia Jax threw a punch that actually connected, and Becky's face imploded. Blood gushed everywhere; her nose left visibly out of place. Her orbital bone fractured. It was a viral moment for Becky that propelled her career to new heights, but there was no way she would be medically cleared for a match by the end of the week.

WWE scrambled to slot in Charlotte Flair as Becky's replacement. We were tossing around ideas when I pulled out a kendo stick, a long bamboo cane used for martial arts training but also occasionally as a prop in pro wrestling.

"You're going to take this, and you're going to break it on me," I said. "And when it breaks I want you to pick up another and keep swinging."

Charlotte's eyes widened. There is no way to break a kendo stick without it hurting like hell.

"I love it," she said.

The crowd did too. We took them from hating to chanting "This is awesome!" In minutes.

My body was covered in huge welts, I limped out of the ring. Our brilliance quickly forgotten, the fans turned their energy and ire to me.

"Fuck you, Ronda!" a fan shouted, coming inches from my face.

Another person leaned over the barricade, flicking me off. "Fuck you, Ronda!"

There was an absolute unrestrained anger directed my way. It was so real in the face of everything else being fiction. Being in my hometown, in the venue where I set the record for fastest submission title defense in UFC history, made it even more personal. The crowd was peppered with signs saying things like "Ronda Go Home!" I *was* home. This was *my hometown*. What they really meant was they wanted me out of the business.

I was bruised, blooded, and booed. I had just let myself get beaten with a kendo stick for their entertainment. I stared back at them, trying my best not to respond with "Fuck you too!"

The predictability of my continued run had bred contempt. The same old "I'm gonna break your arm" promos they kept ordering me to regurgitate and rumors I was already leaving didn't help, but it wasn't just that. I would never be a wrestler to them. No matter what I did, it would never be enough. It didn't matter what I had accomplished or what I had gone through and given up to get there, I represented privilege to them. I wasn't an indie darling they watched grow up like Becky. I was an outsider stealing the spotlight away from those who "paid their dues."

When the WWE fans had welcomed me with open arms, I let my guard down. I wasn't ready for the sucker punch of them turning on me.

Nevertheless, I was back the next night on Raw, determined to show off my welts, deliver a fire promo I wrote myself, and defend my title in another open challenge. It couldn't have gone better. The taping went well, and that was all that mattered—or so I told myself as we left the arena.

We drove back to Riverside from the show, our typically hour-long drive taking more than double that, delayed first by event traffic and then standard LA traffic. When we pulled into the driveway, something seemed off. We got out of the car, walking around the back of the house. Our donkey, Millie, and the goats were hiding in the barn. All of the goats but one.

We discovered the body of our goat Rio, half eaten in a nearby dry creek bed. We had gotten home later than we typically did to put the goats away for the night, giving the coyotes the opportunity to pick off the littlest member of our herd. I collapsed to the ground in tears. *Sweet little Rio.* I had been so caught up in WWE, its fans, and its fake fighting, that I had let it take precedence over everything else in my entire life. My farm. My family. My future.

I called Triple H and told him I was done being a babyface. I was no longer capable of playing the good guy. I was done smiling and shaking hands while being shit on. I wanted to be able to defend myself, to say what was on my mind. It was my turn to turn.

But as hard as I pushed, WWE pushed back. It just wasn't yet time, I was told. We had to build up to it further, the producers said. We needed to better develop the characters. They talked about it as if they were writing scripts for serious actors who wanted to know "what is my motivation for this scene?" and not people who were smashing each other through tables.

I went out every week, night after night, and I sold falls, hits, and cheap shots like a fucking champ for WWE. But the fans hated it. The novelty of my arrival had worn off for everyone—including me—the story that WWE prides itself so much on telling was going nowhere. As months passed, I started to feel like WWE had sold me a bunch of bullshit.

In January, on the day after Royal Rumble, I arrived at the arena to find that now that the "Road to WrestleMania" had begun, the producers realized that we'd have to kick things into overdrive to get to where they wanted the story to go. The longer I spent in WWE, the more I became convinced that in addition to being helmed by a megalomaniac, its creative team was made up of a room full of guys who were the kids in high school who waited until the last night to do a semester-long project. And not the able-to-pull-it-off whiz kid types.

"You're going to do a promo and an open challenge," the producer said, handing me a script. In an open challenge, anyone can request a title shot "right here, right now."

He continued. "Bayley's going to come out and challenge. You'll have a match. And then Becky is going to come out."

As the winner of the previous night's namesake women's rumble—a thirty-person match where the last one in the ring gets to challenge either the Raw or SmackDown title holder for the belt at WrestleMania—it was finally Becky's turn to challenge me.

The writer handed me another page of dialogue. "Then you and Becky are going to have an exchange."

"That's it?" I asked, somewhere between sarcastic and incredulous. Doors had already opened, and fans were filing into seats. There was no way we could rehearse any of this in the ring.

"Um, yeah, I think so. Unless, of course, Vince has any changes."

I looked over the huge blocks of text that I was expected to be able to effortlessly recite in a matter of hours. There was no way I'd be able to memorize all of it plus a match that we hadn't even come up with yet.

I went to find Pam, better known as Bayley. She was describing the match in the hallway, but I couldn't retain anything. As a visual learner, it was just words to me.

"There is no way I can remember all of this," I said candidly. "I need you to know the match. I have to try to memorize and salvage this newest version of this sappy-ass promo in five minutes."

"It's OK," she said. "I'll call it to you out there."

In another, less chaotic moment, I would have been proud of myself for just how far I had come in acknowledging that I couldn't do it all on my own, saying it aloud and letting someone else help. But considering there wasn't time to rehearse, there certainly wasn't any for patting myself on the back over personal growth.

Back in my dressing room, a writer knocked on my door.

"Just a couple of changes to the script," she said, handing it to me.

I looked at the new lines highlighted yellow.

"Do I really have to open with this?" I asked.

"What's wrong?" she asked. "We ripped some of it from your autobiography."

"It just...doesn't fit the situation. Please don't make me say this."

The writer shrugged. "It is beyond my control."

Not even the sounds of Joan Jett could get me excited for what was to come. I walked into the ring and picked up the mic. The crowd booed. I shared their sentiment. I hadn't joined the WWE to become America's sweetheart. I was as over it as the fans were.

Before I'd even gotten out the first lines of dialogue, the crowd erupted in boos until I lowered the mic. Every time I opened my mouth to speak, they booed again.

Guess I should have spent that time memorizing the match instead of this cringeworthy promo, I thought to myself.

After an eternity of embarrassment on the level of a naked-in-class nightmare, Bayley's music hit, and she came running out.

We improvised the entire match, Bayley talking me through it whenever we came close enough for it to look like she was insulting me instead of giving me cues. The crowd hijacked the match, cycling through chants for wrestlers who weren't there. Every time I felt the pain of impact upon hitting the mat for their entertainment, resentment built. But I was trapped. I had no choice but to keep going.

In the moments between movements, I alternated between trying to remember my lines for the promo with Becky that was set to follow and rage over the fact that I couldn't escape this ongoing public embarrassment live on television. I flashed back to the trapped feeling *The Ultimate Fighter* gave me. I wanted out.

Becky came out to thunderous applause. She said her piece. I said mine, a second promo that I had written, not the writers. My voice filled with believable rage and disgust as I channeled my genuine feelings for the crowd into the dialogue. Becky glared back at me, then whispered "good job" under her breath. I could see the pity in her eyes though, looking at me thinking, *Poor naive girl got in over her head*. Becky was a WWE lifer, and I was never more grateful that this was her burden to carry instead of mine. I started to count the days until I could leave.

But my greatest in-ring embarrassment was considered a success since it kept the momentum going for Mania and made the crowd adore Becky even more. I still had to wait another month for my heel turn.

When Triple H had asked me to commit from one WrestleMania to the next, his reasoning had been that WWE builds story lines and rivalries from one Mania to the next. But the longer I had spent in WWE, the idea that there was any kind of planning and forethought when it came to best utilizing talent was as rooted in reality as ninety-pound Alexa Bliss being able to hold her own against me in an actual fight.

The match between Becky and me was finally set for WrestleMania and billed as the main event. It would be the first time WrestleMania was headlined by women, but word came down that Vince didn't believe we could pull it off just the two of us. No reasoning was given as to why he thought that to be the case, but he insisted Charlotte be added to the match.

Charlotte was the epitome of what Vince McMahon thought a woman should be. A tall blonde with enhanced features and impressive lineage (her father was WWE legend Rick Flair), she brought the wrestling IQ and the athleticism to make any match she dreamed up a reality. Driven to emerge from the shadow of her famous father, she had entered the industry with a chip on her shoulder and something to prove. It didn't matter if she was in front of a sold-out NFL stadium or a tiny crowd in Bangor, Maine, she was still going to do a moonsault off the top turnbuckle onto the floor to get everyone, be it 100,000 or 100 people in attendance, to pop.

Charlotte was one of the biggest women's names in WWE. Becky was its biggest rising star, but the two of them had already faced each other for what seemed like every other week for years. Not only that, but they were set to face each other *again* just before Mania.

Charlotte and I were coming off a great match at Survivor Series, but now that Becky was back, the "WWE Universe" (as the company refers to their own fanbase) was dying for a singles match between the two of us, the one they had been promised. However, Vince had declared it, so I sighed and accepted it.

Finally, more than a year after I had made my first WWE appearance and with only a month to go before my run ended, I made my heel turn. As Steph stood in the ring with Becky and Charlotte, I entered enraged. This turn was important to me. WWE higher-ups even let me write it myself.

"I did everything I could to respect this business," I shouted, at Steph and the fans. "I worked my ass off and exceeded every expectation. I poured my heart out and sacrificed my body for your entertainment, and what did you do? You booed me out of the Staples Center in Los Angeles, my home."

It was the least acting I'd ever had to do because I literally meant every word of it.

"I am done pretending," I continued. "I am not your dancing monkey. Damn your fantasy. Damn the man. [A dig at Becky's "The Man" tagline.] Screw the Woo. [A shot at the chant that welcomes Charlotte into every arena.] No more Mrs. Nice Bitch."

Turning, I kicked Charlotte in the stomach. Becky swung the crutch she had been using as a prop for a fake leg injury. I caught it, slapped her, and started beating her in a corner of the ring before dropping her to the canvas and transitioning into an armbar. Charlotte moved as if to re-enter the action, then thought twice as I continued to unleash on Becky.

The ref, who jumped in to "keep us apart," kept relaying messages he was getting from the back via an earpiece under his breath.

"Vince says armbar her again," he said.

So I did. The ref came close again. "Vince wants another armbar."

I wasn't feeling that far removed from the custom match wrestlers who shot matches at Santino's.

The pieces were being rushed into place to set up a showdown between myself, Charlotte, and Becky. What had been sold to me as a masterpiece twelve months in the making was being scaled down to a cheap paint-by-numbers. What they didn't realize is that, while they had long underestimated the women's division, I was a talented fucking artist. We all were.

Over the weeks that followed, all of the attention was on the women's division. It had never been hotter. We continued to hurtle toward Wrestle-Mania. Building the tension between myself, Becky, and Charlotte so that it reached a "breaking point" was key. Fans had to "believe" we wanted not just to fight each other, but to destroy each other.

Yes, Charlotte and I had bad blood ever since she slid in to replace Becky at Survivor Series. Yes, WWE had beyond belabored Becky vs. Charlotte as rivals. But we'd been given two lines and were told to make a triangle. They wedged Charlotte, the SmackDown champion, into the narrative. As I already held the Raw title, the powers that be (i.e., the sycophants who do Vince's bidding) dictated that to raise the stakes and overcompensate for us having vaginas, the winner of our match at WrestleMania would lay claim to not just one, but both titles. The concept felt hastily put together at best. The only good part was that now I had turned heel, I didn't have to pretend that I didn't think everything was bullshit.

The Raw on the Monday before WrestleMania was going to be crucial to set the stage. Becky, Charlotte, and I were set to face off against the Riott Squad in a bit that served solely to segue into a backstage brawl where Becky, Charlotte, and I would be arrested, but even the cops couldn't keep us apart.

At least, that's how it would look to the masses. The backstage would be filmed beforehand and be edited in as if it were live after the tag match. The whole concept had been dreamed up at the last minute by Vince, who was standing backstage giving direction, one of the few times I'd ever seen him out of his office or Gorilla.

Watching him throw it together was a rare glimpse into the genius behind his insanity. He knew where each person and every camera needed to be to execute his vision. It was the kind of sequence that takes weeks to put together for a movie, and Vince slap-dashed it together in a matter of minutes. My role was to be forced into the back of a squad car with Becky, where we'd start kicking at each other until I kicked out the window. After the cops removed Becky, I'd stick my head out the window to yell at Charlotte, who would knee me in the face. While Charlotte and Becky battled, I'd climb still cuffed into the front of the cop car to drive it, hands behind my back, into another cop car. The cops would pull me from the driver's seat, again throw me in the back, and I'd stick my head out shouting back at them as the car drove away.

"Make sense?" the writer asked.

It had been months since anything about this place made sense.

"Kinda," I said, uncertainly.

"Great. We've got about five minutes," a producer said as various crew members rushed to set up to shoot. The sudden urgency wouldn't have been so frustrating if we hadn't been sitting around at the arena for six hours asking about a plan.

A "police officer" whom I recognized from other illustrious roles such as "security guard #3" and "No Way Jose's conga line dancer" cuffed me and shoved me into the backseat of the black sedan that was apparently the best they could do when it came to a last-second cop car fill-in. I rolled onto my back, and as I stared at the window I was supposed to kick out, realized that I knew what I was supposed to do next, but had no actual idea of how I was supposed to do it. Was I supposed to stick my head out of a broken window? There had been no guidance, no rehearsal, nothing.

"We have five minutes" echoed in my head, so I kicked. The glass shattered everywhere, leaving jagged shards jutting up like monster teeth around the frame through which I was supposed to stick my head out and get kneed in the face by Charlotte. The only way to stick my head out safely without risking impaling my jugular was if I kicked the frame out too. I kicked a second time, aiming for the frame, but this time my foot slipped.

I felt the jagged glass slice into my calf like a serrated dagger jabbing into my muscle.

And that's when the producer yelled, "Cut."

"OK, let's set up for the next shot," he said.

I stared in disbelief. *Next shot?* The only thing that tempered the anger rising inside of me was the feeling of blood rushing out of me.

I looked down to see not a gash, but multiple holes in my left leg.

As they reset the shot, I gestured to Paul Heyman, serving as both a producer and in-ring personality and my only anchor to rationality amongst the chaos.

"Hey, so don't freak out and don't let anyone know, but I need a towel," I said, gesturing to my leg.

Heyman calmly relayed the message to my assistant Jenn, who rushed off to find a towel.

Filming resumed, and I stuck my head out of the now frameless window taking Charlotte's knee to the face like a fucking champ.

"And cut," the producer said for a second time.

"Are we done?" I asked.

"Almost. We just need to shoot you stealing the car as you ram it into the other cop car." There was a pause and look of consideration. "We'll just keep your hands cuffed behind your back for that since we're tight on time. Then we'll get you yelling out of the back of the cop car as it pulls away. And that's it." As if these were totally ordinary things to execute without any kind of stunt training or rehearsal.

Hands behind my back, blood dripping down my leg, I slid into the driver's seat and hit the gas until it rammed into the other fake police car in front of me. Moments later, my head missed slamming into the side of a bus by mere inches while I yelled out the window as my car was driven out of the shot.

"Are we done?" I asked again with slightly more urgency.

"Yes, but we need you in the ring in ten minutes for rehearsal. Doors are opening and we're going to lose access to the ring soon," the producer said to my back as I left my bloody towel in the "cop car" to sprint to the trainer's room.

Trailed by drops of blood down the corridor, I burst into the small medical room, panting and pointing. "Can you stitch this up in ten minutes?"

The trainer looked at me with what I imagined to be the expression of a battlefield doctor who has seen enough to know when to ask questions and when to just get to work. He pointed me to the trainer's table and started picking pebbles of broken glass out of my open wound.

"We need fifteen minutes," he said without looking up at either me or the clock.

"Fuck," I said. Jenn had followed me there, and I turned to her. "Tell them I'll be five minutes late for rehearsal."

The trainer was still picking glass out of my leg when the producer knocked on the door.

"We have five minutes," he said.

"You gotta sew me up so that I can walk through this fucking tag," I told the trainer.

With the weariness of a man who long ago accepted his input would be sought but not always followed, he grabbed a suture kit and sewed quickly. I could feel the crunch and sting of the remaining pieces of glass being squished in between my skin and my calf muscle with the tightening of each stitch.

I felt him cut the athletic tape over the protective wrap he wound around my leg, jumping off the table before he even had the chance to say, "Done."

I ran to the ring for five minutes of rehearsal before getting kicked out when the doors opened to let the fans in. We stood backstage talking through the match in a hallway until our music hit. The entrance music for our segment had already started by the time I burst into Gorilla. Emerging from the curtain on the other side, I went out and did the tag match. Unlike the organization, I was goddamn professional. That night would go down as one of the best Mania go home ("go home" referring to the weekly broadcast directly before a pay-per-view) segments ever.

The plan, I had been told in the weeks leading up to WrestleMania, was that we would figure the match out once we got there. What I didn't realize was that when they said, "once we got there," they literally meant when we arrived at the actual event. With the historic first women's main event of WrestleMania on the line, it wasn't until the night before that we even met to start throwing around ideas with a producer.

"And then, maybe from the double armbar, you guys can pick me up for a powerbomb," I suggested at one point. A powerbomb is a move where you lift your opponent so that she is sitting on your shoulders, then you slam her to the ground hard.

"You can't do a powerbomb," the producer chimed in. "The guys are doing a powerbomb before your match."

"Of course," I said in a tone that meant that's bullshit.

It boggled my mind that a men's undercard match could call "dibs" on powerbombs over the women's main event. (We did it anyway.) Even though I had continuously lowered my expectations, it was as if WWE viewed it as a game of limbo, going even lower every time. I realized that on the eve of my pro wrestling swan song, I didn't feel excited, just exhausted.

A few hours later, Trav and I were sitting at the WWE Hall of Fame Ceremony, dressed to the nines. I watched as my friend and fellow wrestler Natalya and her uncle WWE legend Bret Hart accepted the induction on behalf of the Hart Foundation.

Out of the corner of our eyes someone started running toward the ring. A crazed fan was sprinting for Bret. Trav was already on his feet heading up the stairs of the ring before the guy got under the ropes. Trav grabbed the railing to propel himself forward, but in true WWE fashion, it was a gimmick railing that immediately buckled. Trav stumbled to a knee. The fan tackled Bret to the ground, but before anything could happen Trav was back on his feet.

"Get him!" I screamed.

I watched my UFC heavyweight human weapon of a husband rip the fan off Bret and jump on top of him.

"Trav!" I screamed even louder. "Don't kill him!"

Bret was fine. The fan survived. The show went on. But it did not escape me that everyone was so lost in their fantasy world that when shit got real, my husband was the realest motherfucker in the room. Everyone froze. Everyone except Travis Browne. I was reminded of *The Alchemist* where the protagonist goes on a long quest only to find that the treasure he's been searching for had been right next to where he was sleeping the night he dreamed of going on his journey. I looked at my husband in the seat next to me as the shocked murmuring in the crowd faded. I'd finally realized I already had everything I ever wanted. *He* was the treasure. I was ready to go home.

Waking up the morning of my first WrestleMania, I felt like a kid on Christmas morning. This go-round, WrestleMania dawned like Christmas Eve, just get through this one last day. It was a long fucking day. By the time I stormed down the ramp to the sounds of Joan Jett—who WWE had actually flown in to perform "Bad Reputation" for my walkout live, the best part of the entire day—it was after midnight.

I'd love to say that we came out and put on the greatest show anyone had ever seen. That would be a lie. We did our absolute best to sell the hell out of it, but in the end, the match was good but not great. Last Mania had taught me there is a level of excellence that can't be achieved without putting in the preparation it takes to get there.

Halfway through the match, I threw a punch at Becky, but connected with her elbow. It was immediately apparent that I had broken my hand. Since there was nothing I could do, I pushed it out of my mind and kept going. I had one job: lose. Charlotte got me in a leg lock, looking for the win, but Becky broke it up. Together, we put Charlotte through a table, leaving just the two of us, in the match that always should have been. We met in the middle of the ring and let loose with both hands. I was pulling my punches, but it hurt like hell. I moved in on Becky as if I was going to finish her with Roddy Piper's famous Piper's Pit, but she countered, holding my shoulders to the canvas for the win. In order to walk away from WWE, I had to fall to the ground and let Becky pin me for an overly exaggerated count of three. I had reached a point where I could not only accept walking away on a loss but also embrace it.

My entire athletic career had been built not just by me winning, but by other people losing. The fear of losing had driven me to excellence. I had achieved things that no one else ever believed possible. But losing had also crushed me. It haunted me. It had almost broken me. Now, I watched proudly as Becky lifted the titles over her head. As I slipped backstage after that final match, losing provided me a door through which I could quietly exit as I moved onto the next chapter of my life.

13

As soon as I walked out of the ring after WrestleMania, everyone wanted to know if I'd be back.

When I had signed my contract a year and a half earlier, I had assumed wrestling would be a brief, onetime thing. I stayed much longer and accomplished much more than I had ever imagined. But I still couldn't help but feel as if I was walking out of the stadium leaving something unfinished. Maybe our WrestleMania main event fell so short of my own expectations that I didn't want to accept that was how my wrestling career would end. Maybe I saw there were barriers that were still left to be broken. Maybe I just wasn't ready to say goodbye. It felt like there was still more story to tell.

It had been one of the most grueling years of my life. But it had also been one of the most transformative. WWE was not without its flaws (and by flaws, I mean some big fucking problems). But I had come to love pro wrestling in a way I'd never expected. It had given me a new beginning when I thought everything I had ever worked for had come to an end. I would miss it. But I couldn't stay any longer.

More than anything, what I wanted to do was to have a baby. I had it all planned out, we'd go on a series of trips—impregnation vacations, as I'd taken to calling them. A kind of last hurrah where we'd travel to cool places and have lots of unprotected sex. Like a babymoon, but I could still drink wine. It had been the carrot I dangled in front of myself to get me across the finish line.

The only significant post-WWE obligation I had was filming a five-episode arc on *9-1-1*, a network TV drama centered around first responders, slated for late summer. I'd filmed movies before and done a couple of guest spots for TV series, but this provided a chance to experience working on a show as part of a cast without having to fully commit to joining the cast or even leave town since it was filmed in LA.

The four-month hiatus between commitments would give me time to rest up and heal up. I shattered my pinky knuckle clipping Becky on the elbow mid–Mania match, requiring surgery where my doctor shish-kababed my shattered knuckle together with a pin. But I had one final media appearance, promoting the video game *Mortal Kombat 11*, where I was the voice of Sonya Blade, on *The Late Show with Stephen Colbert*. I was driven straight from the hospital to the airport, boarding a flight before the anesthesia had even worn off. Dressed in a black leather jumpsuit, my hand throbbing in my lap, I smiled through my five-minute appearance.

That night, alone in a Manhattan hotel suite, I lay in bed thinking about the future. A seemingly offhand conversation I'd had with Paul Heyman not long before I left WWE floated up somewhere from the back of my mind.

"I'd love to direct you in a movie one day," he said, seemingly out of nowhere.

"What kind of a movie?" I replied.

"Whatever you want."

It was an interesting idea, more of a thinking game than an offer. But it got me thinking. My passion for fight choreography was still there, and WWE made me even better at it. Since my UFC losses, I'd been feeling sorry for myself because no one was handing me my greenlit breakout role. I decided to take my destiny into my own hands. To write my own role. Later that afternoon, I wrote a short summary: "Wanted assassin on the run finds out she's pregnant. Fights her way through enemies to an abortion clinic. But by the time she reaches the clinic, all the threats she overcomes together with her unborn child convinces her she's capable of protecting and wants to have the baby." Then I forgot all about it.

Now, weeks later, lying in bed, trying to will myself to sleep before an early flight home, the opening scene struck me. I ran it over in my mind again and again. My fear of forgetting it was keeping me up.

I sat up in bed. *Fine!* I bargained with myself. *I'll just write down this one damn scene, then I'm getting some rest.*

My motion restricted by my cast, I started typing, using only my thumbs as I poured my ideas into the notes app on my phone. I was still awake and typing five hours later when my car arrived to take me to the airport. I wrote all the way to the airport. As I waited in the airport. On the plane. The in-flight map showed we were somewhere over Nevada when I finally typed the words "The End." I looked at the metrics on my phone. I'd been writing for eleven hours straight.

I had no idea how to write a screenplay, but apparently there was a story in me waiting to be told. I sent the rough sixty pages of block text to my agent, Brad, to see if he could connect me with a real writer to refine it.

He quickly replied. "I hate it when you use the word 'cunt.'"

I read the subtext. I had a lot of work to do, but I was excited to have discovered a passion for something I didn't know was there. Something I never would have discovered if I kept my mind buried in pro wrestling.

Despite my best efforts, being back in the limelight in WWE had brought back my MMA-era obsessive anxiety. My quiet moments were again wrought with intrusive thoughts. This time, instead of trying to distract myself by falling into the destructive rabbit holes of the internet, I channeled that energy into screenwriting, devouring books and interviews on the subject when I wasn't writing. It became an unexpected answer to my disordered thinking. Any time my mind would drift toward self-criticisms or regrets about the past, I would redirect my focus toward my screenplays, harnessing my self-destructive tendencies to create instead of harm.

That summer, as I recovered physically and mentally, catching up on a year's worth of sleep, Browsey Acres continued to grow. In addition to the dogs, chickens, ducks, goats, and donkey, we'd added two wagyu steers in Riverside when our cattle breeder mentioned the ranch next to his in southern Oregon was up for sale. It was a scenic 660 acres, with four ponds, two creeks, and natural springs. But it needed work. The grassland had been taken over by invasive juniper, the pastures overgrazed and mismanaged to the point there was more bare dirt than grass.

Already having the two boys and now planning to bring a baby into the world shifted my perspective when it came to the future. I was no longer just thinking about my future, but theirs. What kind of a world were we creating for our children? Regenerative ranching was one of the solutions I was most enamored with, how the animals are managed to sequester carbon, build soil, make the land into an ecosystem instead of a meat factory.

We took the plunge and bought the land, investing the money I made in WWE into our herd of wagyu. It was the first time since fighting that Trav and I found a new passion we could share.

But before I could go all in on screenwriting, baby raising, cattle ranching, *or* considering a WWE comeback, I had to film *9-1-1.*

A few weeks before shooting was set to start, Trav wanted to go on a hunting trip. He was an avid hunter and had been counting the days until I was done wrestling, when he could leave town for a few days and someone else (i.e., me) could take care of the small menagerie we'd assembled on the Riverside farm.

I was still very much enjoying the novelty of not living out of a suitcase, so I sent him off, assuring him that I would be fine. He gave me that unsaid look between couples that asks, "Do you mean it or is this a test?"

The next week, he headed out before the sun was up, kissing me goodbye before he went. The next few days weren't all that different from the last few months. I slept and ordered delivery. But despite the downtime, I realized that I was suddenly feeling more tired instead of less. I mentioned it to my mom on the phone.

"Maybe you're pregnant," she said offhand.

I laughed. But then it hit me, maybe I was pregnant. Could I be pregnant? I took a drugstore test and waited as a faint line appeared. It was positive.

Gonna have to change that from impregnation vacation to incubation vacation, I thought to myself.

Secretly I was disappointed at getting pregnant so fast. I was looking forward to Trav and I finally getting some "us" time. The window to revel in my freedom passed in a blink of an eye, and I was alone at home without anyone to share the joy of being pregnant with.

The hormones and loneliness got to me. In tears, I called Trav. The words rushed out. How I'd been waiting a year to finally spend time with him and the first thing he does is run off on a hunting trip. How he'd left me alone. How it was so messed up.

"I can come back," he said.

"Just stay," I said, exasperated more at myself than at him.

This too, I reminded myself, was something that I had wanted. Trav had once told me that he hoped when I did get pregnant that I would surprise him with the news and film it. I ordered a onesie with a picture of a sperm on it that said, "Dad's Fastest Swimmer," and hid it. Then, I waited for him to come home.

Two nights later, I heard his diesel engine truck come down the road, then the crunch of its tires pulling into our gravel driveway.

"Hello?" Trav called out as he opened the door tentatively, uncertain as to whether he would encounter the version of me who had enthusiastically encouraged him to go or the one who had yelled at him for doing so.

"Hi!" I said, cheerily. I was trying to play it casual, convinced my face would give everything away. "I got you a surprise. It's in your bow case." I gestured.

"Ahh, babe, you shouldn't have," he said.

He walked over, opened the case, then paused as he saw the onesie.

"We're going to have a baby?" Trav asked. His eyes welled up, making everything feel real.

"We're going to have a baby," I said, a giant smile spread across my face.

He was ecstatic. I was, I realized in that moment, coming to terms with the life-changing enormity of what this meant.

I did all the things you're supposed to do when you find out you're pregnant. I called my doctor and made an appointment. I started taking prenatal vitamins. I stopped drinking alcohol, stopped smoking weed, stopped eating raw fish and deli meat. I downloaded an app that every week updated the size of the baby to a comparable kind of produce.

The first time we heard the heartbeat, I cried. Sitting on the swing on our back porch, we FaceTimed our families and shared the news. I started talking to my stomach and reading books out loud to it. I started imagining what the baby might look like. Whether it was a boy or a girl. I thought ahead to how "we" were supposed to start filming *9-1-1* and how cool it would be to one day tell my kid the story about how I scaled a Ferris wheel with them in my belly.

My first *9-1-1* episode centered around a tsunami hitting Santa Monica and its aftermath. We headed just across the border into Mexico to shoot at the studio that was actually initially built to film *Titanic*, so it had these huge water tanks. First take of the day, I had to open a boat door, step out, and deliver my lines while throwing prop debris off the boat. The door opened up, not out, and I was just a little too short to fully push it up, so I would need to give it a little extra shove at the end. The cameras rolled. I pushed the boat door up. It opened. I stepped through. Just as I walked through the door, it teetered on the edge, but instead of tipping open, it slammed shut again, right down on my hand.

The pain was immediate as I pulled my hand back. I could hear the internal back-and-forth playing out between my body and mind.

"Fuck, that really hurt," I said to myself.

"Don't be a pussy," I replied.

With a skill forged through my judo and MMA careers, I pushed the pain aside and went through the scene as if nothing had happened, delivering my lines without missing a beat, and throwing random things off the boat as the script called for.

The director yelled cut, I looked down at my left hand. My middle finger was being held on by a thread of tendon and the latex glove covering it. Just below the top joint, my finger had been severed from my hand.

I grabbed my hand to hold my finger on, then turned to the director.

"You guys aren't going to like this," I said, my voice completely calm, "but my finger is off."

"What?" he replied.

"My finger is no longer attached to my hand."

"What?!" a chorus of people in the general vicinity exclaimed. The reaction around me was equal parts disbelief and horror as I held up my hand. Several looked away in disgust.

Sitting in the dark in the hospital after surgery, I couldn't believe how selfish and careless I'd been. *How fucking stupid am I?* I berated myself, racked with guilt. *I got pregnant and all I was concerned about was about how I didn't get enough time to dick around beforehand? I was more concerned about how cool I thought I'd be shooting action sequences while pregnant and not about how dangerous it would be for the baby? I'm already the worst fucking mom ever to a clump of cells. How the hell am I going to take care of an actual human?*

The surgeon put me in a removable cast I could take off to finish filming, but it wasn't until I saw the baby's heartbeat on the screen a few days later that I felt any relief.

I was back on set days later. The stitches in my hand throbbed when I removed the cast.

A few weeks later, I was called to the set to film a fight scene. In addition to being a firefighter, my character was involved in an underground fight ring, 'cause, ya know, who isn't? Fortunately, my opponent in the scene was someone who would do whatever he could to make me look like a badass. My character would be taking down a six-foot-seven, 250-pound fighter portrayed by a fighter I knew well because I was married to him. We quickly choreographed and shot the fight scene, I put the cast back on, and we went home. My injured hand throbbed as I rested my good hand on my stomach, rubbing it gently. That night, my stomach cramped.

The next day I started bleeding. I called my doctor in panic. In a calm and kind doctor voice, she informed me that while light bleeding isn't uncommon in the first trimester, it is often the first sign of a miscarriage. Then the cramping worsened. I tried to stay calm, to remain positive, but the more I bled, the more I felt the future I'd started imagining fade away.

I went through every stage of loss within the next few hours. Denial: It's just implantation bleeding. Anger: This is all my fault. Bargaining: Maybe there is something the doctor can do to stop this. Depression: I sat on the floor of the shower, puking and crying, lacking the strength to even stand. And when finally, in the bathroom, I felt the clump of cells slip out, acceptance. I had miscarried. My pregnancy was over.

Travis held me as we stared at the bowl. This clump I had personified, sang to, talked to, and read to for weeks was the physical embodiment of all my hopes and dreams to be a mother. I wiped my eyes and flushed it down the toilet.

My doctor assured me that it wasn't the injury that caused it, that 20 percent of pregnancies miscarry before week 10, which is overwhelmingly due to there being some kind of genetic abnormality that isn't conducive to life. But to this day I feel like it was my fault, that in some way my narcissism had killed my baby. No matter what anyone says, there's a part of me that will never forgive myself.

Production wrapped, and I shut down. In retrospect, but unrecognizable in the moment (which I guess is the definition of retrospect), I handled it the same way I had dealt with my fighting losses. Which is to say, I was devastated and depressed. I hid from the world. I drank a lot and I smoked a lot and I didn't give a fuck. I was angry, mostly at myself. Trav let me be sad but again refused to let me fully withdraw from the world.

"It'll happen," he assured me.

But I felt broken. Time passed, and the ache became worse. Each day was bringing me closer to a due date that would never come. Every notification from the baby-tracking app telling me what size of fruit my never baby would have been made me hate myself until I deleted it.

I moved through the holidays like a ghost. On New Year's Eve, Trav held me close.

"This is gonna be our year, babe," he—like all the other optimistic people on the planet—said as the clock struck midnight. "Twenty twenty is going to be the year."

It was the first week of January when I went to hang the new calendar on the kitchen wall and realized my period was late. I took a pregnancy test, but when the line showed up positive, I felt hesitation, not happiness. Whether it was a second sense or a self-preservation, I knew not to get my hopes up. I wasn't taking good care of myself. There was no reading or talking or singing this time. When the doctor was unable to find a heartbeat at the 10-week checkup, I was simply unsurprised.

After a referral, I found myself sitting in a tranquil waiting room of a fertility doctor, decorated in muted tones that looked as if it were straight off a spa-inspiration Pinterest board as the world outside started talking about this COVID virus. As I waited, I couldn't help but feel I had been misled in every sex-ed class I'd ever had about how easy it is to get pregnant and find yourself unexpectedly with a baby.

I was surprised how nervous I felt, but this new doctor's confidence was contagious.

"I reviewed your records, and from what I see, I don't have any serious concerns about your ability to have a baby," he said.

He had little doubt that if I was a bit more mindful of taking care of myself, I'd have no problem having a baby. "But," he added, "if you want to have three or four kids like you mentioned and you're having trouble now, I would recommend we look at IVF."

I was only in my early thirties, but just a few years away from what the medical field calls a geriatric pregnancy. Because there's no clearer reminder of how society views women than to remind us that as soon as we're past childbearing age, we're basically old and shriveled.

When I left his office, I felt better for the first time in a long time. I had walked in feeling helpless and defeated but had walked out with a plan. As an athlete who had spent decades training, executing plans was my forte.

IVF, as I came to learn, involves a lot of blood drawing, a lot of hormone injections, and a significant amount of having things shoved up your vagina. The point of the process is to get your body to produce as many eggs as possible—not just the standard one it typically releases each month. This is done by jabbing yourself regularly with hormone shots to stimulate your ovaries. Then you go in for them to harvest the eggs. (Scientifically, this is called an egg retrieval, which should serve as your reminder here that this is my IVF recap and not any kind of legitimate medical literature.) During the process, you are put under while they shove some kind of medical vacuum (not the scientific term) up your vagina, through your uterus, and into your ovaries, where they get the eggs. The eggs are then fertilized and ideally turn into viable embryos. Except I would come to learn a lot of them don't.

The first cycle, they were able to get six eggs. Which to me, sounded like a lot. That's six months' worth of trying to get pregnant in a single shot. But the fertilization ended up with just one embryo, and even then my doctor thought it had only a 50 percent chance of developing further. He recommended we take a break for a few weeks, then do a second cycle.

"As many as it takes," I said. The two-hour drives to the clinic and back passed in a blur of Tesla autopilot and *Lord of the Rings* on audiobook.

Four cycles later, we had five girls and three boys, all with a genetically tested clean bill of health.

Now, it was time to transfer one in and wait for a baby. I was equal parts excited and terrified. Everything I had worked so hard for the last year had been leading up to this moment. But it did not escape me that the world was still in the middle of a global pandemic with a new record number of deaths spiking every month. No one yet knew the effects of COVID during pregnancy. I was terrified. Not only that, but a large chunk of the population wasn't.

As I approached pregnancy in a pandemic, it turned out the hermit skills I had been mastering the past few years finally came in handy.

We did the embryo transfer over the holidays, just after the first COVID Christmas. The wait between laying legs in the stirrups, having the embryo inserted via the medical equivalent of a turkey baster shoved up my vagina, and confirmation that the procedure was a success was the longest ten days of my life. Just after the New Year, we got confirmation that the transfer was a success. When at long last I heard the words "Congratulations, you're pregnant!" from my doctor himself, it became real.

The doctor put my due date at September 23, 2021. I did the math immediately to see how long I would have to get back in shape for a return to the ring at the 2022 Royal Rumble.

14

My water broke on my due date, and as Trav and I drove to the hospital, I was adamant that it would be an unmedicated, natural childbirth. It was evening when we arrived at the labor and delivery ward.

"It might be a little while," the nurse said, as she showed Trav how to recline the chair into a bed. After she had left the room, Trav turned to me.

"I'm going to get some sleep," he said. "Tomorrow's going to be a big day."

He smiled at me.

"I love you," he said.

"I love you too," I replied.

He closed his eyes and drifted off. I stared at the ceiling in the dimly lit room, my contractions strengthening. Each one providing a new, more intense answer to the question every pregnant woman asks herself about labor: "How bad could it actually be?" The pain soon escalated until it entered the definitely-hurts-worse-than-getting-your-finger-chopped-off zone.

Trav adjusted his position in the recliner, trying to get comfortable in his sleep. I glared at him. I don't care how much you love your husband, there is a primal sense of the silent resentment and rage that overcomes a woman in labor as she watches her partner dreaming peacefully while she suffers through contractions.

The sun was just coming up when the nurse came in to check how labor was progressing.

"Do you have a name picked out?" she asked, as she moved toward the foot of the bed, pulling up the blanket to check how dilated I was.

"Yes," I said. We hadn't so much selected one as we constructed it over months of discussion with Trav's sisters and the guidance of their dreams.

Trav is Native Hawaiian. Hawaii holds a special place in our hearts. It's where we want to raise our hula-dancing ninja babies, open a small dojo, get old, and eventually be buried together. When I am there, I feel not only happy but at peace.

Shortly after my UFC loss to Holly Holm, when I was still hiding away from the world, Trav had taken me to one of the smaller islands. This was at a point in my life where just getting spotted sitting at In-N-Out in the drive-through incited a mob of people to surround our car taking pictures like I was a mobile aquarium exhibit.

"No one will bother you there," he promised.

One afternoon, we were waiting for our food order at a local counter. A minivan stopped in the middle of the street, reversed, and pulled up next to us. I instinctively tensed, no idea what would emerge from this nondescript van. A whole family piled out.

"Ronda! Travis!" the dad called out. One by one, the parents and kids came over to give us hugs and kisses on the cheek.

"Welcome home," the mom said.

As they pulled away waving, I looked at Trav, through welling tears.

"I love it here," I said.

In Hawaiian culture, women on the men's side of the family name the babies. It's a collaborative deal, not "we picked this name, too bad if you hate it." As important as the name itself is the meaning behind it.

Travis's older sisters Maya and Yoni had named our boys, Kaleo and Keawe, and as soon as I was pregnant, we'd turned to them to name our daughter.

"I think it should be Pō," Maya said one day. It meant, she explained, darkness, but not a scary darkness. It meant darkness like the darkness that bore creation, like the darkness of the bottom of the ocean, like the darkness you need for there to be able to be light.

"It just feels right," she said. And it did.

She sent us a list of names that included Pō and what they meant. There was one name on the list that we loved immediately: Lanipō, which meant a dark, verdant growth. It made me imagine a lush dark gulch in a rainforest. It was perfect.

A few weeks later, Maya called from Hawaii.

"What do you think about including Makalapua?" she asked. "It's Hawaiian for blossom."

"That's really cute," I said. "Lanipō Makalapua."

The only thing about that, Maya explained, was linguistically it wouldn't make sense. The way to phrase it would have to be Makalapuaokalanipō. It was a beautiful name but felt too long for a first name.

"We can make that the middle name," she assured me.

My face fell. I felt like we were being forced back to the drawing board.

"Don't worry," Maya promised. "We'll find something perfect."

She called us, excited, one morning. She had been sleeping on what the name should be and it had come to her in her dream.

"La'akea," she said. "It means a shining, sacred light."

There are different ways to interpret Hawaiian names, she explained. The meaning could even change throughout one's life. I had not yet seen my baby beyond the grainy images of the ultrasound, but when I closed my eyes, I visualized what it meant to me. This bright little flower growing up out of a dark rainforest gulch, rising upward toward the sky under a lush, dense canopy. I envisioned a single beam of light breaking through, finding its way through the vines and trees, shining on this tiny flower in the darkness.

Even though she hadn't yet been born, my daughter was already the light of my life. It was perfect.

Here's the thing about actually giving birth, for all the thinking about it and planning you do beforehand, you have no fucking clue what you're getting yourself into until you're sitting in the hospital stuck at three centimeters after twelve hours of contractions on twenty-four-plus hours without sleep. Plans change. And when plans change, epidurals are one of the greatest inventions of modern medicine. Eventually it was time to push.

After two miscarriages, a year of IVF, hundreds of hormone injections, dozens of doctor visits, all three *Lord of the Rings* books and part of *The Silmarillion* (a lesser-known prequel to LOTR), eighteen hours of contractions and four good pushes, the doctor placed the most beautiful baby I had ever seen on my chest.

Everything I had ever won, done, experienced, or accomplished paled in comparison.

15

Six weeks after my sister Maria was born, my mom made weight and won the US Open.

It was only after I had a baby that I realized how equally badass and borderline insane that was. I was not quite that ambitious. I would be stepping back into the WWE ring exactly four months from when I stepped out of the hospital.

Motherhood was everything I imagined and more, but that didn't mean it wasn't also exhausting. I spent the first blurry days nursing and caring for and sometimes just gazing at this tiny little person we had created. But as I started to come back to some state of awareness, I realized four months to get ready for a full return to WWE would fly by.

Returning for Royal Rumble made the most sense from a storytelling perspective. The winner of the Rumble gets to challenge for the title at WrestleMania.

I had it all planned out. I would return and win the Royal Rumble as I sought to cement a legacy as one of the greatest heels in WWE history. Charlotte and I would meet one more time at Mania in the spring. I wasn't 100 percent physically back from having the baby, and if anyone could carry my postpartum ass, it was Charlotte. As soon as I put away any questions about her ability to beat me once and for all, I would set my sights on Becky. The buildup between the two of us would be epic, and everything the fans wanted to see. It would culminate in not only the greatest women's match in history, but as one of the greatest WrestleMania matches ever.

Besides facing Charlotte and Becky, I wanted to tag team with Shayna. Wrestling at the highest level with her was one of the main reasons I got into the business in the first place. In true pro wrestling style, Shayna would inevitably turn on me. That would set us up for a historic showdown at Summer-Slam, the second biggest event of the year, where she would win and I would walk off into the sunset.

I wanted the singles match between Becky and me to be something special, the kind of matchup that wouldn't just captivate wrestling fans but create new ones. I was inspired by Roddy Piper's Hollywood Backlot Brawl at WrestleMania 12. In that showdown, Roddy and Goldust battled back-and-forth in a (pre-recorded, but meant to look live) behind-the-scenes battle that eventually "spilled out" into the ring where they faced off in WrestleMania. Instead of playing a "package" (the standard highlight reel summary of a feud to catch viewers up to speed before a match), Becky and I could have a backstage brawl interspersed throughout the WrestleMania card. Each clip of the brawl would be more intense than the previous, driven by dialogue recapping our rivalry for new fans. By the time we reached our advertised slot in the show, we'd have been fighting for the better part of the night. "Bad Reputation" would blare, but no one would come out. The announcers would ask each other if there would even be a match.

Then Becky's music would hit. A few more bars, and still no one. The audience, whether watching on the jumbotron or at home, would start to wonder what was going on, and that's when she would throw my ass through the curtain, beating me with a chair all the way down the ramp and into the ring.

It was dramatic and would require high-level production to do it right, but the catchphrase for the event in LA was "WrestleMania goes Hollywood."

I was brimming with ideas and just wanted to get the conversation started. I wanted this to be something that was so great you could tell it came from years of thought from the best minds in the business.

"That's why I wanted to meet with you now," I concluded.

Triple H, Vince McMahon, and Paul Heyman sat in suits around the conference table at WWE headquarters in Connecticut, nodding excitedly as I laid out the entire plan. By the end, we were finishing each other's sentences.

"Fucking love it," Vince said.

That was all I needed to hear.

That was what motivated me as I dragged myself out of bed, half asleep, hair unbrushed, milk leaking from my boobs, back to training. It had been two-and-a-half years since I truly worked out. Contrary to what one might expect, working out isn't something I am particularly motivated to do. Yes, if you happen to come to our house at 5:00 a.m., you will see someone working out hard in the gym we converted our garage into, but it will be my husband. I will be upstairs, asleep in my bed. My entire adult life working out was a major part of my job responsibilities. But no one had been paying me for it since I left WWE, and I had no interest in working for free. When I have downtime, I very much enjoy doing nothing.

Not only had I not been working out, but my body had changed. I knew I wouldn't be able to bounce back into shape the way I used to because I could no longer train the way I used to. I couldn't dehydrate or crash diet my way back into shape. I was breastfeeding and had to keep eating regularly to make sure that Pō was getting enough nutrition

I found that, for the first time in my life, I had anxiety about returning not just to function, but also to form. I had little doubt that, from an athletic standpoint, I would be ready to get back in the ring within four months. Getting back into a sports bra and midriff baring spandex shorts within four months was another story. The idea of being directly compared to how I looked before I had a baby was far more daunting than the idea of storming into an arena in front of 45,000 people and throwing a bunch of chicks around the ring.

But I felt like I had something to prove. And, for the first time in a long time, the person that I was looking to prove something to was myself. In the almost three years that I had been away, I felt like I had lost my athletic self.

More than losing the baby weight, I wanted to make sure that I hadn't completely lost who I was.

The doctor told me I had to wait six weeks before working out to avoid hemorrhaging, meaning I effectively only had two-and-a-half months to get back in shape after years of letting my body turn to mush. My first time back working out, I stepped in a ring and did a forward roll. It's the first thing I learned in judo, and I'd been doing it since I was almost eleven. I felt like I was about to throw my back out. I had trouble lifting five-pound weights. I was shocked at my own regression. I was literally starting at zero.

For the next eleven weeks, every day was a remix of feed the baby, work out in the garage, shower, feed the baby, sleep, work out in the ring, shower, feed the baby, sleep, and repeat. I was exhausted, but grateful to have a goal. Without it I wouldn't have dug so deep to work on myself. My body slowly started to resemble the way I remembered it, my self-esteem along with it.

My return was shrouded in as much secrecy as my debut, so WWE had loaned me a ring that we set up in our backyard. As the Rumble got closer, they sent a couple of match producers out to my house a few days before the event. We brought in some local guys to stand in for the women who didn't even know I would be in the match. My goats watched from the other side of the fence.

Because of the nature of the Rumble itself—a match with thirty wrestlers—you can't rehearse for it the way you would a match with one or two other people. Instead, we were rehearsing just parts. The rolling clothesline. Turning around and jumping off someone's back to the elbow. The plan was that I would be the last entrant, come out, people would lose their minds, I would smash everyone who remained in the ring, point at the Wrestle-Mania sign signifying my return, and go.

Trav, Pō, and I hitched a ride from LA to St. Louis, site of the Royal Rumble, on a chartered flight with the cast of *Jackass*, the guys who had made themselves a name on MTV and a series of movies by subjecting themselves to insane stunts like being Tasered, snapped by mousetraps, locked in a limo filled with bees, trampled by bulls, and smacked by a giant-size high-five hand, just to name a few. WWE had granted Johnny Knoxville a spot in the men's Rumble as he promoted *Jackass Forever*. The guys (Trav excluded) punched each other in the balls, while I nursed my baby in the corner.

We exited from the charter on the tarmac and loaded into the back of a car that took us to a hotel where I'd be able to rehearse with the other women in the match for the first time. Security led us through the service entrance up to the ballroom where a ring had been set up.

"So, there's been a change," the producer said when I walked in.

My eyes widened. "What change?"

"You're going to be coming in at twenty-eight."

"I've been rehearsing to come in at thirty," I said. "What am I supposed to do if I come in at twenty-eight?"

The producer shrugged. "Just look like you're doing something. Keep busy."

"Cool," I said in a tone that I hoped conveyed that I didn't think it was cool.

I left rehearsal, slipped out of the hotel and into the car that was set to take me to my bus.

The bus had been suggested by Stephanie McMahon. Steph and Triple H had spent much of their oldest daughter's early years on the road, and Steph said it was only manageable because they had a tour bus. She recommended that if I came back with a baby that I request one. So I did.

The bus was maroon, silver, and white and—both inside and out—had an aesthetic that can best be described as a tribal tramp stamp. She (vehicles, like ships, are always her) even came with a name: Scandalous. I looked up at her in awe. After having spent my previous run crisscrossing the country in a rented sedan, this bus, despite being a relic from the late 1990s, wasn't just a step up, it was another atmosphere.

"Mike," the bus driver introduced himself, his thick Southern accent evident in just that single syllable.

As I looked around, my mouth dropped.

"Can you believe it?" I asked Trav.

I turned to see him standing in the exact middle line of the hallway, real-izing at that moment, it was the only place on the bus he could fully stand up straight.

The next morning, we drove to the arena, shades down, passing Pō from lap to lap to keep her happy. I went through the match in my head as my glam team started the transformation from postpartum mom to Royal Rum-ble champion.

We pulled in and parked, our bus blocked off by black curtains to shield me from the world. WWE both leaks word of who its surprise appear-ances will be while maintaining an appearance of trying to keep them a secret.

I paced back and forth on the bus, baby in arms, walking through the match, still unsure what to do in the "keep busy" periods. Pō alternated between sleeping and staring at me as if trying to reconcile the heavily eye-linered lady in front of her with the person who gave her milk.

A producer knocked on my door, giving me a heads-up that it was almost time to head to Gorilla. While I was ready to "rumble," I was not ready to put on tiny shorts. Instead of sliding on my traditional tiny belly-button-baring spandex, I found myself instead wiggling into a double layer of Spanx and a pair of jeggings. One step at a time, I told myself. Then I stepped out of the bus and back into my second run in the WWE.

When Joan Jett hit, 45,000 people went wild. I was shocked, even elated. I was expecting outrage at my return. But I didn't smile back. I was return-ing as a heel, meaning my relationship with the crowd was supposed to be antagonistic. It wasn't just an act. I didn't want to give them the satisfaction of knowing they had the power to make me happy.

I stormed down the ramp, focused. There were a half-dozen women in the ring when I entered. I tossed a few out, then "kept busy." I felt awkward, stalling. Then Shayna's music hit, she ran through a few chicks, before taking to the middle of the ring. I stood across from her. The crowd started to buzz as we circled each other. In all this time, we had never shared a ring together. We didn't even touch, but were like two lightning rods connected by a spark.

We felt it. The whole stadium did too. As the crowd reached a fever pitch, we were interrupted by the other women in the ring. The crowd groaned. The moment they hadn't known they wanted already taken away. One woman after another went over the ropes, until in the end it was just me versus Charlotte Flair. I motioned at her to bring it on, and she charged. I grabbed her, throwing her over the top rope for the win, bringing the crowd to its feet.

I raised my arms and pointed at the WrestleMania sign. Pop. Pop. Pop. Pop. A sequence of pyro blasts exploded around the sign.

It might not have looked perfect. I might not have hit every spot. I might have forgotten to emote for the camera at every possible second. I might have needed a third layer of Spanx. My boobs might have been on the verge of leaking milk right through my black jumpsuit. But I had just blown the roof off a sold-out stadium in my return to the ring four months after having a baby.

A few steps outside Gorilla, I passed Shayna, still in her match gear, white and red leggings with a white sports bra emblazoned with her signature spade across the chest.

"Did you feel that out there? They want this!" She gestured to us both.

"And they're gonna get it!"

"Seriously though," she said, her tone shifting from fellow wrestler to genuine friend. "Congrats!"

"Aww, thanks!" I said pseudo-bashfully.

"But did you have to try to burn the whole place down?"

I looked at her confused.

"The WrestleMania sign," she explained. "After you pointed at it and the pyro went off, it caught fire!"

"Really? On fire? It's a sign!" I said. Shayna rolled her eyes at my love of wordplay. She kept going instead of dignifying my corniness with a response.

In the moment, I took it to mean that I was going to set WWE ablaze. But as the fire began to melt pieces of the sign, forcing the fans to evacuate the seats below, I might have misinterpreted what it was foreshadowing.

CREDIT: Cynthia Vance

16

We left the Royal Rumble and headed to Cincinnati to make an appearance on Raw, the official declaration that I was back. Trav flew home from St. Louis as it was our shared-custody week with the boys.

Pō slept nestled in my arms as my rockstar tour bus took me to the next town. I had committed to a year-and-a-half for my second run. I had worn myself out and down the first go-round but was determined this run would be different. In addition to the bus, I had requested a lighter schedule that would give me one week off a month and no live shows unless we needed them to prepare for a big event.

Because I'd been sequestered before the Rumble, it wasn't until I arrived at Raw that night that I saw how much things had changed. The WWE I was returning to seemed almost unrecognizable to the version of it I had left behind at WrestleMania nearly three years before. Backstage felt empty. The pared-down women's locker room seemed almost silent. Everyone seemed jumpier, more on edge. There was no longer laughter or bustle in the arena hallways.

During the pandemic, WWE had made huge cuts, especially on the women's side. And while events had rebounded since the world started opening back up, the slimmed-down rosters remained. There was one unintended positive result of the cuts: the women's locker room was united in a way it had never been before. It was us against the machine. We were determined to steal the show with the scraps of time we were given to do it.

At the same time, a competitor to WWE had begun to emerge in AEW, All Elite Wrestling. It launched in early 2019 as an edgier, less corporate, and grittier alternative to WWE. Independent promotions were nothing new. Vince McMahon had built WWE by buying up competitors and putting them out of business in the 1980s and '90s. In the years since, small indies existed as a platform for amateur pro wrestlers, especially those looking to build their skills in hopes of getting an NXT tryout. But AEW was different. It had money with its own billionaire backer, Tony Khan. It also had talent, much of it developed by WWE itself—either disgruntled former WWE wrestlers who had been cut or in many cases demanded release from the organization. Cody Rhodes, who had left WWE because of "creative differences" (a polite way of saying he reached his breaking point when they made him paint his face and don a gimp suit as a character named "Stardust" instead of wrestling as himself, the son of the legendary wrestler and promoter Dusty Rhodes), was the face of this new organization. WWE's COVID house cleaning had injected AEW with all the talent it needed to reach that next level.

NXT, which had been Triple H's domain, had been caught in the ongoing family dispute between him and Vince McMahon. Vince's unwillingness to give up any control made progress on the main roster all but impossible. But operating out from under Vince's thumb, Triple H had built NXT into a brand that was not only developing WWE's next generation but producing some of the organization's best and most innovative wrestling. People were excited about NXT in a way that they weren't about Raw and SmackDown's constant reliance on rehashing the same formulaic story lines over and over.

As NXT grew and it became apparent that there was the potential to expand and profit from it, suddenly it became attractive to Vince. In fall of 2019, WWE launched a weekly NXT show—slated to go head-to-head on-air with AEW. Now, NXT was on the up-and-up, but so too was AEW. Then Triple H almost died, suffering from heart failure and requiring surgery. He stepped away to deal with his health, and in his absence, Vince's cronies saw an opportunity. NXT was losing the ratings battle to AEW, they whispered to Vince. Changes needed to be made.

Which is how John Laurinaitis, a former wrestler turned WWE executive and all-around dirtbag, ended up running NXT. Laurinaitis had made a name for himself as an average but by no means outstanding wrestler before he moved into playing an in-ring authority figure type and then a producer. He looked and acted like an entitled sixty-year-old former frat boy. Tall, blondish, and with a cleft chin, he always appeared to be scowling, even when he smiled. His raspy voice earned him the nickname Johnny Laryngitis, which was one of the nicer things people called him.

Whereas Triple H looked for talent and potential in NXT prospects, it appeared John Laurinaitis looked for fuckability. He further purged the NXT roster, firing it seemed like everyone over twenty-five and turning recruiting attention away from the indie circuits in favor of blonde sorority-types from places like the Universities of Florida and Tennessee. Putting the blame for the decline on Laurinaitis—which Vince would basically try to do a few months later—would be easy but Laurinaitis was only a symptom of what was wrong within WWE.

Honestly, the actual drama was so much better than anything WWE could ever script.

It quickly became clear to me that the women's division in WWE I returned to had regressed. Women's matches were few, far between, and, I'd soon learn, frequently cut down at the last second to give the men time to run over. Not only that but morale was low. As wildly as WWE had wielded the ax, a lot of the remaining wrestlers were worried they'd be next.

As I looked around what felt like the ruins of what I had been so proud to have been a part of building before, I was left wondering what I had gotten myself into.

———

WrestleMania loomed on the horizon, and it would mark my first solo match back in the ring after weeks of cutting promos and a tag match in

Saudi Arabia. In response to pandemic-related crowd restrictions, WWE had split WrestleMania into a two-day event. Once the restrictions were lifted, they realized they could make double the money by selling twice as many tickets if they kept it across two days, and so a new era of WrestleMania was born.

The initial plan for WrestleMania had been for me to win, but just days before, Vince decided that me winning at Mania was too predictable. I needed to get people to want me to win, not just expect it. At WrestleMania, I armbarred Charlotte and she tapped out for everyone to see. Everyone but the referee that is, as he had conveniently been knocked out—it happens far more in WWE than the average person would find reasonable. When I went to check on the ref, Charlotte blindsided me, ultimately getting the win. That set up a rematch between the two of us a month later.

Which is how I came to spend my first Mother's Day, standing in the designated makeshift hair-and-makeup area backstage, watching as Charlotte's hair steamed in the curler while she and the producers debated what we should do in a match that was slated to be live in less than an hour. My mom passed by holding Pō. My daughter saw me and immediately started screaming and crying as she reached for me. I reached out for her.

"I got her, just handle your business," my mom said, whisking Pō down the hallway and out of reach. The expression on Pō's face broke my heart. Her cries echoed through the corridor.

My eyes welled up. *Worst first fucking Mother's Day ever,* I thought. My blurred gaze fell onto the sign that said "Vince's Office" across the hall. I made a beeline for it, knocking while entering.

Vince was sitting alone next to a monitor in an office chair hunched over his phone. At the surprise intrusion, he gave an expression that likely would have been a raised eyebrow had his face not been heavily Botoxed. He had the appearance of a seedy Vegas mob boss powered by anabolic steroids and Viagra.

"I can't fucking do this last-minute shit," I said. "I need to be able to prepare, rehearse. The match is in an hour and we still don't have it figured out yet"

"Don't be ridiculous. You'll do fine," he assured me.

"I appreciate your confidence in me, but I didn't come in here for a pep talk," I said. "I came in to tell you that performing with zero prep is not only needlessly dangerous, but we're not being enabled to do our best work."

"Don't worry, you ladies are gonna knock it out of the park tonight," he replied.

"Vince, I want to prove you right and be the best investment you ever made," I told him. "But I got in this game too late to ever improvise a five-star match like Bret Hart and Shawn Michaels could. [WWE Hall of Famers known for being able to throw together incredible matches on the fly.] I proved in my debut that if you give me the time and resources to prepare, I can create something really special. But I can't give you my best when forced to constantly throw shit together at the last minute like this."

"We'll see what we can do, but you'll be fine," he said. "Give 'em hell tonight."

I could tell he was just trying to get me out of the room. I had taken my concerns all the way to the top. I didn't know what else I could do. I looked at the clock on my phone. We had forty-five minutes until we were supposed to be in the ring in front of thousands of fans in the stands and millions of people watching at home.

We finished scripting the match thirty minutes before we were supposed to enter the arena. The broadcast had already started. There was no way we could rehearse any of it in the ring.

"There, you have a whole half hour to memorize it. Plenty of time, you'll be fine!" our producer proclaimed with a smile.

I was speechless, shocked at the mayhem everyone accepted as normalcy. That sentiment was exactly the problem. I was striving for great while everyone else was settling for fine.

As watered-down and thrown-together as the match was from what we had initially envisioned, it went down as one of the best "I Quit" matches in history.

I walked back into Gorilla, the title belt over my shoulder.

Vince sat behind a monitor.

"You see?" he said, a look of satisfaction on his face. "You ladies were amazing! Sometimes, it just doesn't come across as visceral if you practice it too much."

I couldn't even bring myself to fake a smile. All I was thinking about was how much better it could have been.

With Charlotte in my rearview mirror, Money in the Bank was next. As a narrative device, winning Money in the Bank provides a big career opportunity, whether by thrusting an up-and-coming star into the spotlight or providing a veteran a segue toward their next planned title run.

Money in the Bank also marked my first title defense. Natalya was challenging me for the belt, a match she would lose, but then cue the music, the winner of the women's ladder match earlier that night would come out, cash in, and take me out.

"Who's that going to be?" I asked.

"Lacey Evans," Paul Heyman told me.

"That will be so great for her," I said.

Equal parts Southern charm and in-ring brutality, she had served in the Marines before getting into pro wrestling. Lacey had a baby just a few weeks after I had Pō and was making her own return to WWE.

Moms are doing it, I thought to myself.

"Does she know?" I asked.

"Not yet," Paul said.

"She's definitely going to get the title?" I asked. "Has anyone told her?"

"Wait a week or so," Paul said. "If nothing changes, you should definitely be the one to tell her. You're the one giving her her first title."

A week passed, nothing changed. I grabbed Lacey when I happened to pass her in a hall. She had been coming up through NXT during my first run. She even helped me develop my Piper's Pit finisher.

"Hey, you know anything around here could change at any minute," I said. She nodded slowly. I continued. "But the plan for the last week or so is that you're going to win Money in the Bank and cash in on me that night."

She broke into a huge grin.

"I wanted to be the one to tell you," I said. "I'm so happy to be giving you your first title."

I could hear the excitement in her voice as she assured me she wouldn't get her hopes up, but it was clear they already were.

Two days later, I was standing in my kitchen washing baby bottles when my phone rang. Paul Heyman's name appeared on the caller ID. I dried my hands on the dish towel and picked it up.

"Hey, Paul, what's up?" I asked.

"So Lacey's out, Liv's in," he said.

I was confused.

"Lacey's hurt?" I asked. I had just talked to her. It didn't make sense.

"No, it's just going to be Liv."

"Why the change?" I asked.

"Vince is just feeling Liv this week," Paul said matter-of-factly.

In any other scenario, I would have been nothing but happy for Liv. We'd made our WWE debuts around the same time. With the exception of Shayna, I was probably closer to Liv than any other woman on the roster. She had more momentum and fan support than anyone. She was clearly the best choice. But I had just told Lacey that she was going to win Money in the Bank and be the champ—and now she wasn't. All I could think was it would have been better if I kept my big mouth shut. That way she'd have never known.

I hung up, throwing the phone on to the counter, immediately regretting it as the noise startled Pō from her nap. I was angry. Angry for Lacey. Angry that WWE had put me in this position. Angry because Lacey probably didn't even fucking know and was out there walking around excited about a moment that would never come. Angry that this old man with our careers and legacies in his hands put no more thought into his decisions than how he was feeling in the moment. Angry that it wasn't Liv's years of back-breaking work, sacrifice, hard-earned fan support, or star power that made this moment happen but the whims of a geriatric billionaire who treated us like action figures. Despite the progress that had been made, our efforts were more frivolous than ever.

Pō started to cry, and it was only then that I realized that tears were also streaming down my face.

I felt like I was being set up to fail. My job was to go out in front of tens of thousands of people in person and millions of people watching on TV and get them to believe a story that some nearly eighty-year-old chauvinist was improvising on the spot. It felt like an impossible task.

Fuck Vince, I said to myself.

My phone rang again. Pō was losing her shit, but I picked up anyway. It was John Laurinaitis, Vince's No. 1 sycophant.

"We're going to need you to jump on a plane between shows this week to hit *Good Morning America* in New York to promote Money in the Bank," he said. "Travel will be in touch with the details."

It wasn't a request. It was an order.

"I can't," I said, juggling Pō in one arm while holding the phone in the other. "I can't put my baby through five cross-country flights in less than a week. When I came back, I was told I wouldn't be required to do that kind of travel."

He made a sound that I could only interpret to mean "I don't care."

"We gave you the title so you could do these things for us," he said.

You gave me the title because it benefits your company for me to carry around your bedazzled logo in belt form on TV every week, I thought. Instead I just said, "I never asked for the title. Give it to someone who will then."

I hung up. *Fuck Vince*, I repeated, adding, *and Fuck Laurinaitis too.* Somewhere out there, it seemed like karma heard me.

The next morning, the *Wall Street Journal* published a story detailing how Vince had paid $3 million to cover up an affair with a paralegal on the WWE payroll. According to the report and to the surprise of absolutely no one backstage, during the affair, Vince had doubled her salary and when he was done with her, he had passed her over to John Laurinaitis. The woman had signed an NDA to keep it all quiet, but a friend of hers had not and emailed the board. Of course, as the board started to dig further in the allegations, they found a whole bunch of other shit because spending a few million on hush money to pay off a paralegal that you and your friend used for blow jobs is typically only the tip of the iceberg.

It turns out that there were a number of other female employees that Vince had sign NDAs and paid settlements—in addition to the numerous women who had previously come forward over the years with claims against Vince for sexual assault, harassment, and discrimination.

You might think that would be enough to push Vince out, or at least to make him lay low. WWE issued a lame statement saying that he was going to step back as CEO and from the board, but that he would still oversee creative. To the outside world, that might have sounded like some kind of repercussion, but internally, the message was clear: Nothing is going to change. Two nights later, Vince went on *SmackDown*, looked straight at the camera, and recited WWE's slogan, "Then, Now, Forever." Fortunately, I had the week off.

17

There was a knock on the bus door.

"Come in," I yelled.

The door opened, and I heard the hesitant footsteps of a writer coming up the four stairs.

"Come in," I said, gesturing grandly. I was sitting in the chair as Abe braided my hair. I pointed the remote at the TV, pausing the seventh season on *RuPaul's Drag Race*. Pō sat on the floor, surrounded by toys as she played with a rock she had brought in from outside.

From the way the writer stood hesitantly in the doorway, as if she did not want to be there, I could tell she had not come bearing good news.

She took a deep breath.

"So, there's been a last-minute change," she said.

I could feel my eyes narrow. I sighed. She was only the messenger, I reminded myself. I stared down at where her tapered suit pants cropped above her Doc Martens boots, attempting to hide the exasperation on my face. WWE required the producers and creative staff to wear suits backstage as if having everyone look like it was a professional organization was the same thing as it being run like a professional organization.

There had been nothing but last-minute changes since Money in the Bank. But the more things changed, the more they stayed the same. As expected, the board of directors' investigation into Vince had yielded more allegations, more NDAs, and more payouts to more women. They determined that the financial threshold between not doing a fucking thing and the appearance of making a change fell somewhere between $3 million and $15 million in hush money. John Laurinaitis took the brunt of the fall, separating from WWE altogether probably with a big fucking check and an NDA of his own. Vince had announced "his retirement," with Triple H tapped to take over creative control. That would have been amazing, *if* it had actually happened.

Instead, Triple H would put together a version of the show two days before the broadcast with the writers. Vince would demand copies of the script, then call up production, change the whole show, and continue requesting changes until the wrestlers walked through the curtain, and sometimes even after.

My first run, there had been a constant tweaking of dialogue and last-minute match changes, but when it came to the story line, everyone *usually* knew where things were ultimately headed from one pay-per-view to another. Under Vince's undisputed authoritarian reign, if worse came to worst, you could cash in one of your unofficial audience-with-the-king chips and stand outside Vince's office until you could appeal to him directly.

This time around, no one knew what to do or who to answer to or who had the final word. My first go-round schedules were made up months in advance. Now, it was often impossible to even know if you were needed on the next show until the day before.

I was supposed to take back my title from Liv at SummerSlam, but Vince had decided that we needed to build Liv up as a champion longer. As he envisioned that match, I'd get Liv in an armbar, she'd tap, but for what felt like the 500th time in a row, the ref wouldn't see it, and I'd got screwed yet again. Even I was bored with that version of the ending, and it was setting Liv up for the crowd to turn on her. We tried to appeal to Triple H, but he said Vince was adamant. This was going to set up the moment I turned. People had to understand why I was angry. They had to believe I was pushed to my breaking point. (And I was, only not because of some bullshit official calls.)

The ending was not embraced by the fanbase. Liv, just a week before the WWE Universe's most beloved champion, was rained down upon with "You tapped out!" chants.

When I brought it up to Heyman, he blamed Liv for getting flustered by it.

"She invited the reaction she got," he said. "Just one fan chanted, she responded. She should have just ignored him. It was her fault."

The attitude within WWE's executive office was sink-or-swim, and if you happened to drown, well, that was fine with them as long as it made good TV.

"If that's the case, then they put her in a situation that exceeded her experience," I argued. "They set her up to fail."

Heyman shrugged. "That's the business we're in," he said, in the tone of someone who had long ago accepted madness as normalcy. I assumed that was the only way to exist in such a world and not be driven mad yourself. But he was right. It was the WWE way. When things go according to last-minute plans, they claim there's a method to the madness. When things don't, they blame the talent.

A few weeks later, I was rehearsing in the ring with some of the other girls before doors opened to the fans, when Liv made a beeline to the ring from Gorilla.

"Have you seen Aliyah?" she asked.

We shook our heads. Aliyah had come up to SmackDown the year before. She had been partnered with Raquel Rodriguez and they'd briefly held the tag team titles, but then Aliyah was sidelined with a shoulder injury.

"I just ran into her, almost hysterically crying," she explained. "She was asking if it's true that none of the talent wants to work with her."

We exchanged confused looks. I didn't know Aliyah well, but I'd had nothing but great interactions with her. She was one of the sweetest girls in the locker room. Not only that, but the women's locker room got along really well, better than ever actually. Backstabbing and double-crossing played out on TV; it couldn't have been farther from the truth in real life.

"Why would she think that?" I asked.

"They wanted her to come back from her shoulder injury right away, but she said she needed more time. That's when Bruce Prichard told her that all the producers were trying to bury her and no one wanted to work with her. She was really upset."

I felt my jaw and fists clench at the mere mention of his name.

Bruce Prichard was another Vince McMahon crony. If "What did you say you do here?" was a person, it would be him. No one knew what exactly his job was or how he got it. He was the type of guy who carries a briefcase just so it looks like he's doing something, yet somehow, he'd wormed his way up to executive producer, handpicked by Vince because he knew Bruce was the kind of guy you could control from a distance through an earpiece.

"Why would anyone say that about Aliyah?" Bayley asked. "Everyone loves her."

Bruce Prichard was loitering behind one of the announcer tables.

"Let's go fucking tell him right now," I said. I stepped between the ropes and out of the ring.

Liv scrambled to catch up with me. Bayley followed.

"You're comin' in real hot," Liv said, with a nervous nasal laugh. "Just let me talk first, 'kay?"

"OK," I said. I took a step back, letting her take the lead.

The women of WWE didn't stand up for each other to upper management in unison often. Even for established talent like Liv and Bayley, there were concerns about repercussions. They stood to gain nothing professionally in sticking up for Aliyah, which made me all the more proud to be standing beside them.

Ten tense steps later, we arrived at the table.

Liv gave a half wave to get Bruce's attention.

"Hi, yes, hello sir," she said hesitantly. "Is it OK if we talk to you about something for a second?"

He looked up at us with the expression of a man who was annoyed to be interrupted by a bunch of chicks until he saw my even more bothered expression. He pivoted to a forced smile. "Sure."

"Sooo ..." Liv started sweetly, cocking her head to one side. She spoke with the accent of a Jersey girl and the cadence of a Valley girl. "Well, we just want to, like, tell you that we heard something and we don't know who's talking, but we really love Aliyah. And we don't know who's speaking for us or anything like that, but any complaints about her are not coming from any of us. We love her. We love working with her, and she's the best."

I stood behind Liv, my arms crossed like an enforcer.

Bruce's strained grin held. He had the air of a failed used-car salesman.

I cleared my throat to send a message, not because I needed to cough.

"And I would really appreciate it if you weren't taking other people's word at face value and speaking for *us*," I said, slowly. "In fact, I would appreciate it if you didn't talk to anyone about what *we* said unless we said it to *you*. You have a question about that, you talk to us."

He nodded too enthusiastically.

"I love Aliyah," he almost shouted. "She's great. Yeah, I have no idea where that came from." He looked around as if he was actually looking for someone to pin the blame on.

The other girls and I exchanged *Can you believe this guy?* looks.

"I'll talk to her," he said, as if to say it was all a misunderstanding.

I nodded, lingering just a little bit longer than the other ladies once they turned to leave. I'd make sure to give Aliyah a hug next time I saw her, I thought to myself. But I never saw Aliyah again. After that night, she all but disappeared, as if she vanished into thin air, even long after her shoulder had healed. It sent a clear message. In the organization's eyes, talent was disposable.

———

Triple H asked me to be patient. He had stepped into a total clusterfuck and was trying to sort it all out.

I reluctantly agreed. I felt I owed him that much. After all, it was because he had been willing to take a chance on me that I was in WWE in the first place. Besides, we were on the same page. He had shown a commitment to the women's division that no one else on the creative side had even come close to demonstrating. He wasn't some women's wrestling Jesus, but he was trying.

I felt like when I spoke, Triple H actually listened. He seemed open to change as long as it was good for business. In a lot of ways, it was reminiscent of the relationship I had built with Dana in the UFC.

Back then, I had refused to refer to my belt as the "women's title" or my division as the "women's division." No one, I pointed out to Dana, referred to it as the men's title or the men's division. I wasn't asking for anything more or different than the way the men were treated.

Dana, who was far from the poster child for the liberal left, having spoken at the Republican National Convention, thought about it for a second.

"Good point," he said.

The next fight card in Brazil two women bantamweights entered the arena to be introduced as simply bantamweights. (Bantamweights referring to the 135-pound weight division.) No one noticed but me. No one at home was left asking, "Wait? What gender are these people? What the fuck am I watching?"

When WWE writers handed me scripts where I was supposed to declare myself the "women's champion," I crossed out the word "women's" and, much to Vince's displeasure—making even a single word change without his approval was not acceptable—addressed myself as "the champion."

"Vince noted you dropped 'women's'," one of the producers mentioned to me one night.

"When the men start calling it a men's title, I'll start calling it a women's," I said.

I raised the issue with Triple H. If the men didn't need to say, "This is for the Men's Intercontinental Championship," why did we have to call it "The Women's SmackDown Title"?

"Good point," he said.

He later told me he had mentioned it to Vince, who was appalled.

"Get out of here with that woke bullshit," Vince had told him. "We're going to call it the women's title because they're fucking women."

Vince, I had learned, wasn't like Dana. Dana still had that poor kid mentality of having something to prove, driven to make as much money as possible to gain the respect of his billionaire cohorts. A true capitalist, it seemed that for Dana, his worth was measured by his net worth.

Vince was an entirely different animal. He was practically born into the billionaires' club and had nothing to prove. He didn't come off as someone whose goal was to make his company as much money as possible, but rather to leverage his wealth and power to impress his worldview on those watching. If the product and bottom line had to suffer for it, so be it. A true dictator, his worth was measured by his influence.

I tried to be patient, but I was also persistent.

Following SummerSlam at the end of July, I asked again about building toward the singles match with Becky at Mania. I didn't want an opportunity for greatness to pass me by again. The tracks were being laid in front of the runaway train that was the WWE and it seemed more and more like we were about to blow past the station.

"We'll get to it after Survivor Series," I was told.

That was almost four months away. Giving us just four months to build Mania. And we still had zero plan for anything.

"We've got plenty of time," Heyman promised whenever I expressed concern about time ticking away. "We'll have plenty of time."

I took the title back from Liv at Extreme Rules in October. In the lead-up, we rehashed the same old bullshit they gave us to say. We figured we'd make up for it in the match itself.

We were adamant that this match have an epic finish. I racked my brain, then it came to me. One of the most iconic weapons in a "extreme rules" match was thumbtacks. A weapon made iconic by the company itself.

"Imagine this finish," I told Liv, then laid it out.

The two of us, grappling on the ground on a ring covered in thumbtacks until I finally get Liv once again in my signature armbar. Echoing back to our previous match, Liv at the same time gets me in a pin. As the ref starts counting the pin, I arch into the thumbtacks to raise one shoulder off the ground. But Liv, refusing to give up, lets me "break" her arm, passing out from the pain instead of tapping again. She falls right on the thumbtacks and me. I would get the title back as WWE's creative team wanted, Liv would come off looking like a badass, and everyone in the audience and at home would be going wild because it was fucking thumbtacks.

Liv paused for a second, biting her bottom lip. I could see her walking through the match in her mind. She got to the end and broke into the biggest smile. "Dude, I fucking love it!"

We took it to the producers.

"Absolutely not," came the reply before we'd even finished the word thumbtacks. "We can't do anything that intentionally breaks the skin."

"What?" we responded in flabbergasted unison.

WWE was notorious for these kinds of stunts. They literally made thumbtacks a universally accepted thing in professional wrestling. Fake thumbtacks were out too.

"What about rubber glass?" I asked, knowing the answer before the words left my lips.

Again, we had to settle for a finish neither of us were too impressed with—and so did the audience.

The next big event, Survivor Series, approached in flashes of half-thought-through/thrown-together-at-the-last-minute mediocrity. Vince and Triple H were jockeying for control, and everyone was caught up in their dysfunctional family feud each week.

We were approaching six months of creative chaos. Promises that things would soon settle down continued. We believed them even less than the dialogue we delivered in the ring.

It had become like one of those toxic workplaces. Producers and/or writers dragged themselves down the hallway, undoubtedly questioning all their life decisions, to tell the wrestlers to scratch the previous changes they'd been given for these new changes. With Vince, still lying low from being Me-Too'ed out of the building, relegated to a role of interfering from the sidelines instead of commanding from the forefront, there were glimmers of incremental improvements. But any progress was lost among the chaos. Even when we had a great show, it was at the expense of days of needless anxiety. Everyone was just trying their best to get through the day unscathed, and it showed. I kept asking myself, *How could they make something so innately fun so fucking stressful?*

I was so caught up in the weekly disorganization, I hardly had time to focus on the upcoming pay-per-view I was supposed to be building toward. Once again the champion after beating Liv, Survivor Series presented perhaps my biggest challenge to date. I'd be paired up against Shotzi. Her punk-rock ring persona and anything-goes attitude made her well liked but not yet well known. For the first time, I'd be the most senior person in the ring. Not only that, but the card we were on was stacked with matches that were going to get the crowd riled up. We didn't want to be the segment where they were let down.

"Your top rope DDT would be a perfect way for us to get to the outside here," I suggested in practice. I'd been watching Shotzi's highlights trying to become familiar with her moveset. In a DDT, you overhook someone's head with one arm, then fall on your back to make it appear as if the other person smacked their head on the ground. There is a wow factor because it looks like a move that can fuck a person up. Done correctly, it's completely safe. Done wrong, someone actually can get seriously hurt.

But when we got to the venue to practice, the ring was encased in a giant steel cage structure. Unable to rehearse the spot, producers sent some guy that I'd never seen before or since to help me with it. As he walked me through the motions, he kept repeating, "Just make sure you put one hand on the waist, the other on her thigh, and guide her to the floor."

"Got it," I replied.

"Hip, thigh, guide her to the floor."

"Guide her to the floor. Got it."

Later when I was in the hallway reciting the match trying to memorize it, he passed by.

"Remember—"

"Hip, thigh, guide her to the floor," I said. "Got it."

"Exactly, good luck out there!"

The time for the match came, and it started out well. The crowd even seemed into it. We got to the DDT spot.

One hand on the hip. Other on the thigh. Guide her to the floor. I walked myself through the steps as I did it. She hit the floor perfectly, safely, but I was so focused on her safe landing that I forgot to bump. Instead of falling flat on my face and pretending the DDT hurt me, I looked completely unscathed. While that was the point, it wasn't supposed to look like that was the point.

Shit, I thought, the deafening lack of audience reaction rang in my ears. *Just move onto the next spot, you'll get them back.*

We moved on, Shotzi jumped over the barricade onto me and several extras planted in the crowd.

"Holy shit!" Chants of approval followed us back into the ring.

All right, we got them back, I thought. I knew what we had left in the match was going to leave my blunder a distant memory. Shotzi started climbing to the top of the turnbuckle.

"Go home!" the ref shouted at me. ("Go home" means go directly to the finish, wrap up the match. The referee has an earpiece and receives direction from the top during the match.)

What? Why? I didn't understand. *We were just getting them back!*

I didn't argue. I countered Shotzi's attack and went straight to the arm-bar finish. Boos rained down on us, I walked up the ramp humiliated, like I was being dragged offstage with a giant cane. I threw back the curtain to Gorilla, heading straight to where Triple H was sitting behind the monitor.

"What happened?" I demanded. "Was it because of the missed DDT? We were just getting them back."

He looked at me slightly confused.

"No, no, no," he assured me. "We're just heavy on time. The guys before you went over by six minutes."

He put his headphones back on and focused back on the monitor.

This is some bullshit, I thought. The non-title men's match went over by three-quarters of our total eight-minute title match time. It put a worrying trend into focus. The time the women were given to wrestle had been getting whittled down more and more all year.

Jenn handed me my phone on the walk to the bus. #FireRonda was trending worldwide because of my botched spot. I rarely made technical mistakes in the ring. When I did, I agonized over them, but as I watched myself go viral, this time I felt something more than just embarrassed, I also felt pissed off.

Two male wrestlers were recently involved in botched spots that spiked them on the top of their heads. Madcap Moss was lucky to walk away with a sore neck. When Big E got spiked on his head, his body went rigid as he fell to the mat with a broken neck. Doctors told him he may never wrestle again. I honestly couldn't tell you who spiked either of those guys on their heads—but I can tell you that there were no #FireWhoeverTheFuck campaigns trending on Twitter because of it. But all of a sudden it's #FireRonda?

This is some REAL bullshit, I thought.

The only upside was we had finally gotten past Survivor Series.

"When are we going to start planning for Mania?" I texted Heyman.

"We'll talk before the New Year," came the reply.

18

I sat alone on the curb, barefoot in a parking lot, staring out at the outline of the trees. The bus was parked behind a hotel next to a swamp in the outskirts of Tampa. The air was so thick with humidity you could see it in the dull glow of the dim streetlights. It was three in the morning. I had given up on going to bed. I couldn't sleep.

Something moved in the bushes next to me, just underneath the sign reading "Warning, Alligators."

If you're planning to attack me, just get it over with, I said silently to whatever lurked in the brush. The rustling stopped. I waited a few seconds to see if I was going to have to wrestle a fucking gator. When nothing happened, I held the joint up to my lips and inhaled. An orange glow pierced the darkness.

This is it, I thought to myself, reflecting on my WWE career as I blew smoke into the darkness of the Florida swamp. *This is the lowest point.*

I had touched down in Miami three days earlier determined to get answers. It was three days after Christmas and more than a month after Survivor Series, and I still hadn't been able to get any clarity or collaboration from anyone as we headed into the final months of my WWE return.

Pō had woken up that morning with a fever, so I left her behind at home for the very first time.

Miami had the vibe of a Caribbean Christmas with holiday lights strung up on palm trees and pink flamingos decked in Santa hats. But I was feeling anything but festive.

"I just want to get some answers," I had told Heyman for the 10,000th time before boarding my flight.

For six months, he kept promising next week we'd have some direction.

"I'm done waiting for next week," I said, exasperated. "A few more 'next weeks,' and Mania will BE next week."

Raquel Rodriguez and I were set to wrestle a full match, an increasing rarity on the women's side. To rehearse, we would do the Miami live show before heading to Tampa for SmackDown. A six-foot-one Latina from Texas, Raquel physically towered over the rest of the women's division. She was muscular, like a former college basketball player, not a competitive bodybuilder. She was the kind of opponent I loved facing in the ring, not only because she looked capable of actually challenging me, but she was so strong I felt safe trying anything with her. Outside of the ring, I just liked her in general. Always smiling, always with an encouraging word, always looking for the good in everyone and every situation, Raquel was a genuinely nice person. She had come up from NXT earlier in the year. She had lost to me in her first-ever title match, an answer to one of my open challenges, a banger despite us never having worked with each other and us throwing it together that same day. Now, she got a rematch and we had time to prepare. She wasn't going to win, but I was happy she was going to get some much-deserved time in the spotlight to show what she was capable of.

I was just about to change into my ring gear for the live show match, when I got a text from Heyman.

"Someone is going to call you in the next hour to tell you the plan until Mania," it read.

To *tell* me. I read it again. To *tell* me. Heyman is a man who has made his entire livelihood around his ability to craft words in a way that they convey exactly what they're meant to convey.

I pulled on my gear and walked into the arena, pacing the nearly empty hallway as I waited for the call, getting angrier with each passing second.

The phone rang.

I answered.

"Ronda, Bruce Prichard," the voice from the other end said. I rolled my eyes so far back they touched my brain.

"Do you have a minute?" he asked.

"I'm just about to have a match with Raquel," I said, which he already knew.

"I'll be quick," Prichard said. "Tomorrow, you're going to have the match with Raquel. After you win, Charlotte is going to come out and challenge you. You're going to put Charlotte over at Rumble. Then you're going to win the Elimination Chamber, and from there, you're going to challenge Bianca, and then put her over at Mania."

I stood there for a moment, trying to compose the "ARRRRGHHH" sounds in my head into words that weren't "fuck." I had toed the company line. I had gone out and done whatever was asked of me. I had let them use my name and face to sell a product that I knew was spiraling because I had thought that I would be given a chance to make things just a little bit better. It had all been for nothing. They never saw me as a partner or even a premier talent. I felt beat down and let down.

"I would really appreciate being part of these conversations instead of hearing about it last minute," I said. "I want to be part of coming up with these ideas. I want to work to put stuff together with you guys. I've been trying to have this discussion for a year now."

"Pshht," Prichard scoffed, adding, "Yeah? Well, we'll try our best to accommodate you." Now, you can misinterpret words or tone. But you can't misinterpret a scoff.

I hung up and turned back to Raquel, who was going over the match one last time a few steps down the hall outside Gorilla.

"Let's handle this shit," I said, just as Joan Jett hit, and the crowd cheered.

I went out that night, fueled by adrenaline and rage, and we put on one of my best matches since I'd been back to a raucous house show crowd. But as soon as I stepped back through the curtain, I was fuming. The next morning,

I woke up on the bus, parked in front of the Tampa arena for SmackDown, livid. I texted Heyman: *New plan. I'm dropping the title to Charlotte. Tonight.* It wasn't an ask; it was a demand. Heyman knew me well enough to read between the lines and relay to creative the part that I had left unsaid: that if I didn't get my way this time, I was going to walk.

I found Charlotte as she was getting ready to rehearse and informed her that she would be walking out of the arena with the title. She didn't have her gear, she pointed out, but she could send someone to make the two-and-a-half-hour roundtrip drive to her house to get it.

"Do it," I said.

That night, to the legitimate shock of everyone in attendance, Raquel and I had the match of the night. For the finish, she had me on her shoulders atop the turnbuckle in the corner of the ring. I looked done for, but then contorted myself into a standing armbar balanced on her shoulders. Raquel held onto the ropes, forced to choose between tapping, letting her arm break, or taking the steep fall behind us. She took the fall. We both crashed down into the center of the ring together, but her valiant effort was in vain. I kept the armbar. She was forced to tap. The crowd gave her a standing ovation as she left the ring. She was an obvious huge star in the making.

Bruised and battered from a hell of a match, I held up the title. Then Charlotte's music hit. The crowd roared. Charlotte, arguably the best wrestler of a generation, had the obvious benefit of nepotism. Despite her consistent excellence, the crowd resented her for her birthright advantages. But not tonight.

Charlotte came out and challenged me for the title that I had taken from her the last time we'd met in the ring. I was in no shape to defend, but my "pride" got the best of me. Shayna, who had been ringside, tried to make me see reason, to rest and recover first. But that's not what a true champion does. I accepted, and quickly lost. The crowd lost their collective minds.

Charlotte reveled in the crowd's adoration. She ran into the audience, embraced by chants and adoration in a way she never had been able to before. I was finally the heel I always wanted to be. Just like Roddy Piper, I felt like

I could get anyone over. I was happy to have been a part of it. But the second I walked back through the curtain from the arena into Gorilla, I returned to the real world, where I was still fucking pissed.

I walked up to Triple H behind the monitors. He shook my hand, congratulating me on a hell of a show.

"Thank you," I replied. "Thank you for trusting us to do it that way. I need to talk to you. When are you going to have time?"

He said he had some network bigwigs to meet with after the show, but he could meet me in his office after.

After the show was over, I stood outside the door marked Paul Levesque. The hallways bustled with people packing our little traveling circus up to move onto the next town. I watched the parade of hard-sided black road boxes and wooden crates roll by, seething. I wasn't going anywhere until I talked to Triple H.

I clenched and unclenched my fists. My lips were twitching.

Finally, Triple H waved me in.

I didn't even wait for the standard pleasantries.

"I feel like I was sold a false bill of goods," I said.

He nodded, indicating that he knew exactly what I was talking about. I wasn't sure if that made it worse or better.

"I thought it was going to be a certain way when I came here," I said. "And it hasn't. And I've been trying to have this conversation all year about Mania, and no one will fucking talk to me. Not only that, but now I'm hearing that it is a completely different plan that you have in mind."

I was waiting for him to cut me off. He didn't.

"I don't care so much about the change of plans. It's the fact that I'm not even allowed to be part of the conversation. No one said anything to me about it until now." I was trying to be professional, but a year's worth of being brushed off and disregarded was boiling over.

"The thing with Becky at WrestleMania," he said, "is we can't get there in time. We don't have time to build to it."

For the second time in as many days, I was not so much at a loss for words but a loss for words that wouldn't get me arrested. I took a deep breath instead.

"We've had a whole year to build it," I said, coldly.

"I'm sorry," Triple H said. I wanted to believe him, then he kept talking. "Anyway, Piper's Hollywood backlot brawl is a classic, but it was booed out of the building. Long cinematic backstages just don't work for a live audience," he added, like he wasn't in charge of the whole goddamn thing.

"Then why not say so instead of nodding emphatically when I came to pitch you guys *years* ago?" I asked. "And what I pitched wasn't a long backstage match like theirs but segments spread throughout the show—and anyway, it doesn't matter, it didn't have to be exactly that. I just wanted to be part of developing something *with* you guys. Remember when I first got here? I had that perfect match with you, Steph, and Kurt. *That's* how I thought it was going to be here, being part of this organization. Instead, I feel like I was given a false representation of what it would be like to work here. It was all an act to get me in the door and to fall in love with this industry. Ever since then, I feel like my love for wrestling has been weaponized against me. But I can't be associated with mediocre shit."

In that moment, I made a decision. I was done. I was done fighting. I was done trying to fix a system that didn't want to be fixed. I was done putting so much time and energy where it wasn't appreciated.

"Listen, I told you I'd be here until SummerSlam," I said. "And I'm a woman of my word, but I'm done after this. All I wanted when I got into this business was to tag with Shayna, have her turn on me, then put her over before I leave. We have until SummerSlam to make that happen. After that, I'm done being associated with this minimum effort lazy-ass shitshow."

I could feel my lip quivering, I was so worked up it took everything I had to hold back tears.

He shook his head like someone who silently shared my frustration.

"OK, I get," he said. "I get it."

I nodded, indicating I had said my piece.

I moved to leave, when he stretched out his hand, I thought to shake mine. Instead, he leaned in, gently touching my arm. He dipped his head, looking up at me. His tone shifted from authority figure to friend.

"But how are you?" he asked sincerely.

I burst into tears. Not just crying, but bawling.

"I'm so tired," I said. "I'm so tired that I feel like it's changing my personality. I'm so much more anxious, stressed, negative, like butter scraped over too much bread."

Triple H looked at me blankly. He obviously hadn't just listened to *Lord of the Rings* as an audiobook driving to and from IVF.

"My ass is struggling, dragging a baby across the country, trying to keep her happy for hours every week in the confines of a single airplane seat, all while Brock, Roman, and even Logan *fucking* Paul are being chartered around for their comfort. And no one fucking cares. All just to do mediocre work. I'm physically so goddamn tired, and mentally even more goddamn tired of this fucking bullshit. I'm over it."

I tried to slow my breathing, so I wasn't hyperventilating as I sobbed.

"But the worst part is I really thought this would be so fucking great, and now I'm just disappointed. Not just disappointed but heartbroken because I had such high hopes that seem so fucking stupid and naive now."

I looked around the room for a tissue, but his office wasn't actually an office, just a random room in a hockey arena where they set up a desk. Triple H looked around, not sure what to do. There was nothing he could say to make it better.

I walked out of the arena knowing that my WWE career would never be what I had envisioned. It would never be what I had hoped.

We left the arena, and Mike parked the bus for the night. I went back to the bedroom and started packing, throwing things angrily into my suitcase. Out of the pocket of my jeans fell a joint that looked like it was from an old-school rap video. Ric Flair, Charlotte's father and one of the original Four Horsemen, had given it to me backstage.

I tiptoed out past the bunks where Maria and Jenn were sleeping, through the kitchen, and stepped outside. My eyes took a minute to adjust, and even then, it was so dark everything beyond the glow of a single street-light just appeared as a silhouette.

I lit the joint, feeling sorry for myself. Until I didn't. Maybe it was the relief of not getting chomped by an alligator. Maybe it was Ric Flair's weed. But, as I sat out there wallowing, I had to admit, that as a low point, this was pretty nice.

I thought back to seven years before. I had been shivering in a tent by myself, making repeated trips to shit in the woods. My skin had been peeling off, my teeth loose, my lip literally split in half. I was sicker than I had ever been in my entire life, mentally and physically. I had been dreading every moment of existence. That was my lowest point. That had broken me.

This, I told myself, as I stood up from the curb and dusted myself off, this was just some make-believe bullshit.

19

After our meeting in Tampa, Triple H agreed to let me set up a weekly meeting with SmackDown's head writer and Paul Heyman three days before the show, a day before they pitched ideas to Triple H. It was by no means a seat at the table. At best, they were letting me stand outside the door of the room where the table was, but it was better than being locked out of the building.

Our first call was the day after the 2023 Royal Rumble. The night prior, Sami Zayn turned on The Bloodline, a faction featuring Vince's anointed WWE king Roman Reigns and his cousins, a culminating moment that had all the hallmarks of Paul Heyman's genius.

"First off, congrats on Sami's turn at Rumble," I said to Paul before the meeting kicked off. "It was fucking perfect!"

"Why thank you," he said, proudly. "A year of planning went into that exact moment."

I froze. The smile dropped from my face into a tight line. It took all my restraint to keep from chucking the phone across the room.

"Must be nice to plan something that far ahead," I said, my words dripping with sarcasm.

As frustrating as it was, I was done letting it bother me. When I accepted that I couldn't change WWE, I decided to focus on myself. There was a huge amount of freedom and reflection that came with accepting the inevitable. I wasn't going to be able to elevate women in WWE the way I had in UFC. So, the question became: What do I want? Why was I banging my head against the wall over *this*?

I had gotten into pro wrestling because it was fun. Because it was a chance to spend time with my friends. Somewhere along the way, I had lost sight of that. So, I went back to the beginning.

Marina and Jessamyn had been cut in the pandemic roster purge, but Shayna remained. I was determined to go out with a bang with my fellow Horsewoman.

"The thing is," Heyman relayed, "Vince doesn't think pairing you and Shayna up would make sense."

I raised an eyebrow.

"This isn't MMA," Heyman attempted to explain. "He thinks no one in the WWE universe knows you and Shayna are friends."

"My first appearance in WWE was with Shayna, Marina, and Jessamyn," I said. "Stephanie McMahon herself introduced us as the Four Horsewomen. You heard the crowd at Rumble last year when we were about to go at it. The fans want this."

"I didn't say it makes sense." It was one of his favorite go-to responses when speaking for Vince.

"I tag with Shayna, or I'm done," I said.

By February, Shayna and I had been brought together as a tag team, by my insistence and some very mediocre writing. Instead of seeing the two of us as an opportunity to turn the tag titles on the women's side into something fans might actually care about, they gave us little attention and even less time. The way I saw it, though, holding the tag titles allowed me to build up Shayna, and other women in the division, two at a time.

The problem was WWE didn't have a women's tag division, just a pair of belts that occasionally switched hands between various girls who seemed to be paired up at random. For us to be champions, we had to build a division, align as many women as possible into teams. We didn't have enough women on the roster to have them specialize in singles or tag the way men were able to. Everyone had to do both for there to be a division. (At any given taping, there were ten or so women each on SmackDown and Raw. There were two to three men on the roster for every woman.) To give the illusion that there was actually a tag team division, I urged the producers to match Shayna and me up against as many women teams as possible.

The idea was met with quizzical looks as if there weren't any other women. I suggested Tegan Nox and Chelsea Green, two wrestlers who had just been promoted from NXT and weren't being used in any story line at the time. When I got to the venue for the first live show in Champaign, I was told we'd be facing Natalya and Tegan. We had just beat Natalya and Shotzi the week before. Facing Nattie again with just a different partner didn't make any sense and it trivialized her alliance with Shotzi. When I raised that point, I was brushed off.

"You said you wanted to face more women. Tegan's a woman," I was told as if I should just shut up and be grateful.

"I said more women's tag teams," I said.

"You requested getting reps on live shows for TV; that's what they're giving you," the producer mansplained. "It's a win."

I was frustrated, but over fighting a losing battle. We were going to do what we always did and make the best of it.

Toward the end of the match, I took the bump from Tegan and slapped the mat hard, popping back up. The pain was immediate. I let it show on my face like I was selling and kept going. After the match, I slid out of the ring, my arm throbbing.

I was used to my elbow randomly dislocating. It was an occupational hazard from never having tapped out in judo. But this time was different. I hugged Shayna one-armed after the match.

"You OK?" she asked, nodding to my arm.

I waved her off, indicating it was nothing. "Elbow just popped out again. Happens all the time."

But back on the bus, I started to think maybe I was wrong. My left elbow was already the size of a grapefruit. I could hardly bend it. Pō stood on the floor, her arms outstretched, crying to be picked up. I tried to lift her, and she arched backward, wiggling and overtired. It hurt too much to hold her. I sat down on the floor, surrounded by her toys, and she crawled up on my lap. I rested my chin on her head, trying to will the pain away, trying to be a good mom. It felt like it was all slipping away.

I didn't have time to be hurt. Shayna and I had just weeks to make this story line believable. The schedule meant I had just two days before I had to be back on the road. The swelling had gone down by the morning, but I was still limited enough that I needed to see a doctor. There was no other way I could get an MRI and have it read on such short notice. I reluctantly reached out to WWE's medical staff.

"I don't see anything concerning here at first glance," the MRI technician said. "But your doctor will take a closer look at you and let you know if anything comes up."

Not my doctor, WWE's doctor, I thought.

There was a reason I avoided their medical staff whenever possible: Their loyalty was to the company. I headed to the airport the next morning without yet having gotten the official results but feeling better. I could move. I was more than capable of wrestling with just one arm. WWE itself had me do it in a match as a gimmick. I just needed to be taped up.

I left Pō at home. She'd already flown enough miles to circle the globe four times in her tiny life. She was past the stage of sleeping in my arms an entire flight, but not yet at the stage where I could give her an iPad and headphones to keep her attention until landing. I just didn't have it in me to chase her up and down the aisles on a cross-country flight to D.C. with a bad arm. When she saw the car coming to pick me up for the airport, she jumped into the car and tried to close the door after her. She sobbed as Trav peeled her off my leg. I sobbed from the backseat as the car pulled away.

In the air, I texted Heyman my thoughts for the segment. We had to wait for medical clearance, he replied.

I rolled my eyes. This was why I hadn't wanted to involve WWE's doctors in the first place. I relayed what the technician had told me about not seeing immediate cause for concern.

Heyman reached out to my segment's writer to share that information.

I looked out somewhere over the Midwest, 30,000 feet below and still covered in snow, waiting for a reply.

On my phone, three dots appeared, then disappeared, then appeared again. The writer's message came through. Heyman copy and pasted a text from one of the corporate shills.

It read: *The Executive Director Bruce Prichard himself declared to me that Ronda is not cleared to work a match tomorrow, per our medical team. I am in the same boat here and want Ronda to be able to work the match, but this is all the information and direction I have.*

I reread the text in my head, only in a British accent accompanied by the sound of trumpets. It was all so fucking ridiculous.

Well apparently, they wanted to tell me last, I wrote back, adding, *after I got on the plane.*

Not only that, but I didn't know what my injury was. Or how long I could expect to be out. Or if there was any kind of treatment I might actually need.

If I had any remaining doubt, it was clear that WWE did not care about me as a person. Bray Wyatt was right. We're just fucking meat to them.

I thought about our ranch in Oregon, the land where our now 300-head herd of wagyu grazed on the land we were healing together. Where herds of antelope passed through and mule deer made their home. Geese and blue herons moved into our ponds. We were being treated worse than I treated meat.

While being injured would keep me out of the ring, they wanted me to be there so they could film a segment where I pretended to get hurt so they could work it into the story line. My radius, I would find out only after a series of phone calls and text messages, showed a hairline fracture. While I was confident I could wrestle with it, I was told it was "too much of a liability to let me wrestle injured."

"When can I return?" I asked Heyman.

"It's up to Bruce," he said. "And medical."

In that order.

That night, as I lay in my hotel room, staring up at a giant white plaster lion head over my bed, I asked myself a question I had never asked myself before: Is it worth it?

I had only ever focused on a goal. I had never really thought about the cost because I had always been willing to sacrifice everything in pursuit of achievement. "Everything" had a different meaning now, and she was at home, 3,000 miles away, wondering where her mama was.

A week before WrestleMania, I was cleared to return to "limited physicality." They gave us just eight minutes for a match featuring eight women. My first run, no one once mentioned "time" to me as a factor in any performance. I was so green I could barely remember the assembled-last-minute choreography let alone know how to hit times. But now the increased pressure of "hitting our time" hung like a sword over the heads of the women in the locker room.

I watched the seven other women in my match rush through the choreography. I was only permitted to sneak in and do an armbar finish on Shotzi at the very end. The crowd erupted in boos.

That's some real heat at least, I thought to myself. ("Heat" being the term for hate you get as a heel.)

The night before at WrestleMania, Rhea Ripley and Charlotte went over their allotted time by TWENTY minutes, putting on arguably the best match of the weekend-long event. There were some murmurs backstage that it was disrespectful of the main event, a men's tag title match, but I thought it was badass that they took the time to tell their story to the fullest and stole the show.

In fact, when they were told to wrap it up so the men after them could perform in front of a fresher crowd, Charlotte and Rhea just kept going like the bosses they were. Instead of running backstage when ordered to do so, they took a stand. I admired them for putting their collective foot down. I wished I was as brave as they were. It gave me hope. I was leaving this shitshow behind, but at least I was leaving it in good hands.

But their act of defiance wouldn't be without repercussions. After Rhea won the title, despite being the most over (fan-favorite) woman in the company, she was only allowed to defend her title twice in over five months. Instead, she spent most of her time escorting the men in her faction, Judgement Day, to and from the ring like a 1990s valet, instead of wrestling herself. The message to the women was clear: if you take time from the men—even if you're the hottest name in the company—the company will make sure to take even more time from you.

After our lightspeed fatal four-way, I stood in the white-painted concrete tunnels that connected backstage to the football field converted into the WrestleMania floor. It had been three months since I had sat across from Triple H in Tampa. Shayna and I had won, but I felt defeated. I stood there still in my spandex fight shorts and sports bra, listening to the crowd cheer for the match after ours. It was my first time performing at the state-of-the-art SoFi Stadium in my hometown, where I hoped for years to create a match that was unforgettable. Instead I shuffled backstage, already forgotten.

A Hall of Fame–caliber wrestler from an era before mine walked past me.

"Hey, there," he said, giving me a hug.

I gave a weak nod.

"What's up?" he asked. While WWE requires acting in the ring, I am horrible at hiding my emotions in real life.

"I'm just so disappointed," I said. "I wanted to do something great..." My voice trailed off.

He looked at me with the rare expression of someone who understood.

"Look around." He gestured. "None of this is real. None of it actually matters. It's a whole bunch of people playing make-believe. It's changed, man. It used to be two guys out there going at it, knowing that it was fake. Laughing about these fucking marks [wrestling fans] eating it up. Everybody used to know it was a work [scripted fiction], but now they've all bought the con. They're not just working the crowd, they're working themselves too."

He laughed.

He gestured toward the invisible crowd, reacting to a match on the other side of the arena walls.

"Don't let it get to you. These people, the wrestlers, the fans, at the end of the day, they're all just a bunch of fucking nerds."

He gave me a heavy pat on the back you'd give a toddler you just picked up after a fall, then continued down the hall.

His words hit me like a much-needed chop to the chest. He was right. Why was I letting this get to me? WWE was a scripted show about a fictional wrestling organization. At best, we were only moderately entertaining people. And yet, I had let myself become almost consumed by it. The rhinestones. The dramatic makeup. The oversized cheetah print coats. The declarations of being the greatest ever. The cheers of the crowd. Applause is a hell of a drug, and I had become an addict. But none of it was real. More than that, none of it mattered.

I had made my way back to my bus but hesitated outside the door.

Snoop Dogg's bus was right next to mine.

I pivoted toward the green glowing light. His security guard clocked my approach.

"Oh, he's gonna wanna see you." The security dipped into the bus, then ushered me in.

Snoop Dogg sat behind a small table in the bus with a line of prerolled fatties in front of him, like a king ready to receive guests. He smiled.

"Ronda." He welcomed me in his iconic, relaxed tone.

"Hey, Snoop," I said like I wasn't fangirling harder than I ever had in my entire life inside my head. "I'd be honored to burn one with you."

He chose the fattest roll in his lineup and lit it.

"You know, everyone says I'm the guy that they wanna smoke with," he said. He took a rip, held it in. "But I got a list of people I wanna smoke with too."

He handed me the lit joint. "And little mama, you're on my list."

As I took a much-needed fat rip at the end of a long day, I watched a shredded, oiled, spray-tanned wrestler dab at his eyeliner in the reflection of the bus window. I laughed to myself.

Fucking nerds.

20

With the satisfaction I was getting from wrestling on a significant decline, my mind started to wander. I kept my anxieties at bay by diving back into screenwriting again, directing my thoughts to plot holes, dialogue, character relationships, how to show and not tell, themes I wanted to get across.

In the years since writing my first screenplay in eleven hours, I learned how to format and structure, yet I doubted anything I wrote would ever be made. Risk-averse studios would never take the chance on me. But the document itself gave me so much satisfaction that I stopped caring if I ever made any of these movies.

Then one day, it hit me. The script that had started it all—now titled *What to Expect When Expecting the Unexpected*—would make a badass graphic novel!

Braced for rejection, I started contacting publishers.

During the WWE-mandated month off to recover from my fractured elbow, the opportunity to go to Mars presented itself. Technically, it was a remote mining town in the Australian Outback called Coober Pedy, chosen because of its resemblance to the red planet. It was for a show called *Stars on Mars*, basically "Celebrity Big Brother Meets Survivor" on Mars—it seemed so ridiculous at first that I turned it down. After *The Ultimate Fighter*, I had sworn off reality shows. However, I was intrigued when producers reached back out emphasizing the Mars and survivalist aspects. I'm a big space nerd. I had held my breath for a month hoping for the success of the James Webb telescope launch. The show doubled its offer, sealing the deal.

But so help me God, if I showed up in the Australian Outback and Miesha Tate walked in, I was fucking out.

The first morning of filming, I was nervous and excited as I waited for the simulated airlock to open. I had no idea who or what to expect. Over the next hour, eleven other "celebronauts" arrived. We were—by casting design—a group that otherwise would have never crossed paths. Looking around the pseudo-space station's mix of athletes, reality stars, and entertainment industry folks, I realized the only way to come out of this experience unscathed was to give everyone a chance.

I had less than flattering preconceived notions when it came to stars of *The Real Housewives* franchise like my castmate Porsha Williams and even less respect for those making a living off the series spin-offs like Tom Schwartz. But sitting in a fake space kitchen and talking to them showed me how self-righteous resentment had crept into my psyche. Instead of putting them in a box and blowing them off like I would have done on Earth, I forged friendships that would transcend imaginary space.

Every member of the group was a joy to be around. It was an unforgettable experience even apart from all the space nerdy goodness. I did football drills with NFL players Richard Sherman and Marshawn Lynch, did figure skating jumps with Olympian Adam Ripon, played basketball with NBA Hall of Famer Paul Pierce, joked with comedian Natasha Leggero, ate food prepared by Iron Chef Cat Cora, and stationary biked with Lance Armstrong. I wrestled everyone!

I realized how much I had been in my own way. Before *Mars*, if you'd have asked me about Lance Armstrong, the most notorious doper in sports history, I would have said, "Fuck that cheater, he's dead to me."

But getting to know him as we worked out alongside each other in the Hab's gym reminded me we are more than our worst day or worst decision. A quote from Nanny, my Venezuelan great-grandma, came to mind: "Of all the crazy things people do, of all unimaginable decisions they make, it was the best they could think of to do at the time."

That doesn't mean there shouldn't be consequences, but you don't forgive people for them. You forgive them for you.

There were certainly times where, by the current standard, I should have been canceled. But I believe I'm a good person capable of doing some dumb shit at times. If I want people to give me that kind of leeway, I have to be willing to give it to others.

My last night, we sat around the table like a family, laughing, joking, refilling our wine. It was one of those moments that you savor as it happens because you know that you will never all be together like that again. I went to bed on my little Martian cot, one last time, with the biggest smile on my face.

I had signed on to the show because it was an opportunity to live out my space geekiness without needing to leave the atmosphere in a little rocket shaped like a penis. But *Stars on Mars* turned out to be that breath of fresh air that I didn't even know I needed.

When we first "arrived" on Mars, everyone laughed at the idea of pretending we were on Mars with its jargon of days as "sols" and the set as the "Hab," refusing to take it seriously. By Sol 10, I watched these same people with no real interest in space debate who should be "mission commander" like they were electing the next president.

Accepting a new reality when you're so immersed isn't a personality flaw, but a human survival trait. I marvel at how adaptable we as people are, but find it equally terrifying how malleable we are.

I would have stayed longer, but I missed my baby so much it felt like a knot in my chest. My medical suspension was over. Shayna and I had a title to win. SummerSlam was edging ever closer. I volunteered myself to be jettisoned out of the make-believe airlock into the vastness of space/the Outback and back to Los Angeles.

Two days later, just in time for Mother's Day, which I swore to myself I wouldn't miss, Pō and I were on a plane heading to North Carolina. We hadn't even reached cruising altitude when my baby-turned-toddler decided she was fucking done.

If you have ever been on a plane with a toddler who decides they are done, you know there is nothing you can do to resolve the situation. It's basically like throwing yourself on a tiny living grenade and just hoping that you're able to shield the people around you from the worst of the explosion. She screamed. She cried. She flailed. She kicked, catching my assistant Jenn, who was sitting next to us, in the face. Jenn's nose started bleeding. Two rows behind us, The Miz, another WWE star and father of two, who happened to be on my flight, gave me a quick look of parental empathy mixed with relief that it wasn't him. My eyes welled with tears.

This is the worst fucking Mother's Day ever, I thought for the second year in a row. *I should have stayed on Mars.*

But as I tried to pin a small person with surprising strength into our shared airplane seat, I didn't have time to wallow.

I'm going back to finish what I started, I told myself, wiping away tears. *One of my closest friends is waiting for me, and we're going to go win the tag team titles.*

———

Liv stood staring up at the TV.

"I'm gonna ask them," she said.

"Don't ask them," I said.

Liv smiled a huge Liv smile.

"Excuse me," she said to the bartender, gesturing up at the TV over the bar that was playing Royal Rumble from 2014. "Umm, do you think you can change it to Money in the Bank? Like the one that just happened? The one we were in."

She pointed to us, innocently tilting her head to the side in a way that made it almost impossible for anyone to say no to her. I flushed red. I also wanted to watch our match again but was too embarrassed to be caught watching myself in public. Liv, Raquel, and Shayna laughed at my awkwardness.

We were standing in Jimmy's Seafood, a dark-bricked seafood restaurant/ sports bar, in Baltimore. Jimmy's was well known among wrestlers as Jimmy himself kept the place open late just for us whenever a show happened to be passing through Maryland.

The bartender messed with the remote for a few seconds, and then there we were. We stood there, staring up at ourselves, just two days before but a literal ocean away in London. Raquel and Liv had faced off against Shayna and me for our tag team titles. We were the overwhelming odds-on favorite to win. (Yes, they actually let people bet real money on fake wrestling.) Then it happened.

Liv was down on the mat, scooting back into the corner. I started slapping my shoulders, moving toward her, indicating that there was nowhere she could go and nothing she could do. Then Shayna, my teammate, one of my best and oldest friends, ran up from my blind spot, elbowing me from behind and knocking me to the ground. Just like me in the ring, the crowd never saw it coming. I rolled to my back trying to understand what had happened, but before it could register, Shayna was on top of me, pummeling me as I tried to protect myself. Shayna grabbed me by the hair, catching me in a choke. Liv watched stunned as Shayna tightened her hold.

It was the biggest pop of the show. They were celebrating my defeat. The betrayal of my best friend. My dramatic "Et tu, Brute?" moment.

I let my body go limp. Shayna threw me to the ground and walked out of the ring. Seeing opportunity, Raquel hit me with her finisher. Liv pounced. I cartwheeled over my elbows, acing the spike DDT sell I made a point to master after the botch with Shotzi. Liv then pinned me for the count of three. She and Raquel celebrated their tag team title win in the ring as I staggered back through the curtain into Gorilla.

Our tag team championship run had been short but sweet. Every match exceeded expectations despite the limits we were working within. Producers were even admitting they should have let me and Shayna tag a long time ago. Now, our run met its bittersweet end.

Afterward, I threw myself around her for a hug in the depths of The O2 Arena.

I turned to the match producer. "Time?" I asked.

"Exactly twelve minutes including entrances," he said. "Pros. You are fucking pros."

Less than twenty-four hours earlier, Liv, Raquel, Shayna, and I had been rolling around in the ring at the now largely unused UK WWE Performance Center. There was just one not-insignificant detail that we needed to be able to shore up our plans: how much time we had for the match.

"I asked for twenty," our producer said in a tone that indicated there was no way we were getting twenty minutes.

When it came to women's matches, asking for time was very different from getting time. We spent the better part of the next three hours mapping things out, while waiting to find how long we might actually get.

"I'd plan for fifteen," the producer said, after checking his phone for the fiftieth time. Still no reply.

"It might change though," he cautioned. "And then you have to factor in walkout time."

"Forget walking out," I said. "We'll run."

All four of us women nodded in solidarity.

The good news was we were slated to be the first segment. That meant it would be impossible for any match before us to run over, and for our time to be cut further as a result. Pay-per-views aren't subject to the confines of live network broadcasts, but production tries to stay on schedule to keep the audience's energy up and the event from running too long. Running over was a common justification when creative made last-minute cuts to match time.

I arrived at the arena the next morning for a final run-through.

Shayna knocked on my dressing room door. It was small, a maybe six-foot-by-ten-foot space in which was crammed a small black loveseat, a folding table, and a couple of metal folding chairs. My team was so squeezed in that Jenn was sitting in the closet.

"Please come in," I said with dramatic flourish.

Shayna looked around as if assessing the room for emergency exits.

"It's cozy," I said in my best Realtor trying-to-sell-you voice.

"Soooo ..." she started in a tone that meant *This is fucked up, but please stay calm*. It was a tone she had used a lot on me over the last few months. "Apparently, London has very strict noise restrictions, and it's hard stop at 11:00 p.m. or else there's a fine."

I rolled my eyes. Whatever the fine was, I was sure as a multibillion-dollar company WWE would be able to cover it.

"Also," Shayna added, "we're second now."

"Second?!" I said.

"And we've got twelve minutes."

"Just twelve?" I asked.

"Twelve minutes, I've been told, as long as the men's ladder match, which is now before us, doesn't go too long," she said, grimacing.

We exchanged a knowing look. In our heads, we could hear the ladder segment producer talking to the guys. "So, we've got twenty minutes, but the good news is, we're now right before the ladies, so if it goes over, we'll just take the time from them."

Together, we headed out to the ring to cut 20 percent of the match. We tore down the house anyway.

I was still on a high the next morning, from the match and a couple of gummies, as my car pulled up to the airport. It felt like for once everything was coming together. My second stint in WWE might not have been a perfect run, but it could at least have a perfect ending.

Initially, I was supposed to fly directly home from London, but the day before we left, Jenn relayed word that they wanted me for Raw that Monday. I found myself heading to Baltimore.

From a storytelling perspective, it made sense. Whenever there's a dramatic turn that makes millions of jaws drop around the world, everyone wants to know why. We had captured people's attention. It was just what we needed to build to SummerSlam.

Sitting next to Shayna as we flew over the Atlantic Ocean, we could hardly believe it was finally happening, this dream that we had shared before any of it seemed possible. Now it was on the verge of coming true. In between playing Zelda on my Switch, I drafted up the promo I planned to cut the next night on TV. *Why?!* I would ask just like the entire WWE Universe was asking. The fans, who were as sick of me as I was of the WWE organization, would pop huge for Shayna. Nothing would make me prouder.

Heyman sent me creative's plan the next morning. It was: Two other wrestlers will be giving a backstage interview. In the background, Shayna walks into the women's locker room. A few seconds later, Ronda walks across the background. We hear shouting from the locker room. Ronda storms out.

"What the actual fuck?" I said aloud as I read and reread Heyman's message. This had to be a joke. Seth Rollins was slated for two entire segments in the ring. To cut a promo. By himself. The Bloodline had been allotted an entire segment for a video recap of their Money in the Bank match and the lead-up to it. Not a single one of them was even in the building.

I called Paul.

"Why am I even here?" I asked.

"It's a starting point," he said, diplomatically.

"It's an insult," I said.

"Well, what do you want to do?" he asked. "It's open to negotiation."

"Good," I said. "Because I'll walk out of this building before we do that backstage bullshit."

"Like I said, just a starting point," Paul said. "How do you see it then?"

Heyman was great at getting me from ranting to working in quick order.

"OK, here's what we're going to do…"

A few hours later, Shayna and I came face-to-face in front of the fans as she unleashed a verbal tirade at me, perhaps even more brutal than her physical attack in London. She was done, she declared. Done being compared to me. Done living in my shadow. Done pretending that we were equals when she was so much better than me. She was sorry, she said. Sorry she ever met me. Sorry to the fans for the role she played bringing me into the WWE.

It was the grains of truth that made the confrontation feel believable. The crowd ate it up. They were behind Shayna like never before.

Wrestlers trickled into Jimmy's after the show. Liv and Raquel were there when I arrived. We were smoking a joint on the patio when we saw Bruce Prichard coming up the patio stairs with several other suits.

"Put it out! Put it out!" Liv blurted in a loud whisper, like a high schooler caught smoking after class by passing faculty. We nodded silent hellos as the executives continued inside and watched them sit right next to our table on the other side of the glass windows.

"Let's just stay out here," I suggested. Our drinks and bags were inside, but we came out to talk shit about upper management, not sit next to them.

"Bro, that's so rude," Liv laughed. "We just can't pick up and move when they show up."

She wasn't wrong, I just didn't care.

I followed the others back inside. The restaurant was so loud we could barely hear each other across the table, let alone have to worry about being overheard as we vented frustrations. I leaned back in my chair. Shayna, Liv, Raquel, and I reveled in the rare win for everyone. This weekend was by far the most fun I'd ever had in that ring, second only to my Mania debut. I'd had an amazing weekend working with some of my favorite women in the company, and now we got to smoke a joint, have a drink, and watch our match while talking shit and eating hot wings. It was pretty close to heaven.

This is why I do this, I thought.

Then, just as we were leaving, when I let my guard down to give people awkward bar-stool hugs goodbye, Prichard emerged from the shadows. He said he'd been hoping to catch us. I tried to force a smile, the corners of my mouth twitched from the effort.

The night's show had been one of the very few nights that neither Triple H nor Vince had been on-site. Triple H was on vacation. I assumed Vince was deep inside the Misty Mountains hoarding the ring of power, either that or a brothel. That had meant that Prichard had been overseeing the show.

Of course, he had no real power, which was why they had left him in charge. There were, Prichard explained, two different phones that he had on the table behind the monitor. One was to Vince and one was to Triple H. I wanted to ask why it couldn't just be one phone that both of them could call, but didn't want to engage him in conversation.

"If either of them goes off during the show, it's always because something bad is happening," he explained. "When your segment happened, they both went off at once."

He paused for dramatic effect, as if telling a spooky story.

"I was really anxious about what they were going to say," he continued. "But they both said the exact same thing. That your segment was fucking awesome!"

He beamed proudly, like he had some part in it.

It took every ounce of self-restraint I have to not scoff and say, "Pshht, well, we're trying our best to accommodate you."

Instead, the four of us staged our exits from Jimmy's so that the kid outside with his dad trying to get autographs wouldn't see we were all friends and have the fantasy ruined.

I got in the car back to the hotel, anxious to get home after a week on the road away from my family but satisfied.

I looked down at my phone, it was a text from my production company partner, Jason. "Dude, AWA comics loved your script. They wanna make you an offer."

I punched the air a few times.

Fuck yeah! I thought. *Could this weekend get any goddamn better?!*

And, for the first time in a long time, I was excited for what lay ahead.

CONCLUSION

I walked up the stone steps, pushed the brightly colored sarape back from over the doorway of the domed structure, and ducked through to enter. My eyes adjusted to the dim, diffused lighting of the ceremonial Mexican sweat lodge. I sat down, leaning back against the clay wall. The warmth radiated through my skin and into my muscles. I rolled my shoulders back and breathed in the fragrant steam.

"This is exactly what I needed," I said.

Half an hour earlier, I had been headed to the gym at my hotel in Mexico City with the sole intention of getting in a quick workout on the elliptical machine. I had agreed to do one last set of live shows to prepare for Summer-Slam, and it just so happened to be on the Mexico tour loop, taking us to Mexico City and Monterrey for two shows in two days. The elevator stopped on the way down, and Santos Escobar walked in. Escobar had moved up from NXT less than a year prior, and while we had briefly been on Smack-Down at the same time, we'd never really crossed paths. When I wasn't in the women's locker room, I was chasing my baby around the bus. We both did that crazy-running-into-you-here double-take, even though it shouldn't have been surprising as everyone on the tour was staying in the same hotel.

"Gym?" he asked.

I nodded.

"Me too," he said.

Then added, "Well, first, the gym. Then, do you know what a temazcal is?"

"I know what mezcal is," I said.

He laughed. The elevator door opened.

"Come, I'll show you," he said. We walked past the fitness center entrance, but instead of turning left, went right. There in what seemed like the quiet tranquil area of a spa reception room was a rounded structure that looked to be made of concrete, brick, and clay. It was painted the faintest pink, with the opening covered in a traditional striped Mexican blanket with shades of red, black, and blueish gray.

"It's traditional," he explained. "It's supposed to be spiritual, like being in a womb from the earth. It's good for detox. This is the only one in the whole city."

"Have you done it?" I asked.

He shook his head. "I've wanted to. However, I have it reserved in thirty minutes, if you want to join me," he said.

"You're asking me if I want to join you in a traditional, ceremonial earth womb that's only located in one spot in Mexico City and we just happen to be here? Ummm, yes!" I said, enthusiastically.

Between judo, fighting, and wrestling, I had spent much of my life traveling the world, but seeing little of it and even less time appreciating it. I have a series of photos of me posed in front of scenic locations—the Acropolis in Athens from the 2004 Olympics, the Pyramids in Egypt from the 2005 World Championships, the Great Wall in China at the 2008 Olympics, the Sydney Opera House promoting my UFC fight in 2015, the Eiffel Tower during a WWE live tour in 2018—but they're just images, not memories. Quick social media snapshots taken so I could say, "I was here," but without actually being in the moment. With tournaments to win and matches to put together, I couldn't spare the time. I had been more focused on gathering the appearance of happiness than I was on actually being happy. I was trying to change that.

The evening before, my sister Maria and I had wandered through the streets of Mexico City, strolling through its Parque Lincoln, ducking into a restaurant serving Oaxacan food, just before a downpour. It's the kind of thing that I would have never done before. For a long while, everywhere I went seemed to spark a near riot, but that was only a small part of it. The real reason was that I was so singularly focused on achieving success that I felt if I took one second to focus on anything else that one second could be the difference between greatness and failure. For more than half of my life, I had been willing to give everything up to achieve just one thing. I had missed out on a lot of living in the process.

A man in a polo shirt who did not look anything like the shaman pictured on the promotional image of the temazcal over the wellness center desk led us into the room with the sweat lodge. He said something about the lodge and the process, at least, I assumed that's what he was saying since it was all in Spanish, then poured herb-infused water on the hot rocks in the center of the room, nodded his head, and walked out.

"Sorry, what is your name?" I asked.

Escobar looked confused.

"Like your actual name?" I said. "Well, I'm guessing your parents didn't name you Santos Escobar. Although if they did, they were basically setting you up to be a wrestler."

"Jorge," he said. "Jorge Luis."

He was, however, born into professional wrestling. In Mexico, perhaps even more than in WWE, professional wrestling is a family affair. The kind of thing that is passed down, the way people come from a family of doctors or lawyers.

His father, he explained, had been a professional wrestler. His uncle was a wrestler. His cousin is a wrestler.

"I've been training for twenty-five years," he said. "Ever since I was fourteen years old."

"That's a long time in this business," I said.

He nodded, then wiped the sweat from his face.

"I love it, but sometimes I feel like I'm chasing the dragon," he said. "Do you know what I mean?"

I understood exactly what he meant. To be forever in pursuit of a level of greatness that is always just beyond reach. To believe that if you just get to that point, if you just catch the dragon, if you just win the next thing, if you just break down this next barrier, if you just... that everything will be perfect. That it will be enough.

I was convinced of that for a long time. Only, no matter what I had achieved, it was never enough. I dangled the promise of "this will be the thing that makes it all worthwhile" in front of myself like a carrot but instead of ever finding happiness, I only felt more and more unfulfilled. No matter how many symbols of happiness I collected, they never added up to the real thing.

There was never going to come a point, no matter how incredible the achievement, where I could say, "OK, I did it!" and just be content in the afterglow forever. I needed to be happy with who I am and the life I have. Not the things I did.

One of the hardest decisions for many athletes and wrestlers is to know when to hang it up. There are far too many examples of those who stayed beyond their prime because they couldn't bear to give up on the dragon. Because they just needed one more win. Because they couldn't imagine life without the applause. Because they didn't know who they were if they weren't this one thing. With my departure from WWE rapidly approaching, I expected to feel *something*, but I hadn't expected it to simply be relief.

I'm one of the lucky ones. Many wrestlers have so few options they don't even have the option of walking away. They're forced to keep going until their body falls apart. It is the only skill some of them have ever had, the only place they have status. For others, it's the only world they had ever known. There are those for whom it is a place to get in, make money, and get out. For me, it was a fun world to visit, but it wasn't where I was truly meant to be. I wasn't a native, I was a tourist. There was some truth to the "Ronda Go Home" signs. This wasn't my home. I enjoyed the escape from reality, but I knew this was the Matrix. I held the red pill in my hand, savoring the final moments of alternate reality before I woke myself up.

Now, we had just a matter of weeks between Money in the Bank and SummerSlam to build up excitement around the match, and there would be limited TV time given to us to do it.

As I lamented the situation, Shayna quoted Triple H from a conversation the two of them had years before. He told her, "We sell stories, not minutes."

"Really?" I asked. "Because one guy's walkout alone is eight minutes, what's the story behind that?"

I waited a beat. Shayna shrugged.

"I'm just saying, there's a reason *The Iliad*'s more than five pages."

Shayna and I wanted to create a match that had never been seen. We wanted to blur the line of real and make-believe. To leverage the truth of our friendship and the fight skills that had brought us into the MMA spotlight, brought us together in the UFC and paved the way for both of us to transition into WWE. To not capitalize on our fight history would be a missed opportunity. Online, fans were already speculating about it.

I got a text from Paul Heyman. It read, "They want to do a fight pit match."

I was hesitant. The WWE fight pit looked like a UFC Octagon birthday cake, that is, a cage topped with a platform with another cage around that.

Our match was supposed to be completely believable, adding climbing up fences ran the risk of pushing it from holy shit to hokey.

"Just wait a second," Shayna said. She pulled out her phone and searched up a fight pitch match from NXT. It was awesome. With the NXT fight pit, the upper level was rimmed by guardrails instead of a second fence. The railings added a danger of falling from eight to ten feet up. In my mind, I saw the moment play out. I would almost fall from the second level, but catch myself, dangling over the edge. In a moment drawn from *The Lion King*, I would beg Shayna to help me up. She'd hesitate. I'd cry for help. She'd pull me up, only then to snatch me up in her rear naked choke, dangling over the edge toward the crowd. It was visual. It was dramatic. It was a perfect ending to my WWE career.

"Can we use the NXT fight pit with the guardrails?" I asked Heyman.

"That fight pit's not safe," Heyman told me. "It's basically held together by Scotch tape."

"It was safe enough to use at least twice before," I said.

"How about a rounds match?" Shayna suggested. A rounds match draws from the combat sports concept of having rounds with breaks in between as opposed to WWE's one-round format. NXT currently had a title just for a rounds format.

"People won't get it," came the reply.

"Tell Vince if we did a rounds match, we could have blonde ring girls with big tits that hold up a sign and walk around the ring like in a fight," I said.

It took Heyman a little longer to shoot that idea down, so I could only assume it was something he thought Vince might at least take into consideration.

We had less than an hour before we had to film our segment in which Shayna was going to set the conditions for our SummerSlam match.

"I don't even know what I'm going to say," she said.

"We'll leave it vague," Heyman said. "You can say, 'I challenge you to a fight. Not a match, but a fight.'"

"Yeah," I added. "A fight. But without a cage. Or rounds. Or blood. Or probably even hitting. We'll call it a fight, but really it will just be a regular wrestling match."

"You can wear the gloves," Heyman said.

"Sorry," I clarified. "A regular wrestling match with gloves."

Twelve days later, after WWE rescinded their offer for a fight pit match because of "logistics," I stood backstage for the final time, waiting for "Bad Reputation" to usher me out. Shayna pulled me in for a hug.

"I fucking love you," she said. "Thank you for everything."

"I fucking love you too. Thank you." I held her shoulders at arm's length, so I could look her in the eye. "I know I don't say it enough but thank you."

Joan Jett's guitar started to blare through the speakers. It was my cue.

"Hey, Rowdy," Shayna said, and I turned my head to look back. "Don't fuck up."

I gave her a wink and pushed through the curtain.

I was met by a chorus of boos as I made my way to the ring after a high-flying men's Battle Royale that had the crowd riveted. They hadn't done us any favors with our placement on the card, but I would have expected nothing less. This time, I didn't care.

I stepped into the ring. For the first time in my career, it wasn't about entertaining the audience. It wasn't about leading a revolution. It wasn't about striving for greatness. It was just about us. It was just for us. Just like we had first dreamed about years ago.

Shayna's black gear was a subtle nod to Horus the betrayer from War-hammer 40K. Her hair was braided in cornrows the way she'd worn it for MMA fights. In a throwback to my fight days, my gear mimicked spon-sors' advertisements, my shorts covered in logos for phony businesses that reflected my love of Dragon Ball Z. The print was so small it was impossible for the crowd to see, but it wasn't for them. I wore my favorite red Fairtex MMA gloves, the Strikeforce ones I'd worn when I beat Sarah Kaufman in my last fight before signing with the UFC. The legendary Strikeforce S was covered in red tape.

We met in the middle, and I reached out my hands to touch gloves. I was never the type to offer my gloves first, but I did for her. She left me hanging as I was known to do to bitches I didn't like.

The match itself drew upon Shayna and my favorite moments in MMA—references a fraction of the people in the stadium would get. It was our love letter to MMA written in the language of pro wrestling.

There was a wink to Anderson Silva's premature knockout celebration. A nod to Bas Rutten and Frank Shamrock trading punches from a double ankle lock. We added a reference to my liver-shot knockout against Sara McMann. We slipped in my flying armbar from my MMA professional debut against Sarah D'Alelio. Hell, we even hailed my own head kick knockout. The entire match was an MMA Easter egg hunt, and only we knew where the eggs were hidden.

The crowd watched, unsure what to do as we whaled on each other.

Nothing we did invited their participation. There were no moments where it was clear fans were supposed to boo. No moves that telegraphed they were supposed to cheer. There was no taking turns punching each other on top of the turnbuckle and letting the crowd count to ten. No holds for applause. We took out almost everything that looked like a "pro wrestling" move, throwing it back to the sport that had brought us to this point.

My step-up knee was the only move that you wouldn't see in a real MMA fight, but Shayna was crazy enough to turn into the knee on purpose, taking it straight to the face. She was probably hoping to get color (bleed for the sake of raising the stakes of the match), but the skin didn't break and her eye swelled immediately instead. For a second, I was worried she was really hurt, then she gave me the iggy (wrestling for "sign") that she was OK. Keeping a straight face, I laughed to myself. She was so damn good she fooled me too.

We swung at each other in the middle of the ring, pulling our punches ever so slightly and aiming for each other's foreheads. Every second slowed down, chopped into a thousand pieces I could examine individually, the way it did when I fought. I missed that feeling.

In that moment, in the ring, every single thing made sense, every motion anticipated and capitalized on, not because it was scripted but because it wasn't. Shayna and I flowed from one spot to the next because we knew how to fight, how to make it real, how to make it make sense. For the very last time, I loved every second of it.

Somewhere in the crowd, I heard the rumblings of "This is boring." But the fans weren't able to sync up from around the stadium and the chant died. I didn't even care. I expected the fans weren't going to understand. They weren't going to appreciate it. If anything, making them sit through it was my last "fuck you" to them and the company.

But it was the match that we wanted it to be. It was a match that I was proud of. That's all that mattered.

From the corner of my eye, in the second row, I locked eyes with Pō. It was a moment she would never remember and a moment I will never forget.

After a series of counters, Shayna wrapped her arm around my neck in her now infamous rear naked choke. I wrenched on her injured arm, but she kept squeezing until she laid me unconscious in the ring. For the first time in my WWE career, I had truly lost clean.

The crowd booed and jeered at me as I walked away from Shayna celebrating in the ring with my hands on my hips and head down. As I headed toward backstage, I wanted so badly to look back, to cheer for her right along with the fans as she raised her arms victoriously.

At long last my creed of "I don't give a damn 'bout my reputation" wasn't something I hoped for but lived by. I paused for a second right before passing through the curtain separating the stadium floor with its spotlights, jumbotrons, fireworks from its backstage concrete hallways, fluorescent lighting, and TV monitors. It was my final walk away from WWE, from the spotlight. It wasn't as bittersweet as I expected it would be. In that moment, all I felt was free.

Backstage, Trav scooped me up into his arms.

I walked out of the building, one arm around my husband, my daughter in the other.

The roar of the crowd faded in the distance. I had lost, and I had never been happier. I hadn't done everything I set out to, but in the end, I had done what it turned out that I needed to do. For the first time in my life, I felt like I had done enough.

As I left WWE, I thought about the words Trav had said to me as I had left my final UFC fight.

I am so much more than a fighter.

I am so much more than a pro wrestler. Than a mother. Than a wife. Than an actress. Than a writer. Than a daughter. There is an entire world out there of so much more that I haven't even started to tackle.

We are much more than the tiny boxes that we put ourselves in. Or allow ourselves to be put in. So much more than the labels that we feel forced to use to identify who we are. We are so much more than our jobs. So much more than our worst days. Than our best days. Than any single moment. We are not merely the things we have done in the past or the things that we might achieve in the future.

The present was everything I wanted it to be. And it was finally enough.

I never won the Olympics in judo like I always hoped, but I learned how to be an absolute badass who could throw down and armbar anyone on earth trying.

I never retired undefeated from UFC, but changed the world, made a small fortune, and found the love of my life trying.

Maybe I'll never make the martial art films of my dreams, but I discovered a love for pro wrestling, screenwriting, and graphic novels trying.

And now I'm walking away from what could have been a Hall of Fame WWE career, but I wouldn't have it any other way.

Because it's impossible to get everything you ever want in life, but trying is the best part anyway.

ACKNOWLEDGMENTS

To my loving husband, Travis Browne, my everything and more. To my beautiful children, Kaleo, Keawe, and Pō, you are the lights of my life.

To Steph McMahon, Triple H, Paul Heyman, and Kurt Angle, thank you for your guidance and belief.

To the Four Horsewomen, Marina Shafir, Shayna Baszler, and Jessamyn Duke, my ride-or-die bitches and future Golden Girls.

To the entire WWE women's locker room, keep fighting the good fight. I believe in you.

To my pro wrestling coach, Brian Kendrick, you're a genius. To my wrasslin' mentor, Nattie Neidhart, you better settle your teakettle!

To Dana White, to whom I am eternally grateful. To Frank and Lorenzo Fertitta. To all my MMA coaches, teammates, and sparring partners, thank you for all the bumps and bruises you've both given and received.

To Abe Esparza, Mariko Hirano, and Hee Soo Kwon, for making me look good literally, and Cynthia Vance and Eric Williams for being there to capture it. To Mike Ponder, the world's greatest bus driver and Southern uncle I never had. To Jenn Novielli, the best coroner-assistant on the planet.

To my fellow celebronauts, there is no one else I would rather live on fake Mars with.

To Mom, who now has to find a new spot to hide her dossier on her enemies. To Eric, Eva, Emilia, and Cal, for bearing with us through this process. To our sisters, for putting up with our shit and loving us anyway. To Dennis.

To Brad Slater and Erin Malone at WME. To our editor, Maddie Caldwell, and everyone on the team at Grand Central Publishing.

To everyone deserving but not listed here, sorry, I was already over the ninety thousand words I was contractually obligated to keep this book under.

And lastly, to my fans, thank you for sharing this journey with me. It's been an honor to be a part of yours.

ABOUT THE AUTHORS

Ronda Rousey has completely transformed the world of martial arts, beginning with a historic bronze medal showing in judo in the 2008 Beijing Summer Olympics and, most notably, a record-setting career as the UFC's first and most dominant female fighter and Bantamweight Champion. She was the first woman inducted into the UFC Hall of Fame, in 2018, the same year she exploded onto the WWE scene, catapulting the women's division toward its first WrestleMania main event in history. The self-proclaimed "Rowdy" Ronda Rousey, Baddest Woman on the Planet, returned to the WWE in January 2022, four months after giving birth to her daughter, La'akea, to win the Royal Rumble. During her time in WWE, she held the Raw, SmackDown, and multiple tag team titles. Rousey is also a *New York Times* bestselling author, the most-followed female athlete on social media, and an actress who has appeared in both *The Fast and the Furious* and *The Expendables* franchises. She is married to former UFC heavyweight contender Travis Browne. They live with their two sons and daughter on their small farm east of Los Angeles, California.

Maria Burns Ortiz is a *New York Times* bestselling author and award-winning sports journalist. Maria spent over a decade in sports media, including seven years as a writer and columnist for ESPN.com, and was the National Association of Hispanic Journalists' Emerging Journalist of the Year. She is a teaching artist on the topic of memoir writing at the Loft Literary Center in Minneapolis, where she lives with her husband and three kids. She is also Ronda Rousey's sister.